T0330276

Labour Market Adjustments in Europe

Labour Market Adjustments in Europe

Edited by

Julián Messina

Economist, European Central Bank, Frankfurt am Main, Germany and Visiting Researcher, CSEF, University of Salerno, Italy

Claudio Michelacci

Associate Professor of Economics, CEMFI, Madrid, Spain

Jarkko Turunen

Economist, European Central Bank, Frankfurt am Main, Germany

Gylfi Zoega

Professor of Economics, University of Iceland, Reykjavik, Iceland and Associate Professor, Birkbeck College, University of London, UK

Edward Elgar
Cheltenham, UK • Northampton, MA, USA

Published by
Edward Elgar Publishing Limited
Glensanda House
Montpellier Parade
Cheltenham
Glos GL50 1UA
UK

Edward Elgar Publishing, Inc.
136 West Street
Suite 202
Northampton
Massachusetts 01060
USA

A catalogue record for this book
is available from the British Library

Library of Congress Cataloguing in Publication Data

Labour market adjustments in Europe/edited by Julián Messina . . . [et al.]
    p. cm.
    'This volume contains a collection of papers and discussions presented at the workshop "What helps or hinders labour market adjustments in Europe?" held at the European Central Bank (ECB) in Frankfurt am Main, Germany, on 28 and 29 June 2004.'
    Includes bibliographical references and index.
    1. Labor market—Europe—Congresses. 2. Labor supply—Europe—Congresses. I. Messina, Julián, 1971– .
HD5764.A6L2722   2006
331.12'042'094—dc22
                              2005050167

ISBN-13: 978 1 84542 609 5
ISBN-10: 1 84542 609 6

Printed and bound in Great Britain by MPG Books Ltd, Bodmin, Cornwall

Contents

Contributors

Sascha O. Becker, Assistant Professor, CES, University of Munich; Research Affiliate, CESifo, Munich; Research Fellow, IZA, Bonn.

Alison L. Booth, Professor of Economics, Research School of Social Sciences, The Australian National University, Canberra; Professor, Department of Economics, University of Essex; Research Fellow, CEPR, London; Research Fellow, IZA, Bonn.

Romain Duval, Principal Economist, Structural Policy Analysis Division, Economics Department, OECD, Paris.

Monique Ebell, Assistant Professor of Economics, Department of Economics and Business Studies, Humboldt-Universität zu Berlin; Assistant Professor, Study Center Gerzensee.

Marco Francesconi, Reader of Economics, University of Essex; Research Fellow CEPR, London; Research Fellow, IZA, Bonn; Research Associate, IFS, London.

Ramón Gómez-Salvador, Principal Economist, Directorate General Economics, European Central Bank, Frankfurt am Main.

Thorvaldur Gylfason, Professor, Department of Economics and Business Administration, University of Iceland, Reykjavik; Research Fellow, CEPR, London.

Pierre Koning, Senior Economist, Centraal Planbureau (CPB Netherlands Bureau for Economic Policy Analysis), The Hague; Postdoc, Department of Econometrics, Utrecht School of Economics (USE), Utrecht.

Adriana D. Kugler, Associate Professor, Department of Economics, University of Houston, Texas; Associate Professor, Department of Economics, Universitat Pompeu Fabra, Barcelona; Faculty Research Fellow, NBER, Cambridge, MA; Research Affiliate, CEPR, London; Research Fellow, IZA, Bonn.

Michiel van Leuvensteijn, Senior Economist, Centraal Planbureau (CPB Netherlands Bureau for Economic Policy Analysis), The Hague.

Nuno C. Martins, Economist, Banco de Portugal; Visiting Assistant Professor, Faculty of Economics, Universidade Nova de Lisboa, Lisbon.

Julián Messina, Economist, Directorate General Research, European Central Bank, Frankfurt am Main; Visiting Researcher, CSEF, Department of Economics, University of Salerno; Research Fellow, IZA, Bonn.

Claudio Michelacci, Associate Professor of Economics, CEMFI, Madrid; Research Affiliate, CEPR, London.

Giovanni Pica, Assistant Professor, CSEF, Department of Economics, University of Salerno.

Karl Pichelmann, Research Adviser, Directorate General for Economic and Financial Affairs, European Commission, Brussels; Associate Professor, Institute d'Études Européennes, Université Libre de Bruxelles.

Hector Sala, Associate Professor, Departament d'Economia Aplicada, Universitat Autònoma de Barcelona; Research Fellow, IZA, Bonn.

Anna Sanz-de-Galdeano, Post-Doctoral Marie Curie Fellow, CSEF, Department of Economics, University of Salerno.

Chiara Strozzi, Assistant Professor, Department of Economics, Università di Modena e Reggio Emilia Modena.

Jarkko Turunen, Economist, Directorate General Economics, European Central Bank, Frankfurt am Main.

Giovanna Vallanti, Research Fellow, Centre for Economic Performance, London School of Economics.

Ernesto Villanueva, Economist, Research Department, Banco de España, Madrid; Assistant Professor, Department of Economics and Business, Universitat Pompeu Fabra; Member of CREA, Barcelona.

Gylfi Zoega, Professor of Economics, University of Iceland, Reykjavik; Associate Professor, Birkbeck College, University of London.

Acknowledgements

We would like to thank all those who contributed to the planning and the organization of the 2004 ECB/CEPR Labour Market Workshop on 'What helps or hinders labour market adjustments in Europe' as well as those who helped produce this collected volume. In addition to the authors and discussants of this volume, we wish to acknowledge the contributions of other workshop participants, including Gabriel Fagan, Francesco Mongelli, Philippe Moutot and Ad van Riet. Our gratitude also goes to the CEPR and the ECB for administrative support. In particular we owe special gratitude to Véronique Genre, Ramón Gómez-Salvador, Ana Lamo, Nadine Leiner-Killinger, Julian Morgan, Roberta Serafini, Melanie Ward-Warmedinger, Molly Schröder and Janet Seabrook whose enthusiastic support made the workshop possible. Finally we would like to thank our assistant editor, Annette Hochberger, for her thorough work in preparing this volume.

Introduction

Julián Messina, Claudio Michelacci, Jarkko Turunen and Gylfi Zoega

This volume contains a collection of papers and discussions presented at the workshop 'What helps or hinders labour market adjustments in Europe?' held at the European Central Bank (ECB) in Frankfurt am Main, Germany, on 28 and 29 June 2004. This was the fifth ECB Labour Market Workshop and the second jointly organized with the Centre for Economic Policy Research (CEPR) in London.

It is now widely accepted that expansionary fiscal or monetary policies alone are unlikely to help Europe's ailing economies. Helping Europe to overcome its economic problems requires the reform of long-lasting economic institutions which influence long-run economic activity and the way the economy responds to macroeconomic shocks, such as changes in the rate of technological progress, the pattern of international trade and changes in oil prices. Examples of economic institutions influencing economic performance include trade unions, which affect real-wage flexibility and the provision of training to workers, employment protection legislation, which discourages firms from firing older workers and also from hiring new ones, the bureaucratic cost of starting up new businesses, which may hamper competition and technology adoption, and the structure of housing market imperfections, which can greatly affect regional mobility.

The volume consists of seven chapters which analyse the effects of institutions on economic performance, from both a theoretical and an empirical perspective. These chapters go beyond the standard approach of exploring the effects of institutions through a narrow focus on aggregate time series. Instead, they contain analyses using microeconomic data and case studies of changes in regulation in specific countries (Portugal, Italy and the Netherlands) to gauge the economic effects of institutions. This has the key advantage of clearly isolating the effects of institutions while other country-specific characteristics remain fixed. We would like to stress that a given institution can improve welfare through some channels and reduce it through others and that the net effect may change over time. Institutions

1

that in one time period may have had a net positive impact on economic performance may in another period, with a changed macroeconomic situation, have adverse effects. The view that emerges from the book is that institutional reforms should explicitly take into account their detailed functioning and the way they affect real activity.

UNIONS AND TRAINING

Chapter 1, 'New monopsony, institutions and training' by Alison L. Booth, Marco Francesconi and Gylfi Zoega, studies the role of trade unions in oligopsonistic labour markets. It argues that unions can help overcome market failures in the provision of training to workers. Firms' market power creates a wedge between wages and the marginal productivity of labour. Thus workers do not appropriate the whole return from their investment in general human capital and they invest too little in it. Firms are willing to pay for part of the investment, but they tend to provide too little training since workers may quit and employ the human capital provided by the current employer at other firms. The authors show that trade unions can help overcome this market failure, provided that trade unions bargain with firms over the provision of training. The chapter provides empirical evidence suggesting that a greater level of trade union coverage and coordination are typically associated with more firm-provided training, which supports the theory.

REAL WAGE CYCLICALITY IN EUROPE

Chapter 2, 'Cyclicality of real wages in the euro area and OECD countries' by Julián Messina, Chiara Strozzi and Jarkko Turunen, analyses the cyclicality of real wages in the euro area and in a group of OECD countries. The properties of real wages over the business cycle are still a matter of some controversy. Even less understood is the effect of institutions on the cyclical volatility of wages. This chapter uses comparable data for a large number of OECD countries and a common methodology to answer these questions. It finds that aggregate real wages have been largely acyclical since the 1970s in the group of countries forming the euro area. In most other OECD countries, in contrast, real wages have been moderately pro-cyclical over the same period. This reflects important differences across countries and in particular the fact that labour market institutions (such as the structure of wage-setting, unemployment benefits and employment protection) affect the cyclicality of real wages.

OLD-AGE PENSION AND EARLY RETIREMENT

The utilization of labour, measured by the total number of hours worked per capita, has declined substantially in Europe over the last three decades, thus contributing negatively to growth in per capita income. Chapter 3, 'Pension systems, social transfer programmes and the retirement decision in OECD countries' by Romain Duval, analyses the impact of pension systems and other social transfer programmes in accounting for this trend. The chapter focuses on the impact of retirement incentives (such as unemployment and disability benefits, and early retirement subsidies) on the retirement decision of older males by using a panel dataset for the OECD countries. The chapter shows that variation in retirement incentives account for a substantial part of the observed decline in older males' labour force participation in OECD countries over the last three decades. A significant part, however, remains unexplained, which suggests that differences in preferences across countries could also play a role. The chapter describes how different institutions affect retirement decisions and proposes several economic policies that could increase labour utilization in Europe.

EMPLOYMENT PROTECTION

Data on labour market institutions are available for just a few countries and exhibit little variation over time. This is why cross-country analyses have not been able to disentangle the effects of labour market institutions on real activity. Chapter 4, 'The effects of employment protection and product market regulations on the Italian labour market' by Adriana D. Kugler and Giovanni Pica, studies the ways in which product and labour market regulations jointly affect the functioning of the labour market. The authors exploit a regulatory change in Italy in the early 1990s, which made Italian firms with fewer than 15 employees experience a rise in firing costs relative to that of bigger firms. This regulatory change provides a natural experiment to identify the effects of firing restrictions and how they interact with product market regulations. The authors find that more stringent employment protection reduces workers turnover and employment. The effect is particularly pronounced for female workers. The rise in employment protection caused a reduction of around 1 per cent in the employment rate of female workers, while the effects on male employment were tiny. When comparing the effects of the reform across sectors, the authors find that the reform reduced accessions most sharply in sectors where the product market was relatively unregulated. This suggests that reforms that liberalize both the labour and the product market are likely to be more effective than isolated reforms in just one of the markets.

Chapter 5, 'On the determinants of job flows in Europe: sectoral factors and institutions' by Ramón Gómez-Salvador, Julián Messina and Giovanna Vallanti, examines differences in job flows for a sample of 16 European countries in the 1990s. The chapter uses homogeneous data for continuing firms in different sectors of the economy. The authors find that sectoral characteristics are important determinants of labour market flows. Across countries, service industries typically exhibit more worker turnover. The authors also analyse the ways in which job flows vary for firms of different sizes, ages and capital intensity. They show that job reallocation tends to be higher among smaller and less capital intense firms. By exploiting cross-country variation, the chapter also documents the ways in which employment protection legislation, labour taxes and unemployment benefits are negatively associated with job reallocation. Interestingly employment protection legislation appears to have stronger negative effects in the industrial sector than in the service sectors. This may partly be the results of the introduction of atypical, more flexible employment contracts in the service sector.

HOUSING AND LABOUR MOBILITY

Chapter 6, 'The effect of home-ownership on labour mobility in the Netherlands' by Michiel van Leuvensteijn and Pierre Koning, investigates the relationship between home-ownership, labour mobility and unemployment in the Netherlands. Owning a house may discourage workers from moving despite a high and persistent unemployment rate. Previous studies based on macroeconomic data document that home-ownership rates tend to be higher in countries with high unemployment and little labour mobility, which may suggest that home-ownership may cause unemployment. The chapter provides new empirical evidence on the effects of home-ownership on labour market performance. It documents a negative relationship between home-ownership and labour mobility in the Netherlands and it examines whether the relationship is driven by unobserved factors that jointly affect home-ownership and job mobility decisions. The main conclusion of the analysis is that, after controlling for these unobserved factors, home-ownership does not appear to constrain job mobility in the Netherlands.

In Southern European countries young adults tend to live with their parents longer than in many Northern countries. For example in Spain, Portugal and Italy the fraction of young adults residing with their parents is around two-thirds. This may explain why in these countries young workers are relatively unwilling to move to another region to escape high local unemployment. Chapter 7, 'The impact of credit constraints on household formation' by Nuno C. Martins and Ernesto Villanueva, proposes a possible explanation for this phenomenon. In particular the authors investigate whether it is partly the result of the fact that young adults are more credit constrained in Southern Europe than in other European countries. Credit constraints could prevent young adults from buying a house, forcing them to remain with their parents. To investigate the role of credit constraints the authors exploit a regulatory change in Portugal: the 1998 reforms of the Portuguese Credito Bonificado programme. The programme subsidizes mortgage borrowing of young individuals whose income is in the lower three quartiles of the income distribution. The '1998 reforms' put a ceiling on the price of a house that could be financed through the programme. This change affected mostly individuals living in areas with high house prices. The chapter shows that the effects of the reforms vary depending on the income of the individual. The effect is basically zero for low-income individuals, while for high-income individuals the reforms led to an increase in the probability of co-residence in the parental home of about 12 percentage points. This suggests that young adults do respond to housing subsidy incentives.

To sum up, the volume provides new evidence about the effects of institutions on an economy's dynamic response to adverse aggregate shocks and on long-run economic performance. The chapters analyse the effects of labour market institutions such as trade unions and employment protection legislation, as well as the effects of a broader set of institutions including product market regulations, housing market imperfections and welfare payments. A number of chapters in this volume exploit microeconomic data and natural experiments, an approach that appears quite promising in extending our knowledge of institutions and their importance for the economy.

1. New monopsony, institutions and training

Alison L. Booth, Marco Francesconi and Gylfi Zoega[1]

1. INTRODUCTION

New monopsony or oligopsony arises when firms face upward-sloping supply curves that cannot be traced to market structure, but instead reflect labour market frictions such as mobility costs. These frictions make it time consuming and expensive for workers to change jobs. In this chapter we present a simple model of oligopsonistic wage determination when workers require work-related general training. Our analysis is motivated by empirical evidence of a positive correlation between trade union presence and work-related training, which represents a challenge to the otherwise competitive labour market model.[2] The predictions of our model are consistent with much of this empirical evidence.[3]

We assume, in common with much of the recent training literature, that employers have some market power in the setting of wages.[4] We define oligopsony – or monopsonistic competition – as a situation in which employer market power persists despite competition with other employers. There are many approaches to modelling such market power. The particular approach we adopt is of idiosyncratic match quality, as will be explained below, and thus some workers randomly change employer after they have been trained. Because of firms' market power, there is a wedge between wages and marginal product and the incentives for workers to invest efficiently in general training are distorted, as we show in the first half of our chapter. Although firms' oligopsony power means that they receive part of the returns to general training and might therefore be willing to pay for it, there is no guarantee that this will be at the efficient level.[5] For this reason it is interesting to see if particular labour market institutions can be thought of as a second-best remedy to overcome the problem of under-investment in general training, and this is what we investigate in the second half of the chapter. An important new result arises from our analysis: we show that training subsidies and labour unions can help reduce and sometimes overcome a market failure in the provision of on-the-job training. The predictions of our model are consistent with much of the available empirical evidence.

Our approach has implications for the trade union literature, which we extend in two ways. First we model an alternative avenue through which unions have the potential to enhance efficiency – through negotiation of training as well as wages – which is distinct from the usual ways discussed in the union literature. Evidence that unions do bargain over both wages and training intensity in Europe is provided in, for example, Mahnkopf (1992) and Streeck (1989). Second, we extend the existing literature on union bargaining structures (see for example Calmfors and Driffill 1988 and Dowrick 1989) by investigating how the choice of bargaining level – centralized versus decentralized – might affect wages and training outcomes.[6]

In the next section we outline the structure of the model and its underlying assumptions. In Section 3 we consider wage and training decisions made by firms that are unconstrained by any institutional rigidities in the labour market – what we term the benchmark case. We also show that the firm is willing to finance the general training that it provides to workers. In Section 4 we compare this sub-optimal benchmark's outcome with the first-best level of hiring and training per worker. This amounts to assuming that there is a social planner who can internalize the training externalities by choosing the number of trainees and their training intensity to maximize the social returns from training. We show that the benchmark case generates the two types of training inefficiency: (i) too few workers are hired into the training sector, and (ii) those workers who are hired receive too little training. In Section 5 we suggest that an appropriately set training subsidy at the sectoral level can remove these inefficiencies. In Section 6 we compare the first-best and benchmark outcomes with that pertaining in a unionized labour market. We show that unions can increase social welfare by increasing training intensity, while reducing welfare by reducing the number of workers trained.[7] Thus unions, while having the standard adverse effect on employment, can in other respects be welfare-improving. Section 7 concludes.

2. ASSUMPTIONS

There is Bertrand competition between two identical firms, $i = 1, 2$, and there are two periods. There is a perfectly elastic supply of workers willing to be hired into the training sector at the start of Period 1.[8] During the initial period, workers who are hired receive training in work-related skills that are general to both firms in the sector. The production technology used by both firms is characterized by constant returns, but firms' maximands are concave owing to the training technology. Throughout we shall consider only symmetric pure strategy equilibria.

Each firm determines how many workers it wishes to train, sets a wage schedule and decides on the level of training per worker. Remuneration is lower in the training period but higher in the post-training period, as will be explained below. The extent to which remuneration is lowered in Period 1 depends on how much time workers spend in training, which also determines the extent to which post-training productivity and wages are augmented in Period 2. Put another way, workers are paid for the time they spend at work and not for the time they spend away from work taking courses. However, the more time they spend away from work in Period 1, the greater is their productivity gain in Period 2. This particular set-up simplifies our model but our general conclusions would not be affected were it to be relaxed.

At the start of Period 2, trained workers may choose either to stay (and produce) with the firm that provided the training, or quit to work in the other firm in the sector. Workers once trained do not leave the skilled sector. The retention probability for each firm is a function of the wage differential between the two firms and individual workers' stochastic preferences. Thus the labour supply curve facing each firm in Period 2 is upward sloping. For simplicity we do not model lay-offs in the face of product-market uncertainty.[9] Because some trained workers may quit, in Period 2 production in each firm will use some internally-trained and some externally-trained workers.

2.1 Training and Training Costs

We make the plausible assumption that there are two types of training and training costs. The first reflects induction training (such as in industry, health and safety), which has an impact on the number of initial hires into the industry but leaves individual productivity unaffected. Thus at the start of Period 1 each firm hires and instantaneously inducts workers at the cost of $c(N_i)$, where N_i is the number of workers trained by firm i, $i = 1, 2$ and $c' > 0$ and $c'' > 0$. The convexity reflects diseconomies of scale in teaching through, for example, the firm hitting constraints of capital equipment required for training as the number of trainees increases. While this induction cost plays a crucial role in determining the number of workers each firm will hire, it does not affect the amount of general training each worker will receive once hired.

Second, each worker hired in Period 1 receives general training in formal courses. The amount of this training per worker – which we term training intensity – is endogenous. Given a finite length to the working week, the opportunity cost of time spent in formal courses is forgone production. Consequently this type of training affects each worker's productivity in both periods. More formally, during Period 1 workers spend a fraction, ϕ, of their time taking courses to acquire further general training, where $0 \leq \phi \leq 1$, and then spend the remaining fraction of their time $(1 - \phi)$ in production. Thus ϕ denotes training intensity. This corresponds to a stylized form of apprenticeship training, where apprentices spend a proportion of the working week in formal courses and the remainder of their time in productive work. Articled clerks offer another example of this form of training.

Each worker has productivity corresponding to one diminished labour unit $(1 - \phi)$ in Period 1, and $g(\phi)$ augmented labour units in Period 2, where $g(\phi)$ is a continuous strictly concave differentiable function with $g'(1) = 0$ and $g'(0) = \infty$, and we impose the normalization that $g(\phi) \geq 1$. The concavity of g reflects diminishing returns to training intensity, an assumption that is supported by survey evidence.[10] Let v denote units of output prior to any augmentation by training and assume this is the same for all individuals (v might also be conceptualized as a worker's innate productivity). It follows that output per labour unit is $(1 - \phi)v$ in Period 1 and $g(\phi)v$ in Period 2.

2.2 The Retention Probability

We assume that workers with identical skills and abilities have heterogeneous subjective preferences over the non-wage characteristics of employers. This gives firms a degree of market power over their workforce, as will be demonstrated. These preferences are not known ex ante but are revealed while working at the firm. This assumption is analogous to that made by, inter alia, Stevens (1994, 1996) and Bhaskar and To (2003), and is a simple way of characterizing imperfect competition in the labour market, as discussed by Bhaskar et al. (2002). Empirical support for this assumption is given in McCue and Reed (1996). This heterogeneity is the only source of uncertainty in our model.

We capture heterogeneity in preferences over the non-wage characteristics of employers by assuming stickiness in the movement of workers between firms – what we subsequently refer to as 'labour market stickiness'. Thus the retention probability (the probability that workers will not quit after training) is a function not only of the wage differential between the two firms but also contains a stochastic component.

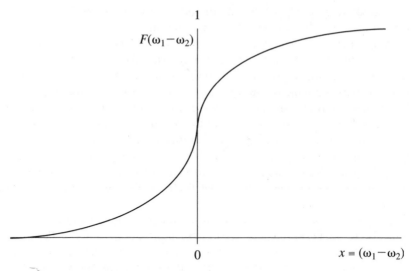

Figure 1.1   The retention function

Following Stevens (1994, 1996, p. 32), we denote the retention probabil-
ity – illustrated in Figure 1.1 – by $F(x) \in [0, 1]$, where $x = \omega_1 - \omega_2$ is the
difference in wage rates between Firms 1 and 2 and $F'(x) \geq 0 \ \forall x$. We assume
the probability density is symmetric about zero, so that $F(-x) = 1 - F(x)$. In
industry equilibrium we have $x = \omega_1 - \omega_2 = 0$ and $F(0) = \frac{1}{2}$. This implies that
half the original workforce is retained.[11] Hence, half the Period 2 workforce
is internally trained and half is trained elsewhere. Furthermore, we assume
that as $x \to \infty$, $F(x) \to 1$, $F'(x) \to 0$, and as $x \to -\infty$, $F(x) \to 0$ and $F'(x) \to 0$.

If workers were perfectly loyal, we would have $F(x) = 1 \ \forall x$. We will see
below that the source of the market failure, and the reason why training
subsidies or unions can play a remedial role if training intensity is on the
bargaining agenda, lies in $F(0) < 1$.

2.3   Timing in the Model

Unskilled workers are trained in Period 1, during which time they can both
engage in production and undergo formal training, where the amount of
formal training is endogenous. In Period 2, trained workers either remain
with the training firm and produce output or quit to the other firm, depending on their heterogeneous preferences for the non-wage characteristics of
firms. The timing is shown in Table 1.1.

Table 1.1   Ordering of decisions

Period 1
A. Firms each set wages, training intensity ϕ_i and new hires N_i and incur induction costs $c(N_i)$.
B. Workers spend ϕ of their time in courses and $(1-\phi)$ in production.
C. Workers learn of their match quality over this period.

Period 2
A. At each firm, FN_i workers stay while $(1-F)N_i$ workers leave.
B. Each firm then produces with a workforce comprising retained workers plus trained workers 'poached' from the other firm.

---

3.   THE BENCHMARK CASE

The training sector comprises two identical firms. Each firm takes the other firm's actions as given and chooses training intensity ϕ_i, wages ω_i and employment N_i in order to maximize profits. The expected profits of firm i, $i = 1, 2$, are

$$P_i = (1 - \phi_i)(v - \omega_i)N_i + RF(\omega_i - \omega_j)(v - \omega_i)[g(\phi_i)N_i + g(\phi_j)N_j] - c(N_i) \tag{1.1}$$

where v is the (inherent) productivity of a worker (which is independent of the total number of workers employed), N_i is the number of workers hired by the i-th firm, ω_i denotes the wage rate paid by firm i and R is the exogenous discount factor. The first term in Equation (1.1) represents the Period 1 profits from employing workers, while the second term represents the discounted expected profits in Period 2 from employing skilled workers, where R is the discount factor. The final term is the cost of giving the N_i workers induction training. The i-th firm will produce in Period 2 using retained internally trained workers plus externally trained workers who quit the other firm.[12]

Notice in Equation (1.1) that the remuneration actually received by a worker is the wage rate multiplied by $(1 - \phi)$ in Period 1 and augmented by $g(\phi)$ in Period 2.[13] Analogously a worker's innate productivity v is multiplied by $(1 - \phi)$ while undergoing training in Period 1 and augmented by $g(\phi)$ in Period 2. (In Appendix 1.1 we demonstrate the robustness of our results to allowing ω_i to vary across time-periods. Since this adds to the complexity of the model without generating additional insights, we continue in the main text with the assumption that ω_i is invariant to time.) Worker remuneration differs across time periods, however, because the remuneration actually received by a worker is given by $(1 - \phi)\omega_1$ in Period 1 and $g(\phi)\omega_1$ in Period 2.

The first-order conditions for the i-th firm – which we now call Firm 1 – with respect to ϕ, ω and N follow.[14] We start with the first-order condition with respect to the training intensity ϕ,

$$\phi_1: \ RF(x)g'(\phi_1) = 1 \tag{1.2}$$

which says that the marginal benefit of increasing training intensity – in terms of the expected discounted second-period return – should be set equal to the marginal cost, which is the sacrificed output in Period 1. Wage rates are also set optimally:

$$\omega_1: \ (1 - \phi_1)N_1 = [Rg(\phi_1)N_1 + Rg(\phi_2)N_2]\{(v - \omega_1)F'(x) - F(x)\} \tag{1.3}$$

This equation shows the marginal benefits of increasing wages due to extra retention and recruitment of workers who might otherwise not be present, denoted by the term $[Rg(\phi_1)N_1 + Rg(\phi_2)N_2](v - \omega_1)F'(x)$. All the other terms denote the marginal cost of increasing wages to workers who would have been retained or poached anyway. Finally, we have a condition for the optimal level of employment:

$$N_1: \ [(1 - \phi_1) + RF(x)g(\phi_1)](v - \omega_1) = c'(N_1) \tag{1.4}$$

The left-hand term represents the marginal benefit of increasing employment – this is expected discounted profits per worker for the two periods – and the right-hand side denotes the marginal cost, which is the cost of giving a new worker the induction training at the beginning of Period 1.

Notice that, given our assumed constant returns production function, the intensity of training on the one hand and both wages and the number of workers hired on the other, are separable because the costs and benefits from acquiring on-the-job training do not depend on wages and the number of workers hired. Due to our chosen specification, both higher wages and higher employment reduce the marginal benefit and the marginal cost of training equally and hence do not affect the firm's training intensity decision.

Given symmetry, in industry equilibrium $\omega_1 = \omega_2$ (the proof of this is given in Appendix 1.2). It also follows that in equilibrium

$$RF(0)g'(\phi_1) = 1 = RF(0)g'(\phi_2) \tag{1.5}$$

so that training intensity is the same across firms in equilibrium.

Consider Firm 1 only, since the equilibrium is symmetric. We obtain from manipulation of the first-order conditions:[15]

$$\omega_1 = v - \frac{F(0)}{F'(0)}\left[1 + \frac{g'(\phi)(1-\phi)}{2g(\phi)}\right] \qquad (1.6)$$

The equation embodies Equations (1.2) and (1.3) and so implies that the marginal profits from increasing training intensity ϕ_1 and wages ω_1 are both equal to zero. Note that ω_1 is invariant to the number of trainees, given the assumed form of our production function. The term $F(0)/F'(0)$ measures the degree of monopsony power of the firm, or labour market stickiness. This result is summarized in Proposition 1.

Proposition 1: *Labour market stickiness, characterized by properties of the retention probability function $F(x)$, drives a wedge between marginal productivity and the wage rate and gives some market power to the firm.*

There are several things to note from Equation (1.6). First, in the limit, as $F'(0) \to \infty$, $\omega_1 \to v$ and the firm does not earn any rent on the worker. This is the perfectly competitive labour market. In this situation the worker would pay for general training through receiving Period 1 remuneration of $(1 - \phi)v$ and be compensated through Period 2 remuneration of $g(\phi)v$. Second, there is imperfect competition if $F'(0) < \infty$ and consequently $\omega_1 < v$. We will show in Proposition 3 below that in this situation workers will not invest efficiently in general training. This is because their returns from any such investment are distorted through the fact that firms set wages oligopsonistically.

Now consider the number of workers hired by each firm in the training sector given by Equation (1.4). The number of workers hired is decreasing in ω_1, which – as (1.6) shows – is a function of the form of the retention function F and the human capital acquisition function g. More workers are hired if the form of the retention function is such that profits are maximized at a low level of wages. This trade-off is shown in Figure 1.2.

Proposition 1 has shown that in an imperfectly competitive labour market the firm is able to extract rents from workers. These rents arise in our model because of workers' heterogeneous preferences or idiosyncratic match values. Although the firm wants to set wages to deter quitting, at the same time it also wants to exploit any surplus from workers who are more likely to stay. The question now arises as to whether or not the firm might find it profitable to use these anticipated rents to finance general training. We therefore next consider sufficient conditions for the firm to finance general training, where the firm's choice of training intensity is denoted by ϕ^c.

MB, MC

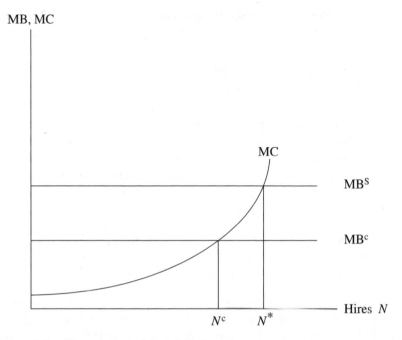

Figure 1.2   Hires in Period 1 in skilled sector

Proposition 2: *In a frictional labour market in which the firm gets rent from the employment relation and there is some probability that the relation will continue into the second period, the firm will invest a positive amount in general training, that is $\phi^c > 0$.*

Proof: Expected profits from a given worker are $\tilde{P} = (1 - \phi)(v - \omega) + F(x)(v - \omega)g(\phi)$, and note that $\tilde{P}'(\phi) = [F(x)g'(\phi) - 1](v - \omega)$. Since $[F(x)g'(0) - 1] > 0$ by assumption, $v - \omega > 0$ implies $\tilde{P}'(0) > 0$.

The firm is here willing to finance its chosen level of general training because it augments workers' productivity in a multiplicative way. As shown in Booth and Zoega (2004), our formulation gives wage compression as defined by Acemoglu and Pischke (1999): increased training raises expected productivity, $F(x)g'(0)v$, by more than expected wages in the two periods, $F(x)g'(0)\omega - (v - \omega)$, as long as $F(x)g'(0) > 1$ and $v > \omega$.

In the following section we show that compared to first-best, the benchmark case developed in this section generates two types of market failure: (i) too few workers are hired into the training sector and (ii) those workers who are hired receive too little training.

4. FIRST-BEST TRAINING INTENSITY AND HIRING

To show the welfare properties of both training decisions – the number of hires and the intensity of training once hired – we examine the outcome were a social planner to maximize the social returns from training S.

Because training is general, the productivity of trained workers is the same in both firms in the industry. Suppose that a social planner maximizes the social returns from training (that is, the value of total output produced by all N trained workers – both those retained by any firm plus those who quit to work in the other firm – less the costs to society of training):[16]

$$\underset{\phi,N}{\text{Max}}\, S = (1 - \phi)vN + Rg(\phi)vN - 2c\left(\frac{N}{2}\right) \qquad (1.7)$$

where $N = N_1 + N_2$. The first-order condition for training intensity is:

$$\phi:\, Rg'(\phi) = 1 \qquad (1.8)$$

which is analogous to that of Malcomson et al. (2003). This condition shows that the socially optimal level of training is such that the level of discounted future output created by spending more time training in Period 1 is equal to output sacrificed during training. This leads to our next proposition.

Proposition 3: *In a labour market in which each firm sets training intensity unilaterally, each worker receives too little training relative to the first-best.*

Proof: Denote first-best training intensity as ϕ^* and training intensity set by the firm as ϕ^c. Where training firms set training intensity unilaterally, the first order condition is given by (1.2) and thus $RF(x)g'(\phi^c) = Rg'(\phi^*) = 1$. It follows that $\phi^* > \phi^c$ given the concavity of $g(\phi)$ since $F(x) < 1$.

The cause of the market failure is $F(0) < 1$. Some workers leave their original employer even when wages are the same everywhere in the industry. If $F(0) = 1$, the benchmark and the first-best solutions would be the same. Thus it is the workers' heterogeneous preferences for firms' non-wage characteristics that drive the results.[17]

The socially optimal number of workers hired is given by the following equation, in which the marginal benefit to the economy from hiring a worker into the sector is equal to the marginal cost:

$$N:\, [(1 - \phi) + Rg(\phi)]v = c'(N_1) = c'(N_2) \qquad (1.9)$$

This leads to our next proposition.

Proposition 4: *In a labour market in which each firm sets training intensity unilaterally, the number of workers hired is smaller than the social optimum.*

Proof: A comparison of Equations (1.9) and (1.4) reveals that, were the social returns to training in the sector maximized rather than firms individually maximizing expected profits, the number of workers trained would be higher ($N^* > N^c$). Intuitively, this is because the social planner does not discount by the retention probability, whereas each individual firm does.[18] Thus too few workers are hired into the training sector.

5.   TRAINING SUBSIDIES

We next address the question of whether or not the socially optimal level of training intensity can be attained under different institutional arrangements for setting wages and training intensity. Perhaps the most direct way of achieving the social optimum is to give firms a subsidy based on the level of training that they provide. From Equations (1.1), (1.2), (1.7) and (1.8) we can derive the required form for this subsidy. When the following function is added to the right-hand side of Equation (1.1),

$$h(\phi) = R(1 - F)\, g(\phi)(v - \omega) \tag{1.10}$$

it follows that Equations (1.2) and (1.8) will be identical. This implies that firms would provide workers with the socially optimal level of training. Note that the hiring subsidy is increasing in the discount factor R, post-training productivity $g(\phi)$, and the markup of productivity over wages ($v - \omega$).

There is another way of giving workers the responsibility for deciding on the level of training. Workers can form trade unions that assume the power to decide on the level of training as well as wages. We now consider two alternative institutions that might affect training efficiency: first, an industry-wide labour union with the power to set wages and training intensity unilaterally, and second, two firm-specific monopoly unions.

6.   UNIONS TO THE RESCUE?

6.1   An Industry-wide Union

Consider an industry-wide monopoly union, which decides both wages and the intensity of training in order to maximize the returns to its membership from training. This differs from the two cases outlined in the previous sections, since here the union sets sector-wide wages and training intensity, but each firm retains the right to determine its number of trainees.[19] At the start of Period 1 each firm decides how many workers to hire and train. After these workers have been hired, the industry-wide union forms, and its membership comprises all N workers in the sector. The union then makes a take-it-or-leave-it wage and training intensity offer to the two firms. We assume that the union sets the wage such that all union members remain employed. For this reason it is concerned about the cost of training the marginal member.

The union maximizes the expected utility U of its representative member with respect to wages and training intensity.[20] We assume that the utility functions are concave in wage income: $u'(\omega) > 0$, $u''(\omega) < 0$.

$$\text{Max}_{\phi, \omega} U = (1 - \phi)u(\omega) + Rg(\phi)u(\omega) \tag{1.11}$$

subject to

$$P_1 = P_2 = 0 \tag{1.12}$$

where the profit functions are defined in Equation (1.1).[21] Since the union's available surplus is declining in firms' profits, it will always choose as a constraint the lowest level of profits commensurate with ensuring the survival of the firm (that is, with making non-negative profits).[22] For this reason, in (1.12) each firm's profit from employing the marginal member net of training costs is set equal to zero. Note that $F(0) = 1/2$ in the case of an industry-wide union. The union cannot affect the retention probability because it only sets one level of wages for the industry. Notice also that $\partial P_1/\partial \phi = \partial P_2/\partial \phi = (v - \omega)(N/2)[Rg'(\phi) - 1]$, using the fact that $N_1 = N_2 = (N/2)$ and $\omega_1 = \omega_2$.

The first-order conditions are:

$$\phi: [Rg'(\phi) - 1]\left[u(\omega) + (\lambda_1 + \lambda_2)(v - \omega)\frac{N}{2}\right] = 0 \tag{1.13}$$

$$\omega: (1 - \phi)u'(\omega) + Rg(\phi)u'(\omega) - (\lambda_1 + \lambda_2)\left[(1 - \phi)\frac{N}{2} + Rg(\phi)\frac{N}{2}\right] = 0 \tag{1.14}$$

$$\lambda: P_1 = P_2 = 0 \tag{1.15}$$

The variable λ_i ($i = 1, 2$), the Lagrangian multiplier in the constrained maximization problem of (1.11), denotes the shadow price of the profit constraint and $F(0) = 1/2$.[23] This brings us to an important proposition.

Proposition 5: *When an industry-wide trade union sets training intensity and wages, training intensity is at the efficient level.*

Proof: In Equation (1.13) it is straightforward to see that the second expression in square brackets has to be positive, and thus the first-order condition can only be satisfied when $Rg'(\phi) = 1$. This is the first-best outcome given in Equation (1.8).

Intuitively, the union is internalizing one of the externalities that arises from the fact that the training firm does not benefit from the higher productivity of workers who quit. Industry-wide labour unions raise the intensity of training because their discount factor is higher than that of firms: workers own their human capital while firms can only hire it.[24]

Proposition 5 survives an alternative specification of the union maximand. In the algebra above, we assumed that the union sets the wage such that all union members remain employed. An alternative maximand might be

$$\text{Max}_{\phi,\omega} \, U = \frac{n(\omega)}{N}(1 - \phi)u(\omega) + \left[1 - \frac{n(\omega)}{N}\right]Rg(\phi)u(\omega)$$

as per the usual monopoly union model, in which $n(\omega)/N$ denotes the proportion of initially hired workers actually employed in the sector after the union forms, and $n'(\omega) < 0$, $n''(\omega) = 0$. It is straightforward to show that, in such a model, training intensity remains at its efficient level (although wages will now be higher and there will be some unemployment of new hires). The reason for this is that the industry-level union always discounts the second period by R unlike the individual firms that discount by $RF(.)$.

6.2   A Firm-level Union

Now consider the case of firm-specific unions. Suppose there are two unions in the industry, one corresponding to each firm.[25] At the start of Period 1, each firm decides how many workers to hire and train. After these workers have been hired, the two firm-specific unions form and the membership of each union comprises all workers hired into each firm. Each firm-specific union then makes a take-it-or-leave-it wage and training intensity offer to the two firms. We assume that the union sets the wage such that all union members in the firm become employed. As workers cannot quit in Period 1 by assumption, they will never work for the alternative firm in that period. However, with probability $[1 - F(x)]$ the trained worker may leave the training firm at the beginning of Period 2 to work for the alternative firm. Because training is entirely general, the productivity of workers is the same in both firms in the industry. The objective function of the Firm 1 union can be written as:

$$\underset{\phi_1, \omega_1}{\text{Max}} \ U_1 = (1 - \phi_1)u(\omega_1) + RF(x)g(\phi_1)u(\omega_1) \qquad (1.16)$$

subject to

$$P_1 = 0 \qquad (1.17)$$

where ϕ_1 is the level of training and ω_1 the wage rate in Firm 1. The first term in Equation (1.16) gives the utility of the representative union member for the time spent in producion in Period 1 and the second term gives the expected discounted utility for working for the training firm in Period 2.

The first-order conditions give the solution for ω_1, ϕ_1 and the Lagrange multiplier λ_1:

$$\phi_1: \ (RF(x)g'(\phi_1) - 1)[u(\omega_1) + \lambda(v - \omega_1)N_1] = 0 \qquad (1.18)$$

$$\omega_1: \ (1 - \phi_1)u'(\omega_1) + RF(x)g(\phi_1)u'(\omega_1) + RF'(x)g(\phi_1)u(\omega_1) - \lambda\psi = 0 \qquad (1.19)$$

where

$$\psi = [(1 - \phi_1)N_1 - RF'(x)(v - \omega_1)\Lambda + RF(x)g(\phi_1)\Lambda]$$

and

$$\Lambda = g(\phi_1)N_1 + g(\phi_2)N_2$$

$$\lambda: \ P_1 = 0 \qquad (1.20)$$

With two identical firms in symmetric equilibrium, the first-order conditions differ from those for the industry union. Most importantly, the firm-specific union does not reach the social optimum with respect to training. The key reason for this is that the function F appears in the union maximand for the firm-specific union. This result depends crucially on unions not caring about the utility level of ex-members, an assumption that is analogous to that made in the union literature that a union does not take into account the utility of its laid-off members (see Pencavel 1991 and Booth 1995).

The equations also show that the firm-level union may set slightly higher wages than the industry-level one because it calculates that there is an indirect positive effect on profits when higher wages reduce quits and raise the number of workers poached. By raising the employer's wages, the firm-level union will ensure that it retains and attracts more workers at the beginning of Period 2. However, there is an offsetting effect in the union's objective function: a union that cares only about its members' welfare and not about the welfare of its ex-members as is the case here – see Equation (1.16) – will not press as hard for wage increases because the marginal benefit of doing so is smaller due to $F(x) < 1$. A comparison of Equations (1.14) and (1.19) reveals that the first effect dominates if $F'(x) > 1 - F(x)$ quits are sufficiently sensitive to wage increases.

Now suppose there is only one firm-specific union in the industry so that the wage in the unionized firm is higher than in the non-unionized one. From Equations (1.18)–(1.20) it should be clear that the retention probability goes up in the unionized firm. The union will as a result ask for increased training. We conclude that unions can also raise training if they affect relative wages and quit rates. But the downside is obvious: quits must go up in the non-unionized firms, and so also must the quitting externality, which reduces training further. On balance, we cannot say whether the average level of training will be higher in the unionized sector than in a non-unionized sector since training goes up in the unionized firm and goes down in the non-unionized firm.

6.3 Empirical Evidence

Microeconometric studies typically show that unionized workers are significantly more likely to receive work-related training than non-unionized ones (see for example Booth 1991; Lynch 1992; Barron et al. 1997; Green et al. 1999; Booth et al. 2003 and Dunstmann and Schönberg 2004). However, some earlier US-based studies have found a negative correlation (see Duncan and Stafford 1980; Mincer 1983; Lillard and Tan 1992; Barron et al. 1987).

This mixture of evidence presents a challenge to the otherwise competitive labour market model, according to which unions should always be associated with a lower general training incidence and intensity.[26] However, these studies are typically based on individual-level data, and hence there is no means of distinguishing the level at which bargaining takes place.

In order to motivate our discussion further we use cross-country aggregate data for European countries to estimate the correlation between training and unions. The dependent variable is the percentage of a country's workforce (aged 25 to 54) in training in the 1990s and this is regressed on union coverage and union coordination. Coordination is defined as either formal or informal coordination between independent unions and employers, frequently at the industry-level. (This should not be confused with centralization; for discussion of these concepts see Boeri et al. 2001, p. 91.) Our results are given in Table 1.2.[27]

Table 1.2   The correlation between training and union coverage and coordination, 1990s

Variable	Coefficient	t-statistic	Mean
Constant	8.52	2.00	1.00
Coverage	−26.38	2.37	70.67
Coordination	5.13	1.79	2.25
Adjusted R²	0.30		

We find that the percentage of a country's workforce in training is declining in union coverage but increasing in union coordination. The latter finding is consistent with our results earlier in this section.

7.   CONCLUSIONS

We have found that, in a model in which the amount of general training is endogenous and wages are set oligopsonistically, workers will not invest efficiently in general training because they will not receive the full returns. However, since firms gain rents from the employment relationship, they may be willing to finance general training although not at the efficient level. In such a situation, we showed that there are several institutions that might help eliminate the inefficiency. First, a training subsidy to firms can achieve first-best. Second, we showed that a monopoly union has the standard adverse effects on employment: by raising wages and making firms raise the intensity of training, the number of workers trained is reduced. But we also obtained a new result: unions can help reduce and sometimes overcome a market failure in the provision of on-the-job training.

When training is general to an industry, firms choose a sub-optimal level of such training since they realize that workers would take with them any human capital when leaving for other firms in the industry. But the human capital is not lost to society, so a market failure arises: private discount rates are higher than social ones. Unions can remedy the market failure in two ways. First, if an industry-wide union has a direct say in the training decision and maximizes the utility of a representative worker, it will choose the efficient level of training intensity (as its discount rate is equal to the social discount rate). The industry-wide union internalizes one of the externalities arising from the fact that the training firm does not benefit from the higher productivity of workers who quit.[28] Second, firm-specific unions can reduce the quitting externality in their firms by raising relative wages, hence reducing quits and the employer's discount rates. While the second effect is known in the union literature, the first effect is new.

APPENDIX 1.1

Investigation of Equilibrium Wages and Training when Wages are Set Separately in each Period

Period 2

Proceed by backward induction. Suppose the firm sets ω_{t+1} at the start of Period 2 before workers decide to quit. Firms want to deter quitting and to exploit any surplus from the workers who are more likely to stay given their stochastic preferences. The firm does not know the preferences of individual workers, only that a proportion of them will stay. Thus it cannot act as a perfectly discriminating monopsonist. (This is done for expositional ease and does not affect the substance of the results. The firm might do this because it is costly, there is moral hazard in verifying workers' outside opportunities, family circumstances and so on.) Then the firm

$$\operatorname*{Max}_{\omega_1} P_{t+1} = N_1 F(x) g(\phi_1)(v - \omega_{t+1}) + N_2 F(x) g(\phi_2)(v - \omega_{t+1}) \quad (1.21)$$

and the first order condition is

$$N_1[F'(x)g(\phi_1)(v - \omega_{t+1}) - F(x)g(\phi_1)] \\ + N_2[F'(x)g(\phi_2)(v - \omega_{t+1}) - F(x)g(\phi_2)] = 0 \quad (1.22)$$

By the symmetry assumption, both firms will behave the same way, so $\phi_1 = \phi_2$ and $N_1 = N_2$.

Thus the first order condition becomes:

$$2F'(x)g(\phi)(v - \omega_{t+1}) - 2F(x)g(\phi) = 0 \quad (1.23)$$

which upon rearrangement yields:

$$\omega_{t+1} = v - \frac{F}{F'} = v - \kappa \quad (1.24)$$

Here the firm is taking advantage of the fact that workers are differentiated by preferences for working in a particular location. Worker remuneration in Period 2 is $\omega_{t+1}g(\phi) = (v - \kappa)g(\phi)$ where ϕ is determined in Period 1 (see below).

We can now write optimally chosen Period 2 profits P^*_{t+1} as:

$$P^*_{t+1}(\omega^*_{t+1}; N_1, \phi, \kappa) = N_1 F(x) g(\phi_1)\kappa + N_2 F(x) g(\phi_2)\kappa \quad (1.25)$$

In the neighbourhood of the optimum

$$\frac{\partial P^*_{t+1}}{\partial N_1} > 0; \frac{\partial P^*_{t+1}}{\partial \phi} > 0 \quad \text{and} \frac{\partial P^*_{t+1}}{\partial \kappa} > 0.$$

Period 1

Now consider Period 1. The firm knows ex ante how it will behave to deter quitting in Period 2 as above, and uses this in conjunction with the incentive compatibility constraint when it sets its Period 1 choice variables. The incentive compatibility constraint is given in (1.27) below. It represents the fact that – to induce workers to participate in the training sector – they must receive at least as much utility as they would get in the alternative sector. The Period 1 profits function is given by:

$$\underset{\phi_1, \omega_1}{\text{Max}} P_1 = N_1(1 - \phi_1)(v - \omega_t) + RP^*_{t+1} - c(N_1) \tag{1.26}$$

subject to

$$\omega_t(1 - \phi) + R\omega_{t+1}g(\phi) \geq \bar{u} \equiv (1 + R)b \tag{1.27}$$

$$\omega_{t+1} = \frac{\bar{u} - \omega_t(1 - \phi)}{g(\phi)}$$

where $\bar{u}$ is alternative utility, and ω_t and ω_{t+1} represent first and second period remuneration respectively (in the sector). This can be thought of as the first and second period 'wage per efficiency unit'. Rearrange (1.27) to obtain:[29]

$$w_t \equiv h(\phi, w_{t+1}) = \frac{[\bar{u} - Rg(\phi)w_{t+1}]}{1 - \phi} \tag{1.28}$$

Notice that (using (1.24)):

$$\frac{\partial w_t}{\partial \phi} \equiv \frac{\partial h}{\partial \phi} = \frac{[\bar{u} - Rg(\phi)(v - \kappa) - Rg'(\phi)(v - \kappa)(1 - \phi)]}{(1 - \phi)^2} \tag{1.29}$$

Differentiation of (1.25) with respect to ϕ yields:

$$-(v - h) - (1 - \phi)\frac{\partial h}{\partial \phi} + RF(x)g'(\phi)\kappa = 0 \tag{1.30}$$

$$\left[Rg'(\phi) - 1 - \frac{\kappa}{v}(1 - F) \right] = 1 \tag{1.31}$$

Notice that if $F=1$ or if $\kappa=0$, then (1.31) collapses to the first best solution of $Rg'=1$. Intuitively this is because it is only the lack of competition induced by the stochastic quits that provides any surplus for training firms – otherwise they would simply not train.

APPENDIX 1.2

Proof of Existence and Uniqueness of Symmetric Equilibrium for the Industry

Profits for Firm 1 can be written as:

$$P_1 = (1-\phi_1)(v-\omega_1)N_1 + Rg(\phi_1)(v-\omega_1)F(x)N_1$$
$$+ Rg(\phi_2)(v-\omega_1)F(x)N_2 - c(N_1) \tag{1.32}$$

Maximization of (1.32) with respect to training intensity ϕ and wages ω respectively gives:

$$RF(x)g'(\phi_1) = 1 \tag{1.33}$$

$$[Rg(\phi_1)N_1 + Rg(\phi_2)N_2]\{(v-\omega_1)F'(x) - F(x)\} = (1-\phi_1)N_1 \tag{1.34}$$

The analogous expected profit equation for Firm 2 is:

$$P_2 = (1-\phi_2)(v-\omega_2)N_2 + Rg(\phi_2)(v-\omega_2)F(-x)N_2$$
$$+ Rg(\phi_1)(v-\omega_2)F(-x)N_1 \tag{1.35}$$

The first order conditions of Firm 2 are:

$$RF(-x)g'(\phi_2) = 1 \tag{1.36}$$

$$[Rg(\phi_1)N_1 + Rg(\phi_2)N_2]\{(v-\omega_2)F'(-x) - F(-x)\} = (1-\phi_2)N_2 \tag{1.37}$$

Now subtract (1.37) from (1.34) to obtain:

$$\frac{(1-\phi_2)N_2 - (1-\phi_1)N_1}{Rg(\phi_2)N_2 + Rg(\phi_1)N_1} = [xF'(x) + 2F(x) - 1] \tag{1.38}$$

Now rearrange (1.38) and define the following function, assumed to be continuous from continuity of the underlying functions:

$$\Psi(x) = [xF'(x) + 2F(x) - 1] - \left[\frac{(1-\phi_2)N_2 - (1-\phi_1)N_1}{Rg(\phi_2)N_2 + Rg(\phi_1)N_1}\right] \tag{1.39}$$

We now show existence of an industry equilibrium by showing that Equation (1.39) only holds for $x = 0$, that is $\omega_1 = \omega_2$.

Case 1: $x \to \infty$
From the properties of the retention function $F(x)$ we know that as $x \equiv (\omega_1 - \omega_2) \to \infty$, $F(x) \to 1$ and $F'(x) \to 0$. Equation (1.39) now becomes

$$1 + \frac{1 - \phi_1}{Rg(\phi_1)} > 0 \tag{1.40}$$

since $N_2 = 0$ when $x \to \infty$. Hence $\Psi(x) > 0$ as $x \to \infty$.

Case 2: $\omega_1 = \omega_2$
Here $F(x) = 1/2$ and the first term in (1.39) disappears. The equation can only hold if the second term is equal to zero also. Since $x = 0$ we can equate (1.33) and (1.36) to obtain $\phi_1 = \phi_2$. Thus (1.39) only holds if $N_1 = N_2$. This implies $\Psi(x) = 0$ if $x = 0$.

Case 3: $x \to -\infty$
As $x \to -\infty$, $F(x) \to 0$ and $F'(x) \to 0$. Equation (1.39) now reads as

$$-1 - \frac{1 - \phi_2}{Rg(\phi_2)} < 0 \tag{1.41}$$

To guarantee uniqueness of the symmetric equilibrium $\omega_1 = \omega_2$, note that

$$\Psi'(x) = 3F'(x) + xF''(x) \tag{1.42}$$

Hence $\Psi(x) < 0$ as $x \to \infty$.

A sufficient condition for uniqueness of solution $\omega_1 = \omega_2$ is $3F'(x) > -xF''(x)$ since $xF'(x) < 0$, $\forall x$.

NOTES

1. Financial support from the Leverhulme Trust and the Economic and Social Research Council is gratefully acknowledged. For their helpful comments, we are grateful to Venkataraman Bhaskar, Ken Burdett, Melvyn Coles, Alan Manning, Abhinay Muthoo, seminar participants at the Australian National University, Essex University, Leicester University, London School of Economics, and the editors of this volume. Address for correspondence: Alison Booth, Economics Program, RSSS, Australian National University, ACT 0200, Australia, E-mail: alison.booth@anu.edu.au.
2. We define as 'otherwise competitive' the situation where the labour market is perfectly competitive except for union presence and the product market is competitive. The

benchmark case is a perfectly competitive labour market without any trade union presence and with a competitive product market.

3. Microeconometric studies show that unionized workers are significantly more likely to receive work-related training than non-unionized ones (see for example Booth 1991; Lynch 1992; Green et al. 1999; Booth et al. 2003). Cross-country comparisons also reveal that workers in Europe receive more work-related training than their counterparts in the USA (see for example OECD 1995).

4. This literature typically utilizes what has become known as the 'new monopsony' theory. Examples include Stevens (1994, 1996), Chang and Wang (1996), Malcomson et al. (2003), Booth and Chatterji (1998), Acemoglu and Pischke (1998, 1999) and Booth and Zoega (1999). In their survey of oligopsony in the labour market, Bhaskar et al. (2002) and also Manning (2003) argue that many otherwise puzzling labour market phenomena (such as wage dispersion and racial pay gaps) can be explained by the assumption that firms have some market power in wage setting.

5. See Acemoglu and Pischke (1999) who also provide references to evidence of firms' financing general training.

6. Most theoretical models of union wage and employment determination typically assume only one union and firm, thereby side-stepping analysis of the impact of the level at which bargaining occurs. And yet unionized industrial economies exhibit a variety of bargaining structures and varying degrees of coordination, which are likely to have an impact on macroeconomic outcomes – as emphasized in Flanagan (1999) – as well as on microeconomic outcomes.

7. Our model differs from that of Booth and Chatterji (1998) who consider how a labour union might affect the number of workers trained where training comprises both specific and general elements. They show how a union acts to reduce the hold-up problem that arises if firms have some monopsony power and labour contracts are not legally enforceable.

8. Wages and productivity in the alternative sector are assumed to be zero for simplicity.

9. See Eguchi (2002) who models lay-offs and in which an additional role emerges for trade unions as commitment devices under contractual incompleteness.

10. See for example Booth et al. (2003).

11. This assumption is for tractability and convenience only. Other distributions would generate similar results provided only that some positive fraction of workers are retained at each firm.

12. Firm i's retention probability for the N_i workers trained by that firm is $F(x)$, while firm j's retention probability for the N_j workers that it trains is given by $F(-x)$. We use the symmetry properties of F, namely $F(-x) = [1 - F(x)]$ to obtain the expression in (1.1).

13. Thus two-period remuneration is $[(1 - \phi + g(\phi)]\omega$. Clearly, for the firm to attract any workers, this must always be non-negative (since the alternative sector wage is set to zero in both periods).

14. The second-order conditions for a maximum are satisfied, since the Hessian matrix is negative definite.

15. Rewrite Equation (1.3), using the industry equilibrium results, to obtain $2Rg(\phi)$ $[(v - \omega)F'(0) - F(0)] = 1 - \phi$. Now substitute into this equation $Rg'(\phi) = [1/F(0)]$ – obtained from Equation (1.2) – in order to give Equation (1.6) in the text.

16. The costs to society of training also include the opportunity cost of production per worker in the alternative sector. This is set to zero throughout the chapter for simplicity, as noted earlier.

17. Since $g'(\phi^*) = 1/R$, we also know from the properties of the training function that $\phi^* < 1$. It is optimal for trainees to spend some time engaged in production in Period 1.

18. Recall that the social planner sets the opportunity cost of labour equal to its true value of zero, and hence this does not enter (1.7) or (1.9).

19. We differ from Acemoglu and Pischke (1999) in a number of respects. First, we allow both training and wages to be the subject of union negotiation. Second, we model the remuneration of workers during training as well as after training. Third, we investigate

the degree to which the outcome varies depending on the level at which bargaining occurs.

20. The retention rate does not enter Equation (1.10) because the worker can transfer all of his or her productivity between the two firms, which are identical by assumption.

21. Note that we could also set up the union maximand so that workers care about their total wage income. In this case, the union objective function would read: $\text{Max}_{\phi, \omega} U = u((1 - \phi)(\omega)) + Ru(g(\phi)\omega)$. This would not affect the results in Proposition 5.

22. The firm has to make non-negative profits otherwise it will not hire the marginal worker, but the monopoly union sets ϕ and ω so that the firm makes zero profits (since union surplus will be reduced if profits are strictly positive).

23. The second-order condition is satisfied so that the determinant of the bordered Hessian is positive.

24. Similar reasoning would lead us to think that firms should pay for the maintenance of machinery, not workers, as they own the machines while workers can only use them while employed and hence have a lower discount rate.

25. While the firm-level union is of limited empirical relevance in Europe, it is more common in the USA (where a company union is unlikely to care about the wages of workers who leave that union/company to work elsewhere – the lapsed members). For an extensive analysis of union objective functions see Pencavel (1991).

26. Some studies argue that, where wages are set collectively by trade unions in an otherwise competitive labour market, wage dispersion is reduced and incentives to invest in general training at the workplace are distorted (for example see Mincer 1983). In particular, workers and firms will not efficiently invest in such training, and there will be a negative correlation between union presence and work-related training (Duncan and Stafford 1980; Barron et al. 1987). Furthermore, the pay returns to training for unionized workers will be lower than the pay returns to training for non-unionized workers.

27. The data are for the twelve European countries for which we could obtain coverage data (Sweden, Finland, Norway, Denmark, Austria, Germany, Belgium, the Netherlands, France, Spain, the UK and Portugal). The dependent variable is the percentage of a country's workforce aged 25–54 years in work-related training in the 1990s (OECD 1999, Table 3.2). The explanatory variables are the percentage of a country's workforce covered by union wage bargaining (from Boeri et al. 2001, p. 80) and the degree of union coordination ranging from one (uncoordinated) to three (highly coordinated) and obtained from Layard and Nickell (1999).

28. But since investment in general training varies considerably across sectors of the economy and so too do stochastic quits, it is unrealistic to suppose that our market failure rationale for union bargaining over wages and training can be used to justify centralized wage and training determination for all sectors of the economy.

29. In principle we could express the IC constraint as: $\omega_{t+1} = [u - \omega_t(1 - \phi)]/[g(\phi)]$ and substitute this directly into the firm's Period 1 maximand and solve for ω_t and ϕ. However, the firm could renege on this contract at the start of Period 2, when workers have established their preferences for staying at a particular firm. The contract represented by (1.28) avoids this hold-up problem.

REFERENCES

Acemoglu, D. and J.-S. Pischke (1998), 'Why do firms train? Theory and evidence', *Quarterly Journal of Economics*, **113** (1), 79–119.

Acemoglu, D. and J.-S. Pischke (1999), 'The structure of wages and investment in general training', *Journal of Political Economy*, **107** (3), 539–72.

Barron, J.M., M.C. Berger and D.A. Black (1997), *On-the-job Training*, Kalamazoo, MI: W.E. Upjohn Institute for Employment Research.

Barron, J.M., S.M. Fuess Jr and M.A. Loewenstein (1987), 'Further analysis of the effect of unions on training, union wages, temporary layoffs and seniority', *Journal of Political Economy*, **95** (3), 632–40.

Bhaskar, V. and T. To (2003), 'Oligopsony and the distribution of wages', *European Economic Review*, **47**, 371–99.

Bhaskar, V., A. Manning and T. To (2002), 'Oligopsony and monopsonistic competition in labour markets', *Journal of Economic Perspectives*, **16** (2), 155–74.

Boeri, T., A. Brugiavini and L. Calmfors (eds) (2001), *The Role of Unions in the Twenty-first Century*, Oxford: Oxford University Press.

Booth, A.L. (1991), 'Job-related formal training: who receives it and what is it worth?', *Oxford Bulletin of Economics and Statistics*, **53**, 281–94.

Booth, A.L. (1995), *The Economics of the Trade Union*, Cambridge: Cambridge University Press.

Booth, A.L. and M. Chatterji (1998), 'Unions and efficient training', *Economic Journal*, **108**, 328–43.

Booth, A.L. and G. Zoega (1999), 'Do quits cause under-training?', *Oxford Economic Papers*, **51**, 374–86.

Booth, A.L. and G. Zoega (2004), 'Is wage compression a necessary condition for firm-financed general training? A comment on Acemoglu and Pischke', *Oxford Economic Papers*, **56** (1), January, 88–97.

Booth, A.L., M. Francesconi and G. Zoega (2003), 'Unions, training and wages: evidence for British men', *Industrial and Labor Relations Review*, **57** (1), October, 68–91.

Calmfors, L. and J. Driffill (1988), 'Bargaining structure, corporatism and macroeconomic performance', *Economic Policy*, **6**, 13–62.

Chang, C. and Y. Wang (1996), 'Human capital investment under asymmetric information: the Pigovian conjecture revisited', *Journal of Labor Economics*, **14**, 505–19.

Dowrick, S. (1989), 'Union-oligopoly bargaining', *Economic Journal*, **99**, 1123–42.

Duncan, G.J. and F.P. Stafford (1980), 'Do union members receive compensating differentials?', *American Economic Review*, **70** (3), 355–71.

Dunstmann, C. and U. Schönberg (2004), 'Training and wages', IZA Discussion Paper No. 1435, December.

Eguchi, K. (2002), 'Unions as commitment devices', *Journal of Economic Behavior and Organisation*, **47**, 407–21.

Flanagan, R.J. (1999), 'Macroeconomic performance and collective bargaining: an international perspective', *Journal of Economic Literature*, **37**, 1150–75.

Green, F., S. Machin and D. Wilkinson (1999), 'Trade unions and training practices in British workplaces', *Industrial and Labor Relations Review*, **52** (2), 179–95.

Layard, R. and S.J. Nickell (1999), 'Labor market institutions and economic performance', in O. Ashenfelter and D. Card (eds), *Handbook of Labor Economics*, Vol. 3, Amsterdam: North-Holland, pp. 3029–84.

Lillard, L.A. and H. Tan (1992), 'Private sector training: who gets it and what are its effects?', *Research in Labor Economics*, **13**, 1–62.

Lynch, L.M. (1992), 'Private sector training and the earnings of young workers', *American Economic Review*, **82** (1), March, 299–312.

Mahnkopf, B. (1992), 'The "skill-oriented" strategies of German trade unions: their impact on efficiency and equality objectives', *British Journal of Industrial Relations*, **30** (1), 61–81.

Malcomson, J.M., J.W. Maw and B. McCormick (2003), 'General training by firms, apprentice contracts, and public policy', *European Economic Review*, **47** (2), April, 197–227.

Manning, A. (2003), *Monopsony in Motion: Imperfect Competition in Labor Markets*, Princeton, NJ: Princeton University Press.

McCue, K. and W.R. Reed (1996), 'New empirical evidence on worker willingness to pay for job attributes', *Southern Economic Journal*, **62** (3), 647–53.

Mincer, J. (1983), 'Union effects: wages, turnover, and job training', in J.D. Reid Jr (ed.), *Research in Labor Economics*, Supplement 2 (New Approaches to Labor Unions), Greenwich, CT: JAI Press.

OECD (1995), *The Jobs Study*, Paris: OECD.

OECD (1999), *Employment Outlook*, Paris: OECD, June.

Pencavel, J. (1991), *Labor Markets under Trade Unionism*, Cambridge, MA: Basil Blackwell.

Stevens, M. (1994), 'A theoretical model of on-the-job training with imperfect competition', *Oxford Economic Papers*, **46**, 537–62.

Stevens, M. (1996), 'Transferable training and poaching externalities', in A.L. Booth and D.J. Snower (eds), *Acquiring Skills*, Cambridge: Cambridge University Press.

Streeck, W. (1989), 'Skills and the limits of neo-liberalism: the enterprise of the future as a place of learning', *Work, Employment and Society*, **3** (1), 89–104.

DISCUSSION

Thorvaldur Gylfason

Which came first: oligopsony in labour markets, or oligopoly? In Europe the historical record seems clear: oligopsonistic employers came first, and for centuries had the upper hand in labour markets, only belatedly to be confronted by trade unions that were formed as workers who felt they had been wronged by their employers turned their backs together in an attempt to undo the injustice and to assert their rights. As the twentieth century progressed, however, labour market power began to shift in the trade unions' favour until in the early 1980s the British government felt that the pendulum had swung too far and that therefore it was necessary to restrict union power by law in order to contain excessive wage increases, make labour markets more flexible and thereby reduce unemployment. Today many observers believe that France, Germany and other continental European countries would benefit from following the British precedent in order to get their unemployment rates down to British, or at least more acceptable, levels. For a long time the debate of the important role of trade unions in labour markets distracted attention from the original phenomenon that set the unions in motion, namely, oligopsony in labour markets (Manning 2003). Even so, the problem never went away. To this day many communities around Europe are company towns with one, two or perhaps three factories that offer the only jobs to be had or thereabouts and use their market power to keep wages low and restrict the number of jobs on offer knowing that the workers have nowhere else to turn. In places where labour mobility is restricted so that the workers are stuck at home, oligopsony among employers imparts a potentially significant bias to labour supply and human capital investment decisions. However, with increased labour mobility the importance of this type of labour market imperfection seems likely to fade with the passage of time. Faced by oligopsonistic employers, some potential workers and parents may decide to forgo education and work and to stay at home with their children, for example, as suggested by Booth and Coles (2004). Hence, in an oligopsonistic labour market, all three are perhaps best viewed as being jointly determined: work and pay, education attainment and fertility. Typically, under oligopsony too little is produced, and valuable education opportunities are lost to parents, while their children may actually gain if parents are able to provide them with better care and training at home than would be available outside the home. Empirical studies suggest that social gains from education exceed private gains especially during the first two years of life

(Blinder 1991; Heckman 1999). Empirical evidence also suggests a strong negative correlation between education and fertility within and across countries.

This paper approaches oligopsony in labour markets from a different but no less interesting angle. Here the main emphasis is laid on oligopsonistic employers who offer too few jobs, too low wages and also too little training compared with a perfectly competitive labour market. Using an elegant game-theoretic framework, the authors suggest that history repeats itself in that training subsidies to firms and welfare-maximizing oligopolistic industry-wide unions that care about training as well as work and pay can restore training intensity – that is, training per worker – to the optimal, competitive level, even if union activity tends to reduce the level of employment – that is, the number of workers with jobs – as earlier literature on oligopolistic trade union behaviour suggests. The results for firm-level unions are less tidy but they still suggest a role for unions in lifting the average level of training under oligopsonistic labour market conditions. Interestingly, the authors note an apparent difference between the results of empirical studies of American and European labour markets indicating that union workers in America are likely to receive less work-related training than non-union workers whereas in Europe union workers are likely to receive more training than their non-union colleagues. The authors present a simple cross-country regression of the percentage of the work force aged 25–54 in training in Europe in the 1990s against two different measures of trade union activity: (i) union coverage that reflects the extent to which labour contracts follow the precedents set in union contracts regardless of the degree of unionization, that is, of union membership, and (ii) union coordination that reflects the degree of coordination between unions and employers at the industry level. The regression results suggest that union coverage – which is perhaps the most representative single measure of union influence available – may significantly reduce training from one European country to another whereas union coordination has a positive effect on training, but the latter effect is not significant; after all, the regression covers only 12 countries, so not much of value can be inferred from the exercise as it stands. More data and more detailed empirical work are needed to settle the issue. Even so, this is good and useful and a well-made chapter that throws new and stimulating light on some of the good things that well-managed trade unions can be expected to accomplish in imperfect labour markets, things that have tended to be overlooked or underrated in some of the recent literature on oligopolistic trade union behaviour.

References

Blinder, A.S. (1991), *Growing Together: An Alternative Economic Strategy for the 1990s*, Knoxville, TN: Whittle Communications.

Booth, A.L. and M. Coles (2004), 'Part-time employment traps and childcare policy', CEPR Discussion Paper 4357, April.

Heckman, J. (1999), 'Policies to foster human capital', NBER Working Paper W7288, August.

Manning, A. (2003), *Monopsony in Motion*, Princeton, NJ: Princeton University Press.

2. Cyclicality of real wages in the euro area and OECD countries

Julián Messina, Chiara Strozzi and Jarkko Turunen[1]

1. INTRODUCTION

Despite the long tradition of empirical research on the cyclical behaviour of real wages there is no consensus view about the direction or the degree of cyclicality of real wages in the euro area or in OECD countries. Indeed, available results appear to be sensitive to differences in the data and the methodology used to measure cyclicality (for a survey see Abraham and Haltiwanger 1995). Lack of comparable evidence limits our understanding of real wage cyclicality and its determinants. Nevertheless, understanding cyclicality of real wages remains central to both economic theory and policy. The original theoretical motivation concerns distinguishing between competing models of the business cycle (see Kennan 1988). More generally, the further development of advanced micro-founded theoretical macroeconomic models, such as Smets and Wouters (2003) for the euro area, relies on empirical evidence to guide modelling choices. In terms of economic policy, the introduction of common monetary policy in Europe makes the response of wages to business cycle fluctuations at the area-wide level a key issue for understanding macroeconomic developments in the euro area (ECB 2004).

Available empirical evidence on wage cyclicality in OECD countries using aggregate data can be broadly classified into two categories according to the empirical methodology adopted in the studies.[2] Studies in the first category analyse the co-movement between real wages and a business cycle indicator by looking at contemporaneous correlations or simple OLS regressions of a (detrended) real wage series and a (detrended) business cycle series.[3] A classification of the major data and methodological differences among some of the studies that belong to this category is reported in Table 2.1a. Studies in the second category analyse the relationship between a (detrended) wage series and a (detrended) business cycle series using dynamic approaches such as Vector Auto Regressions (VAR).

Table 2.1a   Selected studies: static approaches

Authors	Detrending	Wage variable	Deflator	Cycle	Freq.	Sample	Coverage	Countries	Conclusions
Bodkin (1969)	Linear trend	Hourly earnings	CPI	Unemployment rate	A/Q	1900–65 (US) 1921–65 (Canada)	Manufacturing Whole economy	US, Canada	No consistent pattern
Otani (1980)	Growth rates	Hourly earnings	PPI	Industrial production	A	1952–75	Manufacturing	14 OECD countries	Counter-cyclical
Sumner and Silver (1989)	Growth rates	Hourly earnings	PPI	Employment	A	Various	Manufacturing	US	Pro/counter-cyclical depending on time period
Abraham and Haltiwanger (1995)	Linear trend Growth rates HP filter	Hourly earnings	PPI/CPI	Industrial production/ Employment	Q	1949:1– 1993:1	Manufacturing/ Private non-agricultural	US	Pro/counter-cyclical depending on detrending technique, deflator and cycle indicator
Basu and Taylor (1999)	BP filter	Real wages	na.	Output	A	1870–late 1990s	Whole economy	13 OECD countries	Pro/counter-cyclical depending on time period chosen

Table 2.1b   Selected studies: dynamic approaches

Authors	Detrending	Wage variable	Deflator	Cycle	Freq.	Sample	Coverage	Countries	Conclusions
Neftci (1978)	Linear trend	Straight-time wage index	CPI	Hours	Q	1948:1–1972:4	Manufacturing	US	Counter-cyclical
Sargent (1978)	Linear and quadratic trend	Straight-time wage index	CPI	Hours	Q	1948:1–1972:4	Manufacturing	US	Counter-cyclical
Geary and Kennan (1982)	Linear and quadratic trend	Hourly earnings	WPI	Employment	A	1955–78	Manufacturing	12 OECD countries	Acyclical
Abraham and Haltiwanger (1995)	HP filter	Hourly earnings	PPI	Employment	Q	1949:1–1993:1	Manufacturing	US	Pro/counter-cyclical depending on the type of shocks
Fleischman (1999)	Linear trend	Hourly compensation	Implicit price deflator	Output	Q	1955:4–1998:4	Private non-agricultural	US	Pro/counter-cyclical depending on the type of shocks
Balmaseda et al. (2000)		Labour cost	GDP deflator	Output	A	1950–96	Whole economy	16 OECD countries	Pro/counter-cyclical depending on the type of shocks

A classification of the major data and methodological differences among some of the studies that belong to this category is reported in Table 2.1b. Within this category, a number of studies have adopted two-variable VAR models focusing on the dynamic response of real wages to business cycle indicators such as employment or output or use larger structural VAR models with identifying restrictions derived from a theoretical framework.[4] Finally, a more recent branch of literature analyses the behaviour of aggregate real wages over the business cycle using spectral and dynamic correlation analysis.[5]

Overall, despite the extensive amount of empirical evidence no definite conclusion about the cyclicality of real wages in the euro area and OECD countries emerges from these studies. This is due to differences in results depending on data used – such as the wage measure, the deflator, frequency of the data and, last but not least, the sample period – as well as to differences in methodologies, such as the detrending method and the extent to which the dynamics of real wages and output are taken into account.

We contribute to the existing empirical literature by providing consistent evidence of real wage cyclicality in the euro area and in a sample of OECD countries. First, we calculate measures of real wage cyclicality for the euro area, single euro area countries and a large number of non-euro area OECD countries using the same methodologies. The focus on the euro area is motivated by the importance of understanding area-wide real wage cyclicality for the purposes of the single monetary policy. Furthermore, to our knowledge this is the first study of real wage cyclicality using area-wide data. In addition, the analysis of cyclicality in individual euro area countries and, as a comparison, in non-euro area OECD countries gives us additional information that we can use to focus on the role of differences in data and methodology. For the OECD countries, the results are based on a large dataset of quarterly data on real wages and output.[6]

Second, in addition to standard correlation analysis of filtered data we use a VAR methodology proposed by Den Haan (2000) to study real wage cyclicality, thus taking into account the dynamic evolution of output and real wages. This method allows us to distinguish between the co-movement of output and real wages in the short and the long run, a potentially interesting additional dimension of cyclicality. In recent applications of this methodology, Den Haan (2000) and Den Haan and Sumner (2004) find that the dynamics of output and price series matter for the results on cyclicality and that simple correlation evidence may be misleading. Previous studies using this methodology have focused mainly on the cyclicality of price series (Den Haan and Sumner 2004; Vázquez 2002). Den Haan and Sumner (2002) also study real wage cyclicality in the G7 countries, and find a positive correlation between real wages and aggregate output. Third, using the measures of cyclicality derived using the Den Haan method we evaluate statistically whether differences in the results are driven by differences in choices regarding deflators, model specification or time horizon or whether they reflect genuine differences across countries. Finally, we provide some preliminary evidence about the role of labour market institutions as factors affecting real wage cyclicality using simple correlation analysis.

Our findings using area-wide data suggest that, while there is some indication of pro-cyclical real wage adjustment, aggregate real wages in the euro area have been on the whole acyclical since the 1970s. At the same time, real wages in the largest euro area countries and most OECD countries, have been moderately pro-cyclical over this time period. Most OECD countries show a less pro-cyclical pattern than the USA. Overall, these results suggest an important role for cross-country differences. However, we find statistically significant differences depending on the deflator, model specification and time horizon. We find that real wages are more pro-cyclical when the CPI is used to deflate nominal wages, as opposed to the GDP deflator, and more pro-cyclical when the VAR is estimated in terms of first differences, as opposed to levels. There is also some evidence that the correlations tend to become more pro-cyclical when the forecast horizon is extended. Finally, our results suggest that labour market institutions (such as union presence, coordination in wage-setting, unemployment benefits, tax wedge and employment protection) matter for cyclicality of real wages.

The rest of the chapter is organized as follows. In Section 2 we describe the data used in our empirical analysis. In Section 3 we present empirical evidence of wage cyclicality using both static and dynamic methods for the euro area as a whole and a number of OECD countries. In Section 4 we first use factor analysis to identify common sources of variation in wage cyclicality across countries, and then evaluate the importance of different deflators, model specification and time horizons using cross-country regression methods. In Section 5 we provide some preliminary evidence about the link between labour market institutions and real wage cyclicality. Finally, we summarize the evidence and conclude in Section 6 with some suggestions for further research.

2.   DATA

We use quarterly and seasonally adjusted data for the euro area as a whole and a number of OECD countries. Data are available, depending on the country, at most from the 1960s, and at least from the early 1980s, to 2003 (see Table 2.2). The area-wide data is extended backwards from the revised

Table 2.2   Sample coverage

	First observation	Last observation
Euro area	1970q1	2003q4
Australia	1964q1	2003q2
Austria	1965q1	2003q2
Belgium	1980q4	2003q2
Canada	1961q1	2003q2
Denmark	1977q1	2003q2
Finland	1960q1	2003q2
France	1964q1	2003q2
Germany	1970q1	2003q2
Italy	1960q1	2003q2
Japan	1965q1	2003q2
Netherlands	1977q1	2003q2
New Zealand	1970q1	2003q2
Spain	1980q1	2003q2
UK	1960q1	2003q2
USA	1960q1	2003q2

Sources: Quarterly National Accounts and OECD Main Economic Indicators.

area-wide model database (Fagan et al. 2001).[7] Country data have been collected for a number of OECD countries including nine continental European countries (Austria, Belgium, Denmark, Finland, France, Germany, Italy, the Netherlands and Spain), five Anglo-Saxon countries (Australia, Canada, New Zealand, the UK and the USA) and Japan. The data for euro area countries covers more than 90 per cent of total euro area employment and real GDP. The country data are collected from Quarterly National Accounts.

Two measures of real wages are considered: nominal compensation per employee for the whole economy deflated by the GDP deflator, deflated by the Consumer Price Index (CPI) for the country sample and by the Harmonised Index of Consumer Prices (HICP) for the euro area. It is important to notice that, in addition to the hourly wage, nominal compensation includes other components, such as bonuses, overtime earnings and social security contributions that may be cyclical. Furthermore, changes in nominal compensation per employee may reflect changes in average hours worked per person that are likely to be pro-cyclical. As a result, compared to the conceptually more attractive hourly wage measure, using nominal compensation per employee may result in a pro-cyclicality bias. Unfortunately, data on hourly wages are not available for the euro area or for most OECD countries at the whole economy level. Real GDP is used as a measure of the business cycle as is standard in the literature on wage cyclicality.[8]

3.   RESULTS

3.1   Correlation Results from Filtered Data

The simplest and most commonly used measure of wage cyclicality is the unconditional correlation coefficient between the cyclical component of real wages and the indicator of the cycle (see for example Basu and Taylor 1999). The unconditional correlation coefficient measures the strength of the contemporaneous linear association between the two series. The regression counterpart of the contemporaneous correlation coefficient is the coefficient of the cyclical variable in a single equation regression using only contemporaneous values of real wages and the cycle. In order to focus on the cyclical association both the correlation coefficient and the regression coefficient are typically computed after transforming the data either through differencing or through some type of filtering technique. The main disadvantage of this methodology is that it does not take into account the possible dynamic relationship between the series. The chosen filtering procedure also has potentially significant effects on the results (see Canova 1998). Using growth rates in particular does not appear to be appropriate as they tend to contain a significant trend element.

The measure we adopt to analyse co-movement between real wages and the cycle is the correlation between band-pass filtered real wages and GDP. Compared to alternative filtering techniques (simple growth rates or the Hodrick-Prescott filter) the band-pass filter is preferred because in addition to the trend it also removes short-frequency noise from the series. The filtered series is a smooth and non-trending measure of the cycle. For a detailed description of the methodology see Baxter and King (1999). Following standard practice in the business cycle literature, the band-pass filter we adopt removes fluctuations that are too short (less than 1.5 years = six quarters) or too long (less than eight years = 32 quarters) to be considered as cyclical.[9] In order to avoid end-of-sample distortions the first and last 12 quarters of data are deleted after filtering (see Baxter and King 1999).

A visual inspection of the cycle components of real wages and output in the euro area shows that the cyclical behaviour of euro area real wages appears somewhat different both over time and when comparing the two measures of real wages. However, the possibility of long and variable lags in the reaction of real wages makes it difficult to judge both the direction and magnitude of the true cyclical reaction. Table 2.3 presents correlation

Table 2.3   Cross-correlation of GDP and real wages in the euro area

		Correlation of GDP_t with							
Contempo-raneous		W_t							
	GDP deflator	−0.154							
	HIPC deflator	−0.021							
		W_{t-8}	W_{t-7}	W_{t-6}	W_{t-5}	W_{t-4}	W_{t-3}	W_{t-2}	W_{t-1}
Leads	GDP deflator	**−0.241**	**−0.349**	**−0.432**	**−0.461**	**−0.372**	**−0.372**	**−0.293**	**−0.216**
	HICP deflator	0.112	0.043	−0.051	−0.142	**−0.200**	**−0.210**	−0.171	−0.100
		W_{t+1}	W_{t+2}	W_{t+3}	W_{t+4}	W_{t+5}	W_{t+6}	W_{t+7}	W_{t+8}
Lags	GDP deflator	−0.109	−0.069	−0.022	0.042	0.121	**0.200**	**0.266**	**0.312**
	HICP deflator	0.048	0.085	0.093	0.086	0.082	0.091	0.112	0.136

Notes: All data are band-pass filtered. Wages are compensation per employee. Bold type indicates coefficients which are significant at the 5% confidence level.

evidence based on the filtered series. The contemporaneous correlation between the band-pass filtered series suggests that real wages in the euro area are on average acyclical, that is, the correlation is not significantly different from zero, independently of the deflator. Once wages are allowed to adjust to the cycle with some lag, a positive correlation emerges for the real wage deflated using the GDP deflator. Furthermore, the average lag appears to be very large, that is, the largest lagged correlation suggests that the linear association between real wages and the cycle is at its strongest level at up to eight lags, that is, two years.[10] The lagged response of real wages to business cycle conditions is in line with the longer-term nature of wage contracts.

Results of comparable correlation analysis in a number of OECD countries are shown in Tables 2.4 and 2.5. Table 2.4 presents the cross-correlations between GDP and real wages deflated by the GDP deflator. The results reveal significant differences across countries. In five countries the contemporaneous correlation between GDP and real wages is positive and significantly different from zero, indicating pro-cyclical real wages. The correlation is negative and significant for three countries, and not statistically different from zero in the remaining seven countries. Table 2.5 shows the corresponding cross-correlations between GDP and CPI deflated real wages. With this wage variable, the sample contains more countries where wages are clearly pro-cyclical. Furthermore, in each country wages are more pro-cyclical than real wages deflated by the GDP deflator. On the whole, as regards the contemporaneous correlation – the most commonly used measure of real wage cyclicality – the country results seem to suggest that for the whole economy aggregate real wages are mainly acyclical or moderately pro-cyclical.[11] This is in line with the overall conclusion from previous literature on real wage cyclicality (see Abraham and Haltiwanger 1995).

As regards the results for the euro area countries, significant heterogeneity, with correlations ranging from positive to negative, as well as a large number of insignificant coefficients, tend to support the acyclical results from area-wide data. Compared to results for euro area countries, Japan, New Zealand and the USA tend to show more pro-cyclical real wages.

Overall, the correlation analysis shows that wages do not always respond instantaneously to cyclical movements in output; on the contrary, significant leads and lags have been found in the cyclical patterns of wages. In a number of countries a positive correlation emerges some quarters after the corresponding change in cyclical real GDP. These results provide some indication about the importance of dynamic adjustment and suggest that the analysis of the cyclical behaviour of real wages needs to take into account the dynamic response of wages to output.

Table 2.4   *Cross-correlations with real wages deflated by the GDP deflator*

									Correlation of GDP_t with								
	W_{t-8}	W_{t-7}	W_{t-6}	W_{t-5}	W_{t-4}	W_{t-3}	W_{t-2}	W_{t-1}	W_t	W_{t+1}	W_{t+2}	W_{t+3}	W_{t+4}	W_{t+5}	W_{t+6}	W_{t+7}	W_{t+8}
Australia	−0.085	−0.122	−0.148	−0.182	−0.234	−0.285	−0.307	−0.275	−0.183	−0.055	0.068	0.146	0.162	0.125	0.068	0.021	0.002
Austria	0.100	−0.055	−0.174	−0.208	−0.152	−0.041	0.075	0.160	0.200	0.210	0.193	0.151	0.086	0.007	−0.066	−0.111	−0.114
Belgium	−0.748	−0.651	−0.482	−0.294	−0.134	−0.033	0.005	0.001	−0.015	−0.004	0.057	0.168	0.305	0.437	0.548	0.638	0.701
Canada	0.319	0.285	0.222	0.139	0.048	−0.037	−0.109	−0.166	−0.210	−0.238	−0.246	−0.240	−0.227	−0.215	−0.204	−0.183	−0.133
Denmark	−0.368	−0.413	−0.440	−0.448	−0.439	−0.405	−0.336	−0.220	−0.061	0.082	0.206	0.284	0.308	0.298	0.288	0.305	0.347
Finland	−0.231	−0.284	−0.326	−0.357	−0.367	−0.348	−0.294	−0.206	−0.095	0.025	0.142	0.247	0.340	0.422	0.489	0.534	0.545
France	−0.095	−0.094	−0.101	−0.105	−0.097	−0.079	−0.064	−0.059	−0.066	−0.069	−0.056	−0.013	0.062	0.161	0.269	0.372	0.439
Germany	−0.360	−0.452	−0.503	−0.496	−0.419	−0.275	−0.088	0.113	0.298	0.442	0.532	0.560	0.532	0.463	0.368	0.271	0.188
Italy	−0.061	−0.147	−0.189	−0.182	−0.132	−0.067	−0.018	−0.006	−0.027	−0.059	−0.072	−0.050	−0.002	0.053	0.097	0.132	0.171
Japan	−0.318	−0.306	−0.270	−0.205	−0.109	0.013	0.146	0.272	0.368	0.422	0.421	0.379	0.322	0.278	0.258	0.261	0.276
Netherlands	−0.104	−0.107	−0.107	−0.119	−0.149	−0.190	−0.227	−0.244	−0.234	−0.238	−0.197	−0.107	0.025	0.185	0.349	0.494	0.603
New Zealand	0.435	0.376	0.245	0.099	0.005	−0.007	0.064	0.191	0.321	0.395	0.389	0.312	0.204	0.106	0.027	−0.049	−0.137
Spain	−0.413	−0.437	−0.451	−0.449	−0.436	−0.421	−0.410	−0.400	−0.379	−0.328	−0.247	−0.138	−0.009	0.132	0.278	0.425	0.560
UK	−0.152	−0.235	−0.283	−0.302	−0.291	−0.246	−0.172	−0.086	−0.011	0.032	0.059	0.094	0.157	0.246	0.331	0.374	0.354
USA	−0.084	−0.014	0.060	0.146	0.245	0.350	0.446	0.507	0.506	0.431	0.284	0.095	−0.097	−0.255	−0.352	−0.381	−0.352

Notes: All data are band-pass filtered. Wages are compensation per employee. Bold type indicates coefficients which are significant at the 5% confidence level.

42

Table 2.5   Cross-correlations with real wages deflated by the CPI deflator

Correlation of GDP_t with

	W_{t-8}	W_{t-7}	W_{t-6}	W_{t-5}	W_{t-4}	W_{t-3}	W_{t-2}	W_{t-1}	W_t	W_{t+1}	W_{t+2}	W_{t+3}	W_{t+4}	W_{t+5}	W_{t+6}	W_{t+7}	W_{t+8}
Australia	-0.216	**-0.203**	-0.163	-0.126	-0.111	-0.113	-0.107	-0.067	0.011	0.103	0.163	0.153	0.068	-0.059	**-0.172**	**-0.221**	**-0.190**
Austria	-0.091	**-0.176**	**-0.207**	**-0.168**	-0.068	0.060	**0.184**	**0.281**	**0.343**	**0.376**	**0.373**	**0.333**	**0.259**	0.162	0.060	-0.029	-0.092
Belgium	**-0.393**	**-0.254**	-0.089	0.052	0.131	0.135	0.075	-0.013	-0.083	-0.105	-0.058	0.049	0.186	**0.319**	**0.434**	**0.531**	**0.603**
Canada	0.160	0.141	0.112	0.085	0.072	0.073	0.080	0.082	0.073	0.057	0.033	-0.001	-0.050	-0.110	-0.169	**-0.200**	**-0.179**
Denmark	-0.065	-0.129	-0.172	-0.172	-0.135	-0.080	-0.029	0.008	0.038	0.084	0.163	**0.267**	**0.365**	**0.420**	**0.409**	**0.344**	**0.256**
Finland	**-0.246**	**-0.255**	**-0.255**	**-0.237**	**-0.193**	-0.116	-0.008	0.122	**0.258**	**0.385**	**0.489**	**0.564**	**0.606**	**0.615**	**0.591**	**0.534**	**0.444**
France	0.028	0.065	0.094	0.117	0.138	0.157	0.160	0.130	0.061	-0.034	-0.122	**-0.168**	**-0.145**	-0.053	0.075	**0.205**	**0.294**
Germany	**-0.199**	**-0.246**	**-0.281**	**-0.293**	**-0.267**	**-0.192**	-0.066	0.092	**0.254**	**0.390**	**0.483**	**0.518**	**0.501**	**0.445**	**0.364**	**0.272**	0.182
Italy	**-0.308**	**-0.442**	**-0.497**	**-0.446**	**-0.293**	-0.084	0.106	0.218	0.234	0.174	0.101	0.063	0.079	0.134	0.195	0.238	0.265
Japan	**-0.284**	**-0.273**	**-0.239**	**-0.172**	-0.066	0.074	0.237	**0.400**	**0.531**	**0.599**	**0.597**	**0.532**	**0.431**	**0.321**	**0.429**	**0.587**	**0.689**
Netherlands	-0.024	-0.045	-0.085	-0.148	-0.224	-0.290	-0.326	-0.321	**-0.280**	**-0.289**	**-0.245**	-0.137	0.030	0.232	-0.125	-0.142	-0.189
New Zealand	0.234	**0.190**	0.157	0.146	0.157	0.179	0.195	0.186	0.142	0.076	0.001	-0.064	-0.104	-0.120	0.293	0.380	0.461
Spain	**-0.405**	**-0.436**	**-0.475**	**-0.506**	**-0.517**	**-0.499**	**-0.458**	**-0.401**	**-0.336**	**-0.250**	-0.148	-0.033	0.084	0.195	0.381	0.414	0.370
UK	-0.141	**-0.160**	-0.154	-0.133	-0.101	-0.058	-0.008	0.037	0.066	0.074	0.082	0.117	**0.193**	**0.293**	**-0.504**	**-0.526**	**-0.500**
USA	0.131	**0.244**	**0.356**	**0.460**	**0.551**	**0.615**	**0.635**	**0.598**	**0.495**	**0.331**	0.127	-0.087	**-0.279**	**-0.422**			

Notes: All data are band-pass filtered. Wages are compensation per employee. Bold type indicates coefficients which are significant at the 5% confidence level.

Labour market adjustments in Europe

3.2 VAR-based Results

An alternative measure of the degree of co-movement between two series based on correlation between VAR forecast errors at different horizons has been proposed by Den Haan (2000). Contrary to the unconditional correlation coefficient (and its regression counterpart), this measure can take into account the dynamic nature of the variables under consideration through the inclusion of lagged variables in the VAR system. Furthermore, as discussed in Den Haan (2000), the methodology can accommodate both integrated and stationary variables and thus does not require additional filtering. Compared to a fully specified structural VAR model, this method does not require any (potentially controversial) identification restrictions and is simple to be implemented and interpreted.[12]

The measure proposed by Den Haan (2000) can be described in the following terms (see Den Haan 2000 and Den Haan and Sumner 2004 for a more detailed explanation). Consider a two-variable VAR model in standard form:

$$X_t = A_0 + \sum_{i=1}^{m} A_i X_{t-i} + v_t$$

where X_t is a 2×1 vector of random variables, A_0 is a 2×1 vector of constant terms or a matrix of deterministic coefficients, A_i are 2×2 matrices of coefficients, v_t is an 2×1 vector of error terms, and m is the total number of lags included. After estimating the model it is straightforward to calculate the k-period ahead forecasts of the two variables, and consequently their covariance and correlation coefficients. In our empirical analysis, the Den Haan methodology is applied by estimating a number of bivariate VAR models with real wages and output. Similarly to the measure of cyclicality based on band-pass filtered data, we focus both on euro area data and a sample of OECD countries. In order to evaluate the role of model specification in determining the outcome we estimate each VAR twice, using both first differences and the level series. We also calculate the correlation coefficients for different forecast horizons: short run at 1.5 years, medium run at four years and long run at eight years. Bootstrapped standard errors based on 2500 replications were used to construct 90 per cent confidence bands. The lag length in the VAR and the deterministic components were chosen by the Akaike Information Criterion.

Figures 2.1 to 2.4 show the evolution of the dynamic correlation between real wages and output in the euro area for different forecast horizons. In order to evaluate robustness, we show results with VARs in levels and in first differences for the two different deflators. The graphs show the mean of the 2500 replications of the calculation and the relevant lower and upper 90 per cent confidence bands.[13] Confirming the results in the previous section these figures show that real wages appear to be largely acyclical in the euro area. Nonetheless, there are some notable differences across the different models and deflators. In particular, the correlation changes sign for the model in levels using the GDP deflator, whereas the correlation remains positive for the model in first differences. However, the confidence bands are large and mostly indicate that the correlations are not statistically different from zero.[14] Indeed, the only exception to the non-significance result is the positive short-run correlation in the model in differences for the HICP deflated real wages.

The country evidence is presented in Figures 2.5 to 2.8.[15] The figures show the correlation between forecast errors at three different horizons, short run, medium run and long run. Significance at the 10 per cent level is indicated by the stars. Overall, these results point to mostly pro-cyclical real wages. Two countries, Austria and the USA, show statistically significant pro-cyclical real wage adjustment for all deflators, both in levels and differences and for the different forecast horizons. Results for several other countries, including Canada, France, Germany, Italy, New Zealand and the UK, indicate significant pro-cyclical wage adjustment for most results. Only Spain shows consistently counter-cyclical real wage adjustment for all deflators, both in levels and differences and for the different forecast horizons, even if this impact is not significant in all cases. In addition, wages appear counter-cyclical in some cases for Belgium, Denmark and the Netherlands. However, the evidence of counter-cyclicality is not systematic for these countries, including some occasions where the sign of the cyclicality changes from negative to positive, and it is only rarely statistically significant. Overall it is worth noting that a number of results are statistically insignificant even if the apparent correlation between the two forecast error series is relatively large, suggesting that the results of the simple VAR model reflect significant uncertainty for a number of countries.

Results for most countries that have a systematic pattern in the direction of change between the short-run and long-run adjustment suggest that real wages become more pro-cyclical as the forecast horizon is extended. This result may reflect the longer-term nature of wage contracts that allows wages to adjust to changes in business cycle conditions only with a significant lag. Alternatively, following the reasoning in Den Haan (2000), this pattern could be interpreted as evidence of the dominating impact of different types of shocks in the short and the long run. Indeed, there is some empirical evidence that the type of shock matters for the cyclicality of real wages. For example Fleischman (1999) finds that real wages tend to be counter-cyclical in response to labour supply and aggregate demand shocks,

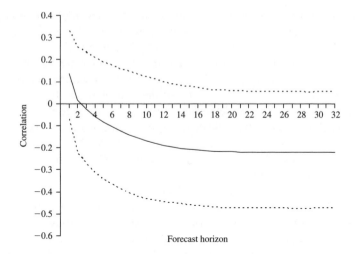

Notes: The correlation at 16 steps ahead is −0.22. The model has two lags and includes a linear and a quadratic trend.

Figure 2.1   Euro area: mean correlation between forecast errors of GDP and real wages deflated by the GDP deflator (VAR model in levels)

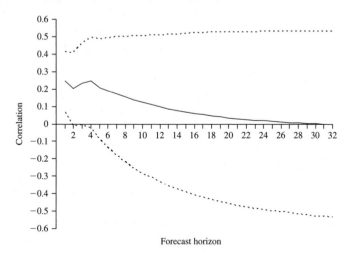

Notes: The correlation at 16 steps ahead is 0.03. The model has four lags and includes a constant.

Figure 2.2   Euro area: mean correlation between forecast errors of GDP and real wages deflated by the GDP deflator (VAR model in first differences)

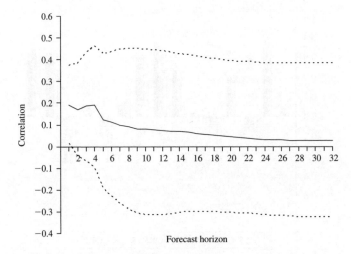

Notes: The correlation at 16 steps ahead is 0.07. The model has five lags and includes a constant and linear and quadratic trend.

Figure 2.3   Euro area: mean correlation between forecast errors of GDP and real wages deflated by the HICP (VAR model in levels)

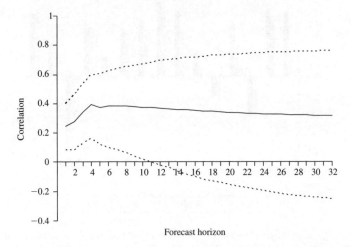

Notes: The correlation at 16 steps ahead is 0.37. The model has four lags and includes a constant.

Figure 2.4   Euro area: mean correlation between forecast errors of GDP and real wages deflated by the HICP (VAR model in differences)

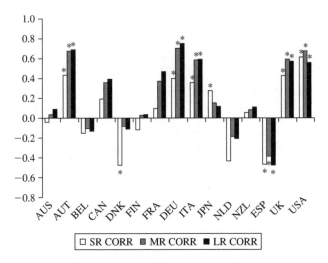

Figure 2.5　*Euro area: mean correlation between forecast errors of GDP and real wages deflated by the HICP (VAR model in differences)*

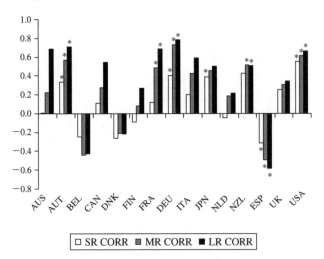

Figure 2.6　*Correlation between forecast errors of GDP and real wages deflated by the GDP deflator in a sample of OECD countries (VAR model in first differences)*

Notes for Figures 2.5–2.8:　Stars indicate significance at the 10% level. SR CORR (short-run correlation) = correlation at 1.5 years; MR CORR (medium-run correlation) = correlation at four years; LR CORR (long-run correlation) = correlation at eight years, Abbreviations: AUS Australia, AUT Austria, BEL Belgium, CAN Canada, DNK Denmark, FIN Finland,

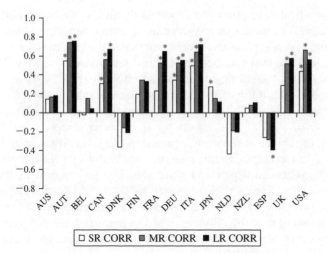

Figure 2.7   Correlation between forecast errors of GDP and real wages deflated by the CPI deflator in a sample of OECD countries (VAR model in levels)

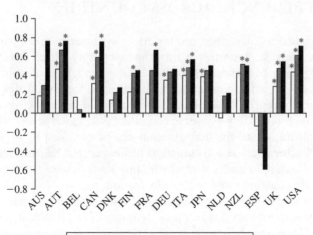

Figure 2.8   Correlation between forecast errors of GDP and real wages deflated by the CPI deflator in a sample of OECD countries (VAR model in differences)

FRA France, DEU Germany, ITA Italy, JPN Japan, NLD Netherlands, NZL New Zealand, ESP Spain, UK United Kingdom, USA United States.

and pro-cyclical in responses to productivity and oil shocks.[16] This would tend to argue for a model where there may be a short-run impact from labour supply and aggregate demand shocks, but that in the long run, the dominant shocks are those that produce pro-cyclical responses to activity. The fact that most (but not all) of the country series extend to the 1970s could suggest that the oil shocks of the 1970s could have a significant impact on the results. To investigate this possibility the analysis was repeated for a shorter sample from 1980 onwards.[17] The results for the shorter sample show that, as expected, the choice of the sample period matters somewhat for individual countries. For example, results indicate that real wages have been clearly more pro-cyclical in Japan and somewhat less pro-cyclical in the USA during the last 20 years than suggested by the results for the full sample. However, no common pattern (across countries) emerges from the comparison, suggesting that the differences across countries are not likely to be driven by different sample sizes or by the impact of common shocks, such as the oil shocks of the 1970s.

4.   IDENTIFYING COMMON SOURCES AND DIFFERENCES ACROSS COUNTRIES

The measures just described are meant to systematize and quantify the differences between countries in real wage cyclicality. Given the variety of measures presented that depend on the deflator, model specification and the forecast horizon, an important question arises: do these measures relate to a common concept? Do we observe consistent differences across different data and methods? Do we observe consistent differences across countries?

A simple answer to the first question can be obtained by using factor analysis. Factor analysis is a statistical technique that helps to reduce the number of variables under study by finding linear combinations of those variables that contain most of the information.

The first step of the factor analysis is an assessment of how many dimensions it takes to produce a reasonable summary of the common variance in the data. This is done by computing the eigenvalues of the principal components decomposition of the correlation matrix of the variables under study. Each eigenvalue divided by the number of variables included in the analysis can be interpreted as the percentage of variance that would be explained by each principal component of the data. Note that deciding the number of relevant factors that adequately describe the underlying phenomenon (in our case wage cyclicality) requires interpretation by the researcher, admittedly a subjective process. Typically, if there is one factor that explains a very large fraction of the variance, and all the others explain only relatively small shares, this is taken as an indication that there is a single source of common variation. If instead there are two factors that explain large and similar shares of the variance this is interpreted as evidence of two sources of common variance and so on.

Once the number of relevant factors has been decided, the next question to be addressed is how each variable relates to this factor. The factor loadings represent an estimate of the correlation of each variable with the hypothetical underlying causes of the common variation. If a variable presents a high loading with respect to a given factor this is an indication that this variable represents relatively well the underlying phenomenon captured by the factor.

We have 12 different measures of real wage cyclicality for each country based on the VAR results. These measures include correlations of forecast errors at three different horizons: the short run, the medium run and the long run from models in levels and in first differences, for two different deflators. We pool these measures to perform principal component factor analysis. The results are presented in Table 2.6. The analysis of the eigenvalues clearly suggests a single important dimension of common variance that explains 83 per cent of the variance. All indicators of wage cyclicality have large and positive loadings on this factor, suggesting the coherence of all measures, regardless of the definition of the deflator, model specification and the forecast horizon.

Table 2.6   Factor analysis

Variance explained			0.83
Deflator	Forecast horizon	Specification	Factor loadings
GDP	Short run	Levels	0.94
GDP	Medium run	Levels	0.94
GDP	Long run	Levels	0.95
GDP	Short run	First diff.	0.86
GDP	Medium run	First diff.	0.90
GDP	Long run	First diff.	0.89
CPI	Short run	Levels	0.91
CPI	Medium run	Levels	0.92
CPI	Long run	Levels	0.92
CPI	Short run	First diff.	0.89
CPI	Medium run	First diff.	0.91
CPI	Long run	First diff.	0.86

Notes: The analysis of the eigenvalues clearly suggested the existence of a single factor explaining the common bulk of the variance.

Having established that all of the correlation measures relate to the same underlying concept, we turn to the next two questions. In particular, we perform standard cross-country regression analysis to statistically evaluate the importance of differences across data, methods and countries. In particular we estimate a regression model with the correlation coefficient as the dependent variable, and a number of indicator variables as the explanatory variables. The indicator variables include dummies for the three different characteristics of measurement as well as the 14 countries (with the USA as the omitted category). The results of the cross-country regression are given in Table 2.7. The results show that there are indeed statistically significant differences in the measured cyclicality of real wages.[18] In particular, real wages are more pro-cyclical when nominal compensation is deflated by the CPI rather than the GDP deflator, when the VAR is estimated in first

Table 2.7   Regression analysis

Variable	Coefficient	t-value
CPI deflator	**0.88**	3.80
Level	**−0.81**	−3.49
Short run	**−0.18**	−5.99
Medium run	−0.04	−1.51
Country dummies:		
Australia	**−0.36**	−5.88
Austria	0.02	0.52
Belgium	**−0.69**	−9.96
Canada	**−0.17**	−3.65
Denmark	**−0.71**	−12.30
Finland	**−0.41**	−9.01
France	**−0.18**	−3.68
Germany	−0.05	−0.95
Italy	−0.09	−1.88
Japan	**−0.28**	−5.16
Netherlands	**−0.67**	−11.28
New Zealand	**−0.31**	−5.10
Spain	**−0.99**	−15.24
UK	**−0.16**	−3.25
Adjusted R^2	0.79	

Notes: The dependent variable is the correlation coefficient. All explanatory variables are dummies. The omitted categories are GDP deflator, first differences, long run, USA.
Standard errors are robust to unknown heteroskedasticity. Coefficients that are significant at the 5% level are indicated in bold.

differences. All these differences are statistically significant. Real wages also become more pro-cyclical when the forecast horizon is extended from the short to the medium run. Differences between the medium and long-run estimates are not statistically significant. The results also point to significant heterogeneity across countries. Confirming the impression in the previous section, as indicated by mostly negative coefficients for the country dummies, real wages are found to be more pro-cyclical in the USA (the omitted country) than in most OECD countries. The observed heterogeneity across countries suggests a possible role for labour market institutions in explaining the cross-country differences.

5.   INVESTIGATING THE RELATIONSHIP BETWEEN WAGE CYCLICALITY AND LABOUR MARKET INSTITUTIONS

As a final step we provide a preliminary assessment of the role of labour market institutions as factors affecting real wage cyclicality. Our procedure is based on a two-stage approach. The first stage consists of deriving country estimates of cyclicality from the correlations between output and real wages from the VAR-based methodology. We use the factor scores from the factor analysis as our summary measures of cyclicality. By using the factor scores instead of the original correlation measures we remain agnostic about the correct data and model specification used to measure cyclicality in the first stage. The second stage consists of simple correlations between this summary measure and the institutional variables. This exercise should be interpreted as a first attempt to link real wage cyclicality and institutions. Rather than testing specific theoretical hypotheses, we follow a fact-finding approach that should serve as input for further analysis. In addition, the empirical approach does not cover all the possible interactions between cyclicality and institutions, excluding factors such as the impact of changes in labour market institutions over time and possible complementarities between institutions.

The institutional variables included in the preliminary analysis come from a variety of sources. Since the focus is on cross-country comparisons, we have taken averages of the institutional indicators for the periods covered by the dataset.

- *Unionization* Union density and union coverage reflect partial aspects of union bargaining power in the labour market. Depending on the set of norms and regulations governing the labour market, there are large differences within countries between the coverage of wages negotiated by unions and the extent of unionization (as measured by the number of union members in the total labour force). Well-known examples are those of France and Spain where collective agreements cover more than three-quarters of the labour force but less than 15 per cent of workers belong to a union. For this reason, the indicator of union coverage is probably a better indicator of the impact of unions in wage negotiations in the case of cross-country comparisons. The main source for union density is Nickell and Nunziata (2001) for all countries except Ireland and New Zealand. Data for New Zealand have been obtained from OECD (1997) and for Ireland from Holden and Wulfsberg (2004). Union coverage data for all countries with the exception of New Zealand, Spain and Ireland come from Golden and Wallerstein (2002). Coverage for New Zealand and Spain is reported in OECD (1997) and for Ireland in Holden and Wulfsberg (2004).

- *Wage-setting institutions* The degree of centralization and the extent of coordination between parties in wage-setting negotiations have proved to be important determinants of labour market performance. We consider an indicator of wage bargaining level developed by Golden and Wallerstein (2002). This indicator is a categorical variable taking values one to five according to an increasing scale in the wage bargaining level. Alternatively, we consider an indicator of wage setting coordination developed by Nickell and Nunziata (2001) which ranks countries in a scale from one to three according to an increasing scale in the coordination of unions and employers associations in the wage setting negotiations.
- *Employment protection* This indicator ranges between zero and two increasing with the strictness of employment protection legislation. Source: Nickell and Nunziata (2001).
- *Unemployment benefits* This indicator reports the first year of unemployment benefits, averaged over family types of recipients, since in many countries benefits are distributed according to family composition. The benefits are a percentage of average earnings before tax. Source: OECD database.
- *Tax wedge* Wedge between the real (monetary) labour cost faced by the firms and the consumption wage received by the employees normalized by GDP. Source: Nickell and Nunziata (2001).

Figure 2.9 shows simple correlations between the summary measures of cyclicality and a number of labour market institutions. All correlations with institutional variables appear with a negative sign. However, only correlations with coordination in wage-setting, unemployment benefits and

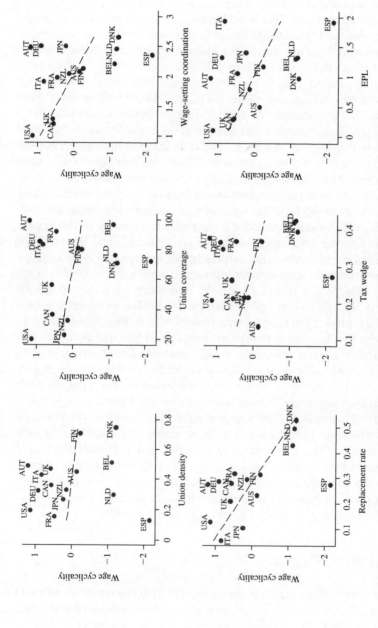

Notes: The values on the vertical axes are standardized factor scores (that is, measured in units of standard deviations from their means). Abbreviations: see Figures 2.5–2.8.

Figure 2.9 Institutions and wage cyclicality

employment protection legislation are statistically significant suggesting that these institutions are associated with less pro-cyclical real wages.

The variable with the strongest negative association is the unemployment benefit replacement rate. This is consistent with the view that more generous unemployment benefits are meant to provide insurance to workers by smoothing out labour income shocks. This institution might reduce the sensitivity of wages to fundamentals and thus dampen real wage cyclicality in a symmetric fashion. Assuming that the underlying tendency is for real wages to be pro-cyclical, more generous benefits would tend to reduce pro-cyclicality. The implications of employment protection legislation (EPL) for wage outcomes have received less attention in the literature, but such institutions can also be viewed as meant to provide insurance (Bertola 2004). These quantity constraints would hardly be binding if wages were free to adjust. Thus, from a theoretical perspective it is reasonable to think that institutions such as more coordinated bargaining systems and binding minimum wage floors limit the sensitivity of wages to fundamentals, thus reinforcing the insurance provided by quantity restrictions. In this framework, the negative association between wage cyclicality and the extent of wage-setting coordination is not surprising. More surprising is the negative association between employment protection and wage cyclicality. One plausible explanation relates to the the interaction of institutions with changes in the composition of the workforce over the business cycle (not controlled for here). For example, it is possible that more stringent employment protection legislation reinforces composition bias that in turn masks pro-cyclicality of real wages. It is well established that stringent EPL imposes barriers to the incorporation in the labour market of workers with lower reservation wages such as women and young workers (Bertola et al. 2002). In such segmented labour markets one could observe higher pro-cyclicality of participation of younger and female workers, which in turn would contaminate the measure of wage cyclicality calculated here through the composition bias outlined above. Overall, more detailed analysis is clearly needed before firm conclusions can be made about the role of institutions as factors affecting real wage cyclicality. However, these preliminary results show that labour market institutions matter for the cyclicality of real wages and provide a basis for a more detailed investigation.

6. CONCLUSIONS

The literature on business cycle characteristics in the euro area and OECD countries remains inconclusive about the cyclical adjustment of real wages over the business cycle. This is partly due to the heterogeneity in data characteristics and methods used in the various investigations of wage cyclicality. In this chapter, we have contributed to the existing empirical literature by providing consistent evidence of real wage cyclicality in the euro area and in a sample of OECD countries.

We calculated measures of real wage cyclicality using the same methodologies for the euro area, single euro area countries and a large number of non-euro area OECD countries. In addition to calculating standard measures of co-movement, that is, correlation coefficients from band-pass filtered data, we used a VAR methodology to take into account the dynamic evolution of output and real wages. Finally, using the measures of cyclicality derived using the VAR-based method, we evaluated statistically whether differences in the results are driven by differences in choices regarding deflators, model specification or time horizon or whether they reflect genuine economic differences across countries.

The results confirm that the evidence based on simple correlation measures that omit the impact of dynamics may be misleading. Our findings using area-wide data indicate that aggregate real wages in the euro area have been on the whole largely acyclical since the 1970s. Taking into account the dynamic evolution of output and real wages in the euro area during this time period, we find some weak evidence of real wage pro-cyclicality. However, given the large confidence bands for the euro area model, the positive correlations are not statistically significant. At the same time, while no clear pattern emerges from the correlation analysis, the VAR-based evidence suggests that real wages in most OECD countries, including a number of euro area countries, have been moderately pro-cyclical over this time period. Confirming the common assumption that the wage-setting process is more responsive to business cycle fluctuations in the USA than in European countries, most OECD countries show less pro-cyclical wages than those in the USA.

In terms of the differences in cyclicality due to differences in deflators, model specification and time horizon, we find statistically significant differences. We find that real wages are more pro-cyclical when the CPI is used to deflate nominal wages, as opposed to the GDP deflator, and when the VAR is estimated in terms of first differences rather than levels. Finally, there is some evidence that the correlations tend to become more pro-cyclical when the forecast horizon is extended. This may reflect the longer-term nature of wage contracts that allow wages to adjust to changes in business cycle conditions only with a significant lag.

Overall, these results suggest an important role for cross-country differences in terms of average cyclicality of real wages. While it is possible that some of the cross-country differences reflect different shocks as causes of business cycle fluctuations, it is also likely that the measures of average cyclicality over the long time period covered in this study relate to more structural determinants of real wage adjustment. Compared to the role of institutions as determinants of other labour market variables (such as unemployment), little is known about their role as factors affecting average real wage cyclicality. We provide the first evidence that suggests that labour market institutions indeed matter for cyclicality of real wages. Our results suggest that higher coordination in wage-setting, higher unemployment benefits and stronger employment protection legislation tend to be associated with a reduction in the pro-cyclicality of real wages. However, given the simple analysis presented here, more research is clearly needed to further pin down the role of labour market institutions as factors affecting real wage cyclicality. In particular, further work is needed on the role of changes in institutions over time, complementarities between institutions and changes in the composition of the workforce.

In addition, the current set of results could be extended in various other dimensions. First, band-pass results could be calculated for different periodicity bands to obtain short-run and long-run correlations, an approach that is closely linked to the VAR-based methodology already applied here (see Den Haan and Sumner 2004). A possible alternative to this approach would be to calculate measures of cyclicality using spectral analysis (closely related to the band-pass methodology: see Forni et al. 2001). Second, additional analysis for the manufacturing sector could help to further pin down causes of the differences across studies of real wage cyclicality. For example, results using total compensation per employee for the whole economy may reflect both important sectoral differences and the impact of variation in hours worked per worker. While data for hours worked are typically not available at the whole economy level, this issue could be investigated using data for the manufacturing sector.

NOTES

1. The views of this paper reflect those of the authors and not those of the European Central Bank. We would like to thank the participants at the ECB/CEPR Labour Market Workshop 'What helps or hinders labour market adjustments in Europe?' and the AIEL conference in Modena for their comments. We would also like to thank Gilles Mourre for valuable discussions and contributions to a preliminary version of the paper as well as for the construction of a first version of the dataset, and Neale Kennedy and Geoff Kenny for comments on a previous version of the paper. E-mail addresses: julian.messina@gmail.com; strozzi.chiara@unimore.it; jarkko.turunen@ecb.int.
2. Another branch of literature is concerned with estimating wage cyclicality using micro data. This allows controlling for changes in the composition of the workforce over the business cycle (Solon et al. 1994). These studies typically find that composition bias masks a pro-cyclical variation in the data. The main disadvantage of studies in this category, particularly relevant for cross-country comparisons, is the lack of homogeneous

data for a large set of countries and over long time periods. Our main interest here is related to achieving a better understanding of the behaviour of aggregate wages over the business cycle and the differences and similarities across countries and not on the response of individual wages to business cycle fluctuations. Therefore, these studies are not included in this review.

3. This group of studies includes Bodkin (1969), Otani (1980), Sumner and Silver (1989), Abraham and Haltiwanger (1995), Basu and Taylor (1999) and Hart and Malley (2000). A related class of papers adopts the static approach to focus on more disaggregated or industry data, for example, Chirinko (1980), Bils (1987) and Swanson (1999).

4. See, for example, Neftci (1978), Sargent (1978), Geary and Kennan (1982), Kennan (1988) and Mohammadi (2003). The structural VAR approach is adopted, for example, by Blanchard and Quah (1989), Gamber and Joutz (1993), Mocan and Topyan (1993), Fleischman (1999) and Balmaseda et al. (2000).

5. See Malley et al. (2002).

6. Recent cross-country analysis of real wage cyclicality in OECD countries can be found in Balmaseda et al. (2000), Basu and Taylor (1999) and Christodoulakis et al. (1995). The focus in Basu and Taylor (1999) is on the description of business cycle facts using historical annual data. They measure real wage cyclicality using the contemporaneous correlation of band-pass filtered series pooling together data from a number of countries. Balmaseda et al. (2000) estimate structural VAR models in an attempt to characterize the effects of shocks to labour markets. Christodoulakis et al. (1995) analyse the correlation between Hodrick-Prescott filtered real wages and GDP in a number of European countries. Compared to these studies we provide more comprehensive evidence of real wage cyclicality by comparing different data and methods, and documenting country heterogeneity after controlling for these differences.

7. Prior to filtering the data were extended forwards using forecasts to cover the period from 1970q1 to 2005q4. All data are seasonally adjusted.

8. Alternatively, employment as a measure more closely linked to labour market developments could be used. Indeed it is likely that the response of wages to changes in employment is different from the response to changes in total output. Investigating this dimension is left for further research.

9. The cycle is meant to correspond roughly to the growth cycle, that is, to deviations from potential growth. The choice of the cycle length is largely based on the literature on the US business cycle and, in particular, on the description of the NBER business cycle dating committee. The results of the CEPR business cycle committee indicate similar business cycle lengths for the euro area (see www.cepr.com).

10. As a robustness check we have compared these results with results that emerge using two alternative methods of filtering the data: the (annual) growth rate (that is, calculated as the four-quarter difference of the log series) and the Hodrick-Prescott filter. From a simple graphical inspection it emerges that the growth rate series shows trending behaviour that is likely to affect the results. Furthermore, as expected, both the growth rate and the Hodrick-Prescott filtered cycles show short-term movements that are likely to reflect noise rather than cyclical movements. Correlation analysis reveals that using the band-pass filtered and Hodrick-Prescott filtered data the correlations are very similar. In contrast, the contemporaneous correlation using growth rates is clearly positive.

11. As a robustness check we also computed the correlation analysis with the Hodrick-Prescott filtered series, and the results are broadly consistent with the band-pass filtered data. In particular with the Hodrick-Prescott filtered data there are more cases where the contemporaneous correlation between wages and GDP is positive and significant. This evidence is also confirmed by the results of Christodoulakis et al. (1995), who analyse the correlation between Hodrick-Prescott filtered real wages and GDP in European countries. Their overall conclusion is similar to our evidence based on the band-pass filtered series. To further test the robustness of our results, we have also computed the correlation analysis between band-pass filtered series using a different sample period, that is, from 1980 onwards. Results for the shorter sample show that, as expected, the

choice of the sample period matters for individual countries. For example, results indicate that real wages have been more pro-cyclical in Japan during the last twenty years than suggested by the results for the full sample. However, no common pattern (across countries) emerges from the comparison. Results are available upon request.

12. For recent applications of the methodology see Camacho et al. (2004) and Vázquez (2002).
13. The mean of the replications coincides closely with the result from the model for the full sample.
14. Note that in general the confidence bands depend also on the uncertainty related with the estimation of the underlying VAR model. Thus, in addition to a possible lack of co-movement between the two series, the large significance bands may also point to problems with the specification of the simple VAR for the euro area.
15. Note that there is some variation in the number of lags and the deterministic variables included in the country models as indicated by the Akaike criterion. In addition, while the same criteria were used to select model specifications in both cases, the country models generally include significantly more lags than the models using area-wide data shown before.
16. For empirical contributions focusing on the role of the type of shocks on real wage cyclicality see also Balmaseda et al. (2000) and Abraham and Haltiwanger (1995).
17. Results are available upon request.
18. Note that the dependent variables are estimated in the first step, and that as a result the t-statistics may be biased upwards in the second-stage regressions (see Feenstra and Hanson 1999). However, it is unlikely that the message from the regressions would change after this correction given the relatively small size of the standard errors in the regressions.

REFERENCES

Abraham, K.G. and J.C. Haltiwanger (1995), 'Real wages over the business cycle', *Journal of Economic Literature*, **33**, 1215–64.

Balmaseda, M., J.J. Dolado and J.D. López-Salido (2000), 'The dynamic effects to shocks to labour markets: evidence from OECD countries', *Oxford Economic Papers*, **52**, 3–23.

Basu, S. and A.M. Taylor (1999), 'Business cycles in an international historical perspective', *Journal of Economic Perspectives*, **13** (2), 45–68.

Baxter, M. and R.G. King (1999), 'Measuring business cycles: approximate band-pass filters for economic time series', *Review of Economics and Statistics*, **81**, 575–93.

Bertola, G. (2004), 'A pure theory of job security and labor income risk', *Review of Economic Studies*, **71**, 43–61.

Bertola, G., F.D. Blau and L.M. Kahn (2002), 'Comparative analysis of labor market outcomes: lessons for the US from international long-run evidence', in A. Krueger and R. Solow (eds), *The Roaring Nineties: Can Full Employment be Sustained?*, New York: Russell Sage.

Bils, M. (1987), 'The cyclical behavior of marginal cost and price', *American Economic Review*, **77** (5), 838–55.

Blanchard, O. and D. Quah (1989), 'The dynamic effects of aggregate demand and supply disturbances', *American Economic Review*, **79**, 655–73.

Bodkin, R.G. (1969), 'Real wages and cyclical variation in employment: a re-examination of the evidence', *Canadian Journal of Economics*, **2** (3), 352–74.

Camacho, M., G. Pérez-Quirós and L. Saiz (2004), 'Are European business cycles close enough to be just one?', Documento de Trabajo 0408, Banco de España, Servicio de Estudios.

Canova, F. (1998), 'Detrending and business cycle facts', *Journal of Monetary Economics*, **41**, 475–512.

Chirinko, R.S. (1980), 'The real wage rate over the business cycle', *Review of Economics and Statistics*, **62** (3), 459–61.

Christodoulakis, N., S.P. Dimelis and T. Kollintzas (1995), 'Comparisons of business cycles in the EC: idiosyncrasies and regularities', *Economica*, **62**, 1–27.

Den Haan, W. (2000), 'The comovement between output and prices', *Journal of Monetary Economics*, **46**, 3–30.

Den Haan, W. and S. Sumner (2002), 'Additional results for the comovement between real activity and prices in the G7', mimeo, University of California, San Diego.

Den Haan, W. and S. Sumner (2004), 'The comovemens between real activity and prices in the G7', *European Economic Review*, **48**, 1333–47.

ECB (2004), *The Monetary Policy of the ECB*, Frankfurt am Main: ECB.

Fagan, C., J. Henry and R. Mestre (2001), 'An area wide model for the euro area', ECB Working Paper 42.

Feenstra, R. and G. Hanson (1999), 'The impact of outsourcing and high technology capital on wages: estimates for the United States, 1979–1990', *Quarterly Journal of Economics*, **114** (3), 907–40.

Forni, M., L. Reichlin and C. Croux (2001), 'A measure of the comovement for economic variables: theory and empirics', *Review of Economics and Statistics*, **83**, 232–41.

Fleischman, C. (1999), 'The causes of business cycles and the cyclicality of real wages', Board of Governors of the Federal Reserve Bank Finance and Economics Discussion Series 99/53.

Gamber, E.N. and F.L. Joutz (1993), 'The dynamic effects of aggregate demand and supply disturbances: comment', *American Economic Review*, **83**, 1387–93.

Geary, P.T. and J. Kennan (1982), 'The employment-real wage relationship', *Journal of Political Economy*, **90** (4), 854–71.

Golden, M., P. Lange and M. Wallerstein (2002), *Union Centralization among Advanced Industrial Societies: An Empirical Study*, dataset available at http://www.shelley.polisci.ucla.edu/data.

Hart, R.A. and J.R. Malley (2000), 'Marginal cost and price over the business cyle: comparative evidence from Japan and the United States', *European Journal of Political Economy*, **16**, 547–69.

Holden, S. and F. Wulfsberg (2004), 'Downward nominal wage rigidity in Europe', CESifo Working Paper 1177.

Kennan, J. (1988), 'Equilibrium interpretations of employment and real wage fluctuations', in S. Fischer (ed.), *NBER Macroeconomics Annual*, Cambridge, MA: MIT Press, pp. 157–216.

Malley, J., R.A. Hart and U. Woitek (2002), 'Manufacturing earnings and cycles: new evidence', University of Glasgow Department of Economics Working Papers 2002–16.

Mocan, H.N. and K. Topyan (1993), 'Real wages over the business cycle: evidence from a structural time series model', *Oxford Bulletin of Economics and Statistics*, **55** (4), 363–89.

Mohammadi, H. (2003), 'The cyclical behaviour of real wages in the United States:

a historical perspective', Illinois State University Department of Economics Working Paper, April.

Neftci, S.N. (1978), 'A time-series analysis of the real wages-employment relationship', *Journal of Political Economy*, **86** (2), 281–91.

Nickell, S. and L. Nunziata (2001), 'Employment patterns in OECD countries', CEP Discussion Paper 448.

OECD (1997), 'Economic performance and the structure of collective bargaining', in *Employment Outlook*, Chapter 3, Paris: OECD.

Otani, I. (1980), 'Real wages and the business cycles revisited', *Review of Economics and Statistics*, **48** (7), 301–4.

Sargent, T.J. (1978), 'Estimation of dynamic labor demand schedules under rational expectations', *Journal of Political Economy*, **86** (6), 1009–44.

Smets, F. and R. Wouters (2003), 'An estimated dynamic stochastic general equilibrium model of the euro area', *Journal of the European Economic Association*, **1** (5), 1123–75.

Solon, G., R. Barsky and J.A. Parker (1994), 'Measuring the cyclicality of real wages: how important is the composition bias?', *Quarterly Journal of Economics*, **109** (1), 1–25.

Sumner, S. and S. Silver (1989), 'Real wages, employment and the Phillips Curve', *Journal of Political Economy*, **97** (3), 706–20.

Swanson, E.T. (1999), 'Measuring the cyclicality of real wages: how important is aggregation across industries?', Board of Governors of the Federal Reserve System Working Paper 99–52.

Vázquez, J. (2002), 'The co-movement between output and prices in the EU15 countries: an empirical investigation', *Applied Economics Letters*, **9**, 957–66.

DISCUSSION

Karl Pichelmann

Commenting on the chapter by Messina, Strozzi and Turunen has turned out to be a very pleasant task assignment. The authors provide a considerable body of evidence on the degree of real wage cyclicality in the euro area, single euro area countries and a number of non-euro area OECD countries. In addition to standard correlation analysis of detrended real wages and aggregate output, they also use a VAR approach to better capture the dynamics in the co-movement of the two series. Moreover, the authors take a lot of care to test whether the differences in the estimated degree of real wage cyclicality are driven by choices regarding deflators, model specification and time horizon, or whether they reflect genuine cross-country differences. Finally, they attempt to relate the cyclicality of real wages to a number of labour market institutions, but – as acknowledged by the authors themselves – this part of the analysis remains still rather preliminary.

Obviously, the brief discussion possible here cannot do full justice to the wealth of the empirical findings. Thus, I will concentrate on a limited number of measurement and methodological issues which may bear upon the interpretation of the empirical findings in the chapter.

(i) Wages per hour or per worker? Data limitations force the authors to use nominal compensation per employee as the relevant wage series in the analysis. Obviously, this may introduce a pro-cyclicality bias, since average hours worked tend to increase in a boom and vice versa. Perhaps more important in the context of the chapter is that the cyclicality of hours worked is likely to be affected by labour market institutions such as overtime regulations, short-time work schemes temporary lay-off practices and so on. However, regulations of this sort are themselves likely to interact with other labour market institutions analysed in the chapter and probably also with the wage-setting process proper. This already points to a subtle and fairly complex relationship betwen labour market institutions and the cyclicality of real wages.

(ii) Consumption wages or producer wages? In general it is hard to say whether it is more appropriate to use a consumer price deflator or a producer price deflator to construct the real wage series. The choice is not made easier in the present chapter by the fact that the labour market institutions analysed here are likely to impact upon both the labour demand and the labour supply schedule. Note though, that under the stylized assumptions of a simple competitive model with independently distributed labour supply and demand shocks and some other factor that affects the wedge between producer and consumer prices, the consumption wage will be more pro-cyclical than the production wage (Abraham and Haltiwanger 1995).

(iii) Choice of the sampling period? The choice of time period under investigation is probably very critical, since shocks of different types can have very different implications for the cyclicality of the real wage. For example, as pointed out by Abraham and Haltiwanger, technology shocks that induce business cycle slumps will tend to produce pro-cyclical real wage behaviour, whereas nominal shocks of the textbook variety will generate counter-cyclical real wage movements. It is not unreasonable to assume that over the past 35 years or so some cyclical episodes were driven more by shocks to the labour supply schedule, while others were driven more by shocks to the labour demand schedule. In consequence, it is highly likely that the nature of the co-movement between real wages and output has fluctuated over time. Clearly, labour market institutions have also changed quite significantly over time in most countries.

(iv) How to interpret the empirical findings? In my view, the major problem with this type of measurement of aggregate real wage cyclicality is the almost complete lack of a theoretical structural framework that would allow the attachment of an unambiguous economic meaning to the empirical results. In the absence of such a framework, it is impossible to identify the driving mechanisms and to link the degree of real wage cyclicality to the relative intensity of the shocks that shift the labour supply and demand schedules. Yet the temptation is high: For example, from the observation that real wages in most OECD countries have been less pro-cyclical than in the USA, the authors jump to the conclusion that the wage-setting process in the USA is more responsive to business cycle fluctuations than in Europe. While this is certainly a possible and perhaps even plausible interpretation, it is just one out of many other explanations that could be given. Indeed, the role of labour market institutions needs to be better explored. We have a fairly good understanding in a standard new Keynesian imperfect competition framework of how they affect the average mark-up wages over the competitive wage; however, we know much less about the impact of labour market institutions on the cyclical variability of the wage mark-up. Needless to say that we have to get price-setting behaviour into the full picture as well, since counter-cyclical price mark-ups could easily yield pro-cyclical real wages.

Reference

Abraham, K. and J. Haltiwanger (1995), 'Real wages and the business cycle', *Journal of Economic Literature*, **33** (3), 1215–64.

3. Pension systems, social transfer programmes and the retirement decision in OECD countries[1]

Romain Duval[2]

1. INTRODUCTION

Over the future decades, population ageing will induce a substantial 'greying' of the working-age population in OECD countries. Given their currently low labour market attachment compared with prime-age workers, aggregate participation and employment rates would decline and old-age dependency ratios would rise. These evolutions, combined with the growth slow-down associated with lower growth rates of the working-age population, would put increasing pressure on living standards and the fiscal sustainability of social expenditures. Increasing the labour force and employment of older workers, not least by raising effective retirement ages,[3] could help alleviate the burden of ageing populations by increasing output and curbing the projected increases in spending on old-age pensions, while at the same time generating higher tax revenues to finance them. More broadly, as this chapter will make clear, there is evidence that higher labour force participation of older workers would be welfare-enhancing in many countries.

Despite the potential gains associated with later retirement, the steep decline in the effective retirement age that has prevailed since the first oil shock has been at best reversed slightly in a few OECD countries during the 1990s, and has simply come to a halt in most others. As a result, effective retirement ages remain significantly lower than in the early 1970s. However, there is considerable variation across countries in terms of both current levels of participation rates of older workers and the magnitude of their past declines. In 2001 the participation rates of males aged 55–64 ranged from under 40 per cent in Belgium, Hungary and Luxembourg to over 80 per cent in Iceland, Japan, Mexico and Switzerland, and the cross-country dispersion was even larger for females. Starting from comparable levels in the late 1960s, the participation rates of older males remained broadly stable in Japan until the mid-1990s while they declined by almost 40 percentage points in Finland and the Netherlands.

A broad range of factors identified in the literature may account for the trend decline and the cross-country variation in effective retirement ages. Some of these primarily affect labour supply, such as wealth effects associated with rising living standards, increased demand for leisure, and policies that distort retirement incentives, including through the design of welfare systems. Other factors affect supply indirectly via labour demand, such as: (i) declining relative productivity and wages of low-skilled older workers in times of rapid technological change (Peracchi and Welch 1994; Lee 2003), (ii) insufficient training, (iii) rigid age–earnings profiles – supported by specific institutional arrangements of which some reflect policies (high minimum wage, stringent employment protection legislation) reducing the employment opportunities of the older unemployed, thereby discouraging them to remain in the job market – and (iv) temporary negative demand shocks leading to irreversible labour force withdrawal. Some of these demand-side influences tend to reinforce each other. For instance, rigid age–earnings profiles can provide insufficient incentives to engage in training, thereby magnifying the decline in productivity of older workers. At the same time they can hinder the wage response to this productivity decline. As a result, demand for older workers declines and unemployment increases, thereby encouraging older workers to leave the labour market.

The focus of this chapter is mainly on early retirement incentives embedded in pension systems and a number of social transfer programmes used de facto as early retirement schemes. This relatively narrow focus on social protection systems is adopted for various reasons. First, in reasonably well-functioning labour and product markets supply-side factors should be the major long-run determinants of labour force participation, even though in practice market imperfections may also assign an influential role to demand-side factors. In this chapter, demand-side policies, such as tax wedges, minimum wages, employment protection legislation or active labour market policies, are indirectly taken into account – to the extent that they affect labour force participation indirectly via their impact on unemployment ('discouraged worker' effect) – but not explicitly explored. Second, reducing early retirement incentives may to a certain extent contribute to easing labour demand constraints, for example by lengthening the pay-back period for investment in training. They may also reduce the risk that temporary negative demand shocks induce some older workers to withdraw irreversibly from the labour market, thereby leading to permanent labour supply effects. Third, other supply-side factors, such as living standards and/or demand for leisure, cannot account a priori for the large differences in effective retirement ages observed in the OECD area, and even less so for the fact that these differences have widened over time.[4] This hints at a significant impact of retirement incentives embedded in social systems. Finally, adjusting these systems to better cope with ageing populations is a main policy target in OECD countries and is the main instrument available for policymakers to raise labour force participation of older workers.

The remainder of this chapter is organized as follows. Section 2 presents descriptive results regarding early retirement incentives embedded in pension schemes and other welfare systems – such as unemployment, disability or special early retirement benefits that have been used as pathways into early retirement – both across countries and over time. Section 3 presents preliminary cross-country econometric evidence about the overall impact of these schemes on labour force participation of older males. Section 4 provides more in-depth econometric analysis, based on panel data estimates. Section 5 sums up the main findings and concludes.

2.   ASSESSING EARLY RETIREMENT INCENTIVES EMBEDDED IN OLD-AGE PENSION SYSTEMS AND THEIR EVOLUTION OVER TIME

Three main characteristics of old-age pension systems, presented each in turn below, can affect the retirement decisions of older male workers: (i) standard and early ages of entitlement to pension benefits, when associated with liquidity constraints and/or 'customary' effects, (ii) the generosity of pension benefits, and (iii) the implicit marginal tax attached to them.

2.1   Standard and Early Ages of Entitlement to Old-Age Pension Benefits

In theory, retirement eligibility does not per se induce effective retirement. Under a certain set of assumptions, standard and early ages of entitlement to benefits would even have no direct effect on the retirement decisions of older workers, over and above their indirect impact via pension wealth levels and implicit taxes on continued work (see below). When trading-off between consumption and leisure/retirement over their life cycle, forward-looking individuals could always set their retirement age at the optimal level chosen to maximize their welfare by borrowing or lending in capital markets. Since there is a priori no reason for the optimal retirement age to be equal to the standard age, the latter should not per se affect the retirement decision.

However, there is ample evidence that actual retirement decisions do not conform to standard life-cycle models on this specific point. Indeed, a common feature of empirical studies of the retirement decision is that even fairly detailed microeconomic models cannot explain the large jumps in retirement rates occurring at early and standard retirement ages (Gruber and Wise 2002). At least four factors may account for this apparent impact of standard and early entitlement ages on the effective retirement age: (i) some individuals are 'liquidity-constrained', which makes them unable to borrow in order to retire before pension benefits are available, (ii) custom or accepted practice induce people to retire at 'customary' ages (Lumsdaine et al. 1996), (iii) workers are myopic or information-constrained, that is, they do not assess accurately actuarial incentives/ disincentives to continued work embedded in pension systems and thus tend to retire at the earliest age at which benefits become available, and in some cases, (iv) individuals may not be allowed to continue working after the standard retirement age.

The standard age of eligibility to pension benefits differs substantially across OECD countries (Table 3.1). It is currently set at 65 years in two-thirds of them, but ranges from a low of 60 in a few countries (France, Korea, Slovak Republic and Turkey) to a high of 67 in some Nordic countries (Denmark, Iceland and Norway). There is somewhat wider cross-country variance in standard ages for females because this is still lower in several countries than ages for male retirement (Austria, Belgium, Czech Republic, Poland, Slovak Republic, Switzerland, Turkey and the UK). However, in most of these countries gradual convergence towards male levels has already started or is scheduled in the future. There are even greater cross-country differences in early eligibility ages than in standard ages, but interpreting their impact on retirement incentives is not straightforward because pension penalties for early withdrawal also differ considerably.

In the majority of OECD countries, standard and – to a lesser extent – early ages have remained constant since the late 1960s. In those countries where changes have occurred, a general pattern of cuts emerges in the 1970s to the 1980s (Canada, Finland, Germany, Ireland, the Netherlands, Norway, Spain and Sweden), followed by a few increases (Finland, Italy, New Zealand and Sweden) since the beginning of the 1990s. In New Zealand, the rapid transition from 60 to 65 in the standard retirement age during the 1990s was accompanied by a pick-up in the labour force participation of the 55–64 age group by over 15 percentage points – a larger rise than in any other OECD country over the past three decades.

2.2   Replacement Rates and Pension Wealth Levels

Under a certain set of conditions labour force participation should be independent from replacement rate levels. According to standard life-cycle theory a Pay-As-You-Go (PAYGO) scheme that pays pension benefits

Table 3.1 Standard and early ages of entitlement to old-age pension benefits

	Males								Females			
	Early age				Standard age				Standard age			
	1969	1979	1989	2003	1969	1979	1989	2003	1969	1979	1989	2003
Australia	65	65	65	55	65	65	65	65	60	60	60	62.5
Austria	65	65	65	65	65	65	65	65	60	60	60	60
Belgium	60	60	60	60	65	65	65	60	60	60	60	63
Canada	66	65	60	60	66	65	65	65	66	65	65	65
Czech Republic	–	–	–	58.5	–	–	–	61.5	–	–	–	59.5
Denmark	67	67	67	65	67	67	67	65	67	67	67	65
Finland	65	65	60	62	65	65	65	65	65	65	65	65
France	60	60	60	60	65	65	60	60	65	65	60	60
Germany	65	63	63	63	65	65	65	65	65	65	65	65
Greece	60	60	60	60	60	60	65	65	55	55	65	65
Hungary	–	–	60	62	–	–	60	62	–	–	55	62
Iceland	67	67	67	65	67	67	67	67	–	–	67	67
Ireland	70	65	65	65	70	66	66	66	70	66	66	66
Italy	55	55	55	57	60	60	60	65	55	55	55	65
Japan	60	60	60	60	65	65	65	65	65	65	65	65
Korea	–	–	60	55	–	–	60	60	–	–	60	60
Luxembourg	62	62	60	60	65	65	65	65	62	60	65	65
Mexico	–	65	65	65	–	65	65	65	–	65	65	65
Netherlands	65	62	60	60	65	65	65	65	65	65	65	65
Norway	70	67	67	67	70	67	67	67	70	67	67	67

New Zealand	60	60	65	65	60	65	65	65	60	65
Poland	—	—	65	65	—	—	65	—	—	60
Portugal	65	65	55	65	65	65	65	65	62	65
Slovak Republic	—	—	60	60	—	—	—	—	—	57
Spain	65	60	60	65	65	65	55	65	65	65
Sweden	63	60	61	65	65	67	67	65	65	65
Switzerland	65	65	63	65	65	62	62	62	62	63
Turkey	60	55	60	60	55	65	55	50	50	55
UK	65	65	65	65	65	65	60	60	60	60
USA	62	62	62	65	65	65	65	65	60	65

Notes: Australia: minimum retirement age (that is, age at which superannuation savings can be drawn) will increase to 60 over the period 2015–25; standard age for women to be increased from age 62.5 to age 65 between 2003 and 2013. Austria: early age of eligibility does not incorporate special early retirement for long insurance years, which will be progressively phased out (following the 2003 reform) but could still be accessed from age 61.5 in 2003 (60 in 1969, 1979 and 1989). Standard age for women to be increased from age 60 to age 65 between 2024 and 2033. Belgium: standard age for women scheduled to rise to age 65 by 2009. Czech Republic: standard and minimum retirement ages are scheduled to rise gradually to reach age 62 for men and age 61 for women (with no children) in 2007. Greece: standard age is 62 for men and 57 for women who first started to work before 1992. Iceland: early retirement age in 2003 is still 67 for the basic pension. However most occupational pension schemes, which are progressively maturing, set the minimum retirement age at 65. Italy: minimum retirement age is the minimum age of eligibility to a seniority pension, also equal to the minimum retirement age in the new pension system. Standard age is 60 (instead of 65) for women who first started to work before 1996. Korea: standard age scheduled to rise from age 60 to age 65 between 2011 and 2033. Luxembourg: early age of eligibility does not incorporate the special early retirement scheme ('pré-retraite'), which can be accessed from age 57 with 40 years of contribution. Norway: early age of eligibility does not incorporate the special early retirement (AFP) scheme, which can be accessed from age 62 in 2003. Poland: standard age is 55 for women with 30 years of insurance. Slovak Republic: standard age for women will be 64 in 2005. Turkey: standard age for women will rise from age 60 to age 65 over 2010–20 period. Switzerland: standard age for women varies between 53 and 57 according to number of children raised. Switzerland: standard age for women will be 64 in 2005. UK: standard age for women who first started to work before 1990. UK: standard age for both men and women scheduled to rise to age 67 over 2000–22 period.

Source: US Department of Health and Human Services, *Social Security Programs Throughout the World*, various issues.

equal to the amount of contributions (or other taxes in flat-rate pension systems) paid (in present value terms) should have no effect on consumption or labour supply as long as the taxes imposed are no greater than the amount that the person would have saved voluntarily and the real interest rate equals the rate of growth of total real wages (Aaron 1982, Chapter 2; Disney 1996, Chapter 7).[5] Indeed, such quasi-funded or fully-funded schemes would simply reduce personal saving during working life by the amount of contributions paid, that is, the savings rate would be low if contributions and replacement rates were high, and vice versa.[6]

In practice, however, redistributive elements in schemes, changes in scheme provisions as well as demographic changes, lack of information and short-time horizons imply that public pension systems affect the distribution of income and wealth both across and within generations, thereby creating 'wealth effects' on the retirement decision (Disney 1996). Indeed, the future stream of benefits to which older workers are entitled can be regarded as their old-age pension wealth, which is a share of their total wealth. Hence, an unexpected[7] increase in the level of pension benefits of older workers not offset by an increase in their tax payroll creates windfall gains in the value of their retirement and total assets. The resulting increase in their demand for both consumption goods and leisure pushes them to retire earlier than expected, in so far as retirement is a form of leisure concentrated at the end of the working life.[8] Assuming no further institutional or demographic shocks, these participation effects then fade over time as new cohorts, unaffected by redistribution between past generations, replace older ones.[9]

The most straightforward indicator of the generosity of pension benefits is the replacement rate, which corresponds to the ratio of annual benefits to earnings just prior to retirement.[10] However, there is no obvious method to compute this indicator because its level varies depending on a large number of factors.[11] For the purpose of this chapter, replacement rates have been constructed for illustrative cases under a set of common simplifying assumptions.[12] They are defined here as average *expected* replacement rates over a future five-year period, and are computed at ages 55, 60 and 65 for 22 OECD countries (Appendix 3.1).[13]

At present,[14] average expected gross replacement rates at ages 60 and 65 differ noticeably across OECD countries (Figure 3.1). At age 60, they range from 0 in those countries where the early age of eligibility is at least 65 (Austria,[15] Iceland, Ireland, Norway,[16] New Zealand and the UK) to over 70 per cent in several countries where people can claim generous old-age pension benefits in their early sixties (Korea, Luxembourg, the Netherlands,[17] Portugal and Spain). At age 65, they range from less than 40 per cent in Ireland and Norway to as high as 100 per cent in Hungary and Luxembourg.

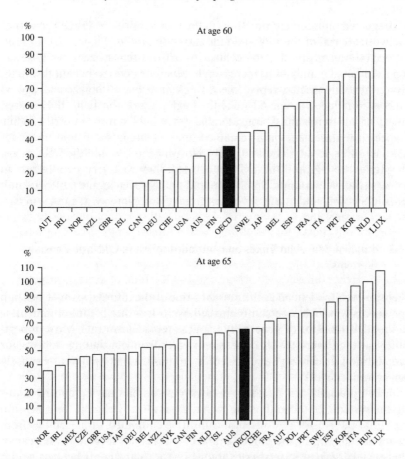

Notes: For the Netherlands, the calculation at age 60 is based on a 'typical' early retirement (VUT) scheme. For Czech Republic, Hungary, Mexico, Poland and Slovak Republic, the calculations are done only at age 65 for a single worker with average earnings. Abbreviations: AUS Australia, AUT Austria, BEL Belgium, CAN Canada, CZE Czech Republic, FIN Finland, FRA France, DEU Germany, HUN Hungary, ISL Iceland, IRL Ireland, ITA Italy, JAP Japan, KOR Korea, LUX Luxembourg, MEX Mexico, NLD Netherlands, NZL New Zealand, NOR Norway, POL Poland, PRT Portugal, SVK Slovakia, ESP Spain, SWE Sweden, CHE Switzerland, GBR United Kingdom, USA United States.

Source: Author's estimates.

Figure 3.1   Average expected replacement rates over next five years in current old-age pension systems, average across six situations (three earnings levels and two marital statuses)

Expected replacement rates rose in the vast majority of OECD countries between the end of the 1960s and the end of the 1980s (Figure 3.2). The rise at age 60 was mostly due to declines in early retirement ages, while at age 65 it stemmed mainly from increasingly generous pension benefit formulas. By contrast, expected replacement rates have been stabilized at age 65 and even reduced at age 60 since the beginning of the 1990s.[18] However, these broad trends mask considerable differences across countries. While expected replacement rates remained fairly stable in some countries over the last three decades (Ireland, Italy, Norway, the UK and the USA at age 60; Italy, the UK and the USA at age 65), they rose very significantly in others (the Netherlands, Spain, Finland and Sweden at age 60;[19] Finland, Spain, Sweden, and to a lesser extent Ireland and Norway, at age 65) in particular at early ages.

2.3   Implicit Marginal Taxes on Continued Work in Old-Age Pension Systems

Pension wealth, defined as the present value of the future stream of pension payments to which a person is entitled over his or her life in retirement, is a broader indicator of generosity than the replacement rate. Most importantly, at each age, *changes* in pension wealth from continuing working for an additional year can be regarded as an implicit marginal tax or subsidy on continued work.

More precisely, working for an extra year implies paying contributions to the system. Provided that the individual is already eligible for a pension and that the receipt of a pension cannot be combined with earnings from work, remaining in the labour market also implies forgoing one year of benefits. If the cost in terms of forgone pensions and contributions paid is not exactly offset by an increase in future pension benefits, the pension system is said to be 'actuarially non-neutral' and carries an implicit tax on continued work. Formulating this definition in terms of pension wealth, actuarial non-neutrality arises when the change in pension wealth from working for an additional year is less than the value of contributions paid.

In theory, labour supply effects of implicit taxes on continued work created by pension schemes are ambiguous (Mitchell and Fields 1984). As suggested by Lazear (1986), over and above the usual wage rate, the implicit tax/subsidy on continued work can be regarded as an additional component of the 'true wage'. From this perspective, a rise in the implicit tax on continued work – due for instance to a cut in the pension accrual rate – is equivalent to a fall in the wage rate, producing opposite substitution and income effects: the lower financial gain from postponing retirement reduces the opportunity cost of retiring earlier (negative substitution effect), but at

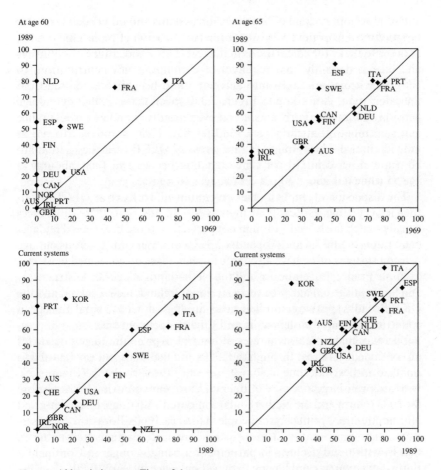

Notes: Abbreviations: see Figure 3.1.

Figure 3.2   Historical changes in average expected replacement rates in old-age pension systems, average across six situations (three earnings levels and two marital statuses), in percentages

the same time provides lower income for each future year of work, thereby inducing later retirement (positive income effect). In practice, however, there is overwhelming empirical evidence that the substitution effect dominates (Lazear 1986; Lumsdaine and Mitchell 1999). Therefore high implicit taxes on continued work tend to bias the retirement decision towards early labour market withdrawal.

In this chapter, implicit taxes on continuing working for five more years are computed (for a single worker with average earnings at ages 55, 60 and 65) for both normal old-age pension systems and other social transfer programmes (Appendix 3.2). As for the computation of replacement rates, in order to make the calculations manageable for a wide range of countries and time periods, the tax treatment of earnings – only contributions to pension schemes are taken into account – and benefits are omitted from the calculation. According to Figure 3.3, implicit taxes created by old-age pension systems are fairly small, and even negative in a few cases (France and Luxembourg) at early ages, but they have a clear tendency to rise as individuals age. The average tax rate across 22 OECD countries is found to be below 5 per cent (10 per cent excluding France and Luxembourg) at age 55 while it is above 30 per cent at ages 60 and 65.[20]

The dispersion of implicit taxes on continued work across OECD countries is very large, especially at high ages.[21] In addition, these differences usually match fairly well – though not perfectly – those in expected replacement rates (Figure 3.4 and Appendix 3.3):[22] countries with generous old-age pension systems often have also large implicit taxes on continued work (for example France, Luxembourg and the Netherlands at age 60; Austria, Italy and Spain at age 65) and vice versa (Iceland, Ireland, New Zealand and the UK). Broadly speaking, implicit taxes are high in Continental European countries compared with Nordic and English-speaking ones.

Like expected replacement rates, although less pronounced, implicit taxes on continued work rose through the 1970s and the 1980s, but have started to stabilize and even decline in some cases since the early 1990s (Figure 3.5). Increases were large in some Continental European countries (France before the 2003 reform and the Netherlands) compared with English-speaking and Nordic countries, primarily for people in their early 60s. Both of these observations are consistent with historical labour force participation patterns, that is, with trend declines in participation being stronger in Continental European countries and having flattened out since the early 1990s.

2.4 Implicit Marginal Taxes on Continued Work in Other Social Transfer Programmes

In a number of OECD countries, relatively easy access to various social transfer programmes has often enabled certain categories of older workers to withdraw from the labour market before the early age of entitlement to old-age pension benefits. Such schemes, which include special early retirement provisions as well as unemployment-related and disability benefits (Blöndal and Scarpetta 1998; Casey et al. 2003), often entail high implicit taxes on continued work for two main reasons: replacement rates are usually high and pension rights continue to accrue, even if, in some cases, at a reduced rate.

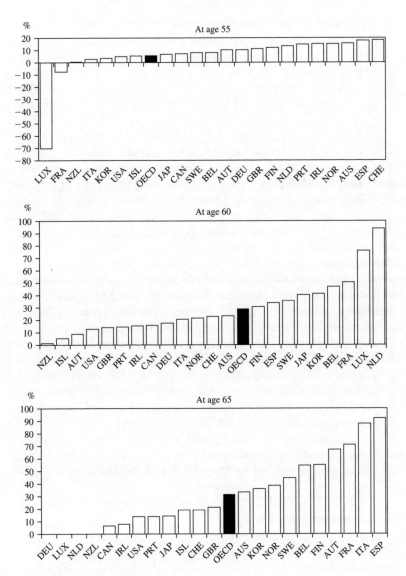

Notes: Abbreviations: see Figure 3.1.

Source: Author's estimates.

Figure 3.3   *Average implicit tax rates on continued work over next five years in current old-age pension systems, single worker with average earnings*

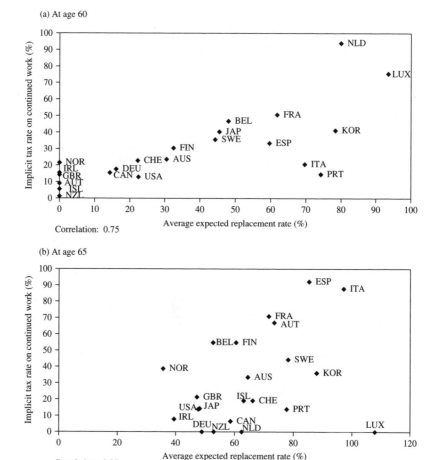

(a) At age 60

Correlation: 0.75

(b) At age 65

Correlation: 0.37

Notes: Abbreviations: see Figure 3.1.

Source: Author's estimates.

*Figure 3.4   Average expected replacement rates and implicit tax rates on
continued work in current old-age pension systems*

No attempt is made here at being comprehensive in the coverage of these
programmes. Rather, in order to provide a rough assessment of early retirement incentives arising from them, a 'typical early retirement route' is modelled along the following lines:

● In those countries where unemployment-related benefits can be used
de facto[23] to bridge the time until people are entitled to an old-age

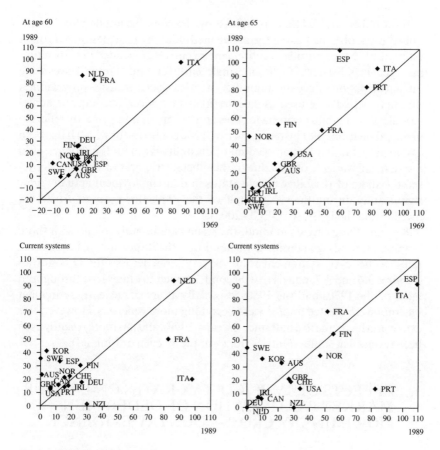

Notes: Abbreviations: see Figure 3.1.

Source: Author's estimates.

Figure 3.5 *Historical changes in average implicit tax rates on continued work in old-age pension systems, single worker with average earnings*

pension,[24] implicit taxes on continued work are computed for the same illustrative cases as for old-age pension schemes.

- Where unemployment-related schemes cannot be used effectively as an early retirement device but other schemes are available,[25] the latter are considered.
- Where no social transfer programme can be used to withdraw from the labour market before the minimum pensionable age,[26] the 'early retirement route' is simply the old-age pension pathway into retirement.

It should be stressed that, for at least two reasons, the implicit tax on continued work obtained using the above methodology provides only a rough estimate of the magnitude of retirement incentives embedded in early retirement schemes. First, the focus on a single 'early retirement route' leaves aside the participation effects of a number of other social transfer programmes that may actually be used as early retirement devices. Second, the actual strictness of eligibility criteria for these programmes is imperfectly reflected in the calculations. For instance, even in those countries for which it has been assumed that retirement on account of disability is not, or is no longer, as in Sweden, an available option due to the official strictness of eligibility criteria, the share of disability benefit status in non-employment actually grew significantly during the second half of the 1990s (for example Australia, Sweden and the USA; see OECD 2003).

Keeping these caveats in mind, the results are broadly in line with those obtained for old-age pension schemes. First, the dispersion of implicit tax rates in the 'early retirement route' is very large across OECD countries (Figures 3.6 and 3.7, panels (b)). Second, implicit tax rates rose throughout most of the 1970s and the 1980s, especially at age 55, as early retirement schemes were created and/or were becoming more generous. However, this expansion has come to a halt since the early 1990s, and has more recently even been reversed in some countries (for example Sweden or Finland).

3.　EFFECTS OF IMPLICIT TAX RATES ON LABOUR MARKET PARTICIPATION OF OLDER MEN: PRELIMINARY CROSS-COUNTRY EVIDENCE

The implicit tax on continued work is the key summary indicator of early retirement incentives embedded in pension schemes because it also captures some of the effects of both eligibility ages and the generosity of benefits. The higher the replacement rate, the higher is the 'opportunity cost' of and the implicit tax on continued work, *ceteris paribus* (Appendix 3.3). Similarly, the higher the minimum pensionable age, the lower is the implicit tax on continued work before this age, *ceteris paribus*.[27] Thus there is a rationale for focusing primarily on implicit taxes on continued work when assessing participation effects of retirement incentives embedded in pension schemes. In any event, the strong correlation between the replacement rate and the implicit tax on continued work raises a multi-collinearity issue, thereby excluding the possibility of including both variables in cross-country and/or panel data regressions using macroeconomic data.[28]

As an illustration of potential participation effects of retirement incentives embedded in 'regular' pension schemes, panels (a) in Figures 3.6 and

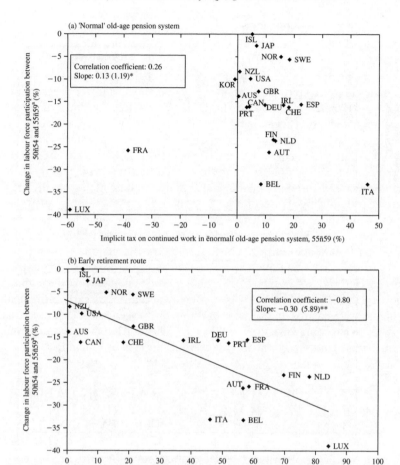

Notes: t-statistic in brackets; * significant at 5% level; ** significant at 1% level;
[a] (Pr 55–59–Pr 50–54)/Pr 50–54, per cent; [b] the early retirement route is modelled as the
unemployment benefits/assistance pathway into retirement with the exception of Ireland,
where the modelling refers to the pre-retirement allowance, and Luxembourg, where
disability benefits were considered given their widespread incidence among pensioners.
In those countries where it was considered that no early retirement scheme could be widely
used to withdraw from the labour market before the minimum pensionable age (Australia,
Canada, Iceland, Italy, Japan, Korea, New Zealand, Norway, Sweden, Switzerland and the
USA) the retirement scheme considered in the figure is simply the 'regular' old-age pension
system. Abbreviations: see Figure 3.1.

Source: Author's estimates.

Figure 3.6 *Fall in male labour force participation between 50–54 and*
55–59 and implicit tax rates on continued work (single worker
with average earnings, 1999)

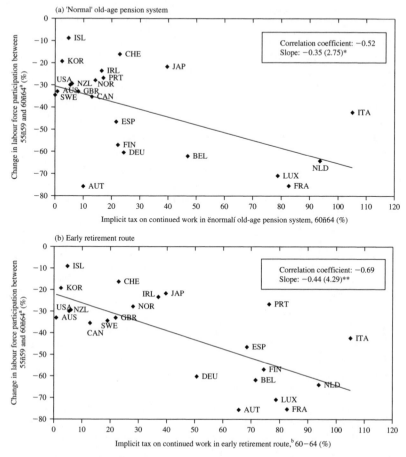

Notes: t-statistic in brackets; * significant at 5% level; ** significant at 1% level; [a] (Pr 60–64–Pr 55–59)/Pr 55–59, per cent; [b] the early retirement route is modelled as the unemployment benefits/assistance pathway into retirement with the exception of Ireland and the Netherlands, where the modelling refers to the pre-retirement allowance and a 'typical' early retirement (VUT) scheme, respectively, and Luxembourg, where disability benefits were considered given their widespread incidence among pensioners. In those countries where it was considered that no early retirement scheme could be widely used to withdraw from the labour market before the minimum pensionable age (Australia, Canada, Iceland, Italy, Japan, Korea, New Zealand, Norway, Sweden, Switzerland and the USA) the retirement scheme considered in the figure is simply the 'regular' old-age pension system. Abbreviations: see Figure 3.1.

Source: Author's estimates.

Figure 3.7   Fall in male labour force participation between 55–59 and 60–64 and implicit tax rates on continued work (single worker with average earnings, 1999)

3.7 plot the fall in male labour force participation for two age spans (55–59 and 60–64) – an implicit measure of labour market withdrawal against the corresponding implicit tax on continuing working for five more years.[29] The fall in labour force participation over the age span 55–59 appears to be unrelated to the implicit tax on continued work between ages 55 and 60 (Figure 3.7, panel (a)). This finding should come as no surprise, in so far as implicit taxes in regular pension schemes are usually low and fairly similar across countries at age 55, while differences in participation rates are large. A slightly positive, but insignificant relationship even emerges due to the position of France and Luxembourg where participation rates are low despite large implicit subsidies on continued work embedded in 'regular' old-age pension schemes between ages 55 and 60. By contrast, there is a significant bivariate correlation between the fall in male labour force participation over the age span 60–64 and the implicit tax on continued work between 60 and 65 (Figure 3.7, panel (a)). Both labour market withdrawal and implicit taxes are generally higher in Continental European countries than in Japan, Korea, English-speaking and Nordic countries.

While no clear link emerges between the fall in male labour force participation over the age span 55–59 and the implicit tax in 'regular' pension systems (Figure 3.6, panel (a)), a robust relationship emerges when the early retirement route is considered (Figure 3.6, panel (b)). For the 60–64 age group, taking into account early retirement schemes brings a more limited improvement to the cross-country relationship between labour force participation and implicit tax rates (Figure 3.7, panel (b)). These results hint at larger participation effects of early retirement programmes on workers in the 55–59 age group than on those in the 60–64 age group whose retirement decision seems to be comparatively more influenced by regular pension schemes. This finding refines those of previous studies which had already pointed to comparable cross-country correlations for broader age groups (55–64 age group in Blöndal and Scarpetta 1998; 55–69 age group in Gruber and Wise 1999a).

4. PANEL DATA ECONOMETRIC ANALYSIS OF THE LABOUR FORCE PARTICIPATION OF OLDER MALE WORKERS

4.1 Previous Studies

A broad range of microeconometric studies of the retirement decision have been conducted over the past decade for a number of OECD countries (for a summary of individual country results see for instance Blöndal and

Scarpetta 1998; Gruber and Wise 1999b, 2002). They confirm that among a variety of factors such as individual and household characteristics, economic variables such as wage earnings and retirement incentives embedded in old-age pension and early retirement schemes affect the labour supply of older workers. This result is also supported at the macroeconomic level by a variety of country case studies (see for instance the country-specific papers in Gruber and Wise 1999b). The latter are based on the idea that historical changes in old-age pension benefits rules offer 'natural experiments' to study the participation effects of early retirement incentives. For instance, when early and standard retirement ages are lowered and/or when early retirement benefits are allowed or extended, the wealth of older workers and the implicit tax on continued work tend to rise. Therefore, historical experiences showing the effective age of retirement plummeting following benefit extensions (such as Germany and France respectively in the aftermath of the 1972 and 1981 reforms) or, conversely, soaring following benefit restrictions (New Zealand during the 1990s), can be interpreted as evidence of a powerful effect of retirement incentives on the labour supply of older workers.

In comparison, panel data macroeconometric evidence remains fairly limited. Blöndal and Scarpetta (1998) find effects of old-age pension and early retirement schemes on the labour force participation of older men aged 55–64 in a panel of 15 countries from 1971 to 1995. Johnson (2000) investigates old-age pension systems only and reaches similar conclusions for males in the 60–64 and 65+ age groups in a panel containing data for 13 countries at approximately ten-year intervals from 1880 to 1990. However, in both studies the magnitude of the participation effects of early retirement incentives is relatively moderate: for instance, for the 60–64 age group Johnson estimates that only around 11 per cent of the decline in average participation rates from 1920 to 1990 can be explained by old-age pension variables.

The econometric analysis presented below combines the respective strengths of both studies, and as a result should, a priori, improve the estimates and allow richer analysis of the participation effects of retirement schemes. As in Johnson (2000), the calculation of implicit tax rates takes proper account of the possibilities of combining work with the receipt of a reduced or full pension. For instance, when benefits are not income-tested and no contributions to the pension system have to be paid, the implicit tax is simply zero because the stream of future payments is the same whether individuals keep working or not (Appendix 3.2). For instance, less strict income testing has been traditionally at the root of low implicit taxes on continued work in the Swedish and Japanese pension systems – two countries with significantly above-average participation rates of older workers. Also as in Johnson (2000), separate analysis is undertaken for the 55–59, 60–64 and 65+ age groups, while only the aggregate 55–64 age group was studied in Blöndal and Scarpetta (1998). There are several advantages associated with breaking up older males into three different age groups: (i) the narrower the age band considered, the smaller the 'demographic bias' involved in older males' participation trends,[30] (ii) isolating the 55–59 age group allows more precise analysis of the participation effects of early retirement schemes, because the latter affect, a priori, to a lesser extent the 60–64 age group, and (iii) the implicit horizon for the retirement decision is shorter and thus probably more realistic in practice (individuals are implicitly assumed to decide whether they retire immediately or remain in the labour market for five additional years, rather than ten as in Blöndal and Scarpetta 1998). Finally, as in Blöndal and Scarpetta (1998), early retirement schemes are covered, which should significantly improve the analysis of the labour force participation of the 55–59 age group and to a lesser extent the 60–64 age group, compared with Johnson (2000).

4.2 The Estimated Equation

The equation adopted, which is estimated separately for each of the 55–59, 60–64 and 65+ age groups, can be expressed as follows:

$$\Delta(PRM)_{it}/PRM_{it} \times 100 = \beta_1 \times TAX_{it} + \beta_2 \times (STANDARD\ AGE)_{it} + \beta_3 \times UR_{it} + a_i + \gamma_t + \varepsilon_{it}$$

where i and t are country and time suffices, $\Delta(PRM)_{it}/PRM_{it} \times 100$ is the difference in male labour force participation rates between two consecutive age groups (in per cent), TAX is the implicit tax on continued work, $STANDARD\ AGE$ is the standard retirement age and UR is the unemployment rate of prime-age workers.

In each of the three equations, the dependent variable is the same as in Figures 3.6 and 3.7, that is, the difference in labour force participation rates of older men between two consecutive age groups. Therefore these equations implicitly model withdrawal from the labour market and thus the retirement decision rather than the level of participation per se, which may be influenced by a number of other factors including irreversible withdrawal from the labour market at earlier ages.[31]

The main explanatory variable characterizing early retirement incentives is the implicit tax on continued work in the 'early retirement route' defined above. As mentioned in Section 3, focusing on this variable is justified on two grounds. First, it sums up various dimensions of retirement incentives such as the availability and generosity of benefits or the pension accrual rate. Second, in any event, the strong correlation between the replacement rate and the implicit tax rate raises a multi-collinearity issue, thereby excluding the possibility of identifying separately the participation effects of both variables within the same regression.

Even though the labour force participation equation estimated in this chapter is not directly derived from an option value model *à la* Stock and Wise (1990), it is implicitly consistent with such an approach. Indeed, in practice, most of the cross-country and time-series variance of the option value of postponing retirement actually comes from corresponding variance in implicit taxes on continued work, to the extent that changes in wage rates and preferences are likely to be comparatively smaller and less frequent. However, no attempt is made below at estimating a full option value model, mainly because of data limitations, particularly in a cross-country dimension.[32]

In order to test for the existence of 'customary' and/or 'liquidity' effects, the standard retirement age is introduced as a separate explanatory variable in the regressions for the 60–64 and 65+ age groups.[33] Other potential influences on the retirement decision are controlled for in two ways. First, potential discouragement effects among older workers associated with low employment opportunities are captured by the unemployment rate. Since the latter is jointly determined with participation, a potential endogeneity issue arises which is addressed by using the unemployment rate of prime-age workers instead of the old-age unemployment rate. In so far as the unemployment rate is counter-cyclical, this variable also captures business cycle effects, in addition to discouragement effects. Second, as in Johnson (2000), secular retirement trends, such as increasing demand for leisure over time and/or wealth effects stemming from rising living standards, are captured by time dummies.[34] These time-fixed effects may also absorb all shocks common to all countries, such as irreversible withdrawal from the labour market by laid-off workers in the aftermath of the two oil shocks of the 1970s.

All other determinants of older males' labour supply, which may vary across countries, are not explicitly covered by the analysis. These factors, such as insufficient training or rigid age–earnings profiles, affect the retirement decision indirectly by pressuring older workers' wages and/or by reducing their employment opportunities. To a limited extent, part of their influence may be captured indirectly by other variables in the regressions. For instance, the rigidity of age–earnings profiles is supported by specific/ institutional arrangements (high minimum wage, stringent employment protection legislation and so on) that may also affect the unemployment rate of prime-age workers, a variable included in the regressions. Similarly, the low incidence of training for older workers may partly result from the fact that high implicit taxes lower the expected retirement age. In any event, some omitted variable bias cannot be completely ruled out of the regressions below.[35] In addition, implicit taxes are measured with error, not least because of the number of simplifying assumptions underlying the calculations (Appendix 3.2), but also because the illustrative worker considered in the modelling may not be representative of the typical worker.[36, 37]

4.3 Econometric Results

For each of the 55–59, 60–64 and 65+ age groups, Table 3.2 presents three alternative regressions. All are estimated on an unbalanced panel dataset of 22 OECD countries over the period 1967–99.[38] Model A incorporates country-specific time trends rather than common time-fixed effects in order better to capture country-specific retirement trends.[39] As expected, implicit taxes on continued work and the unemployment rate of prime-age males are negatively signed and statistically significant. The standard retirement age appears to have a positive effect on the labour force participation of workers aged 65 and over, but it is not significant for the 60–64 age group. However, there is evidence that despite their statistical significance, country-specific time trends unduly capture part of the participation effects of implicit taxes on continued work. Indeed, a simple regression of the estimated coefficients of country-specific time trends on a variable[40] representative of the magnitude of implicit taxes yields significant results at the 5 per cent level for each of the three age groups: the larger the incentive to retire early in a country, the larger the estimated coefficient of its (negative) specific time trend. This finding can be imputed to the fact that changes in participation rates induced by abrupt changes in implicit taxes are usually gradual, and may thus be better captured by simple time trends. Since Model A probably understates the coefficients of implicit taxes on continued work, in Model B country-specific time trends are replaced by common time-fixed effects. All variables remain correctly signed and significant (including the standard retirement age for the 60–64 age group), but the coefficients of implicit taxes are larger and do not differ across age groups at the 5 per cent level. The latter finding comes as no surprise, given the difficulty of capturing the complex influence of early retirement schemes on the retirement decision through a single quantitative variable. Finally, Model C is the same as Model B, except that it corrects for countrywise heteroskedasticity (using feasible generalized least squares) rather than for individual heteroskedasticity (using the Huber–White sandwich estimator of variance as in Model B). The econometric results remain broadly unchanged, except that the coefficients on implicit taxes are somewhat smaller.[41]

The magnitude of estimated participation effects of implicit taxes on continued work is consistent with existing panel data estimates at the macroeconomic level. In particular, they are fairly similar to those estimated for the 60–64 age group in Johnson (2000) and are somewhat larger than in

Table 3.2 Panel data estimates of the labour force participation of older workers

Model A

Dependent variable	(Pr 55–59–Pr 50–54) /Pr 50–54 (%)	(Pr 60–64–Pr 55–59) /Pr 55–59 (%)	(Pr 65–69–Pr 60–64) /Pr 60–64 (%)
Implicit tax on continued work	−0.06 (4.23)**	−0.06 (3.54)**	−0.13 (5.43)**
Unemployment rate	−0.16 (2.97)**	−0.77 (7.85)**	−0.34 (3.32)**
Standard retirement age		−0.14 (0.39)	2.41 (6.08)**
Country-fixed effects	Yes	Yes	Yes
Country-specific time trends	Yes	Yes	Yes
Time-fixed effects	No	No	No
Observations	431	431	431
R^2	0.93	0.95	0.87

Model B

Dependent variable	(Pr 55–59–Pr 50–54) /Pr 50–54 (%)	(Pr 60–64–Pr 55–59) /Pr 55–59 (%)	(Pr 65–69–Pr 60–64) /Pr 60–64 (%)
Implicit tax on continued work	−0.11 (7.15)**	−0.17 (4.88)**	−0.15 (4.88)**
Unemployment rate	−0.12 (1.88)	−0.90 (5.95)**	−0.53 (3.98)**
Standard retirement age		1.63 (3.29)**	1.17 (3.70)**

Country-fixed effects	Yes	Yes	Yes
Country-specific time trends	No	No	No
Time-fixed effects	Yes	Yes	Yes
Observations	484	471	471
R²	0.92	0.89	0.80

Model C

Dependent variable	(Pr 55–59 - Pr 50–54) /Pr 50–54 (%)	(Pr 60–64 - Pr 55–59) /Pr 55–59 (%)	(Pr 65–69 - Pr 60–64) /Pr 60–64 (%)
Implict tax on continued work	-0.09 (8.98)**	-0.12 (5.16)**	-0.10 (5.65)**
Unemployment rate	-0.15 (3.25)**	-1.07 (10.28)**	-0.29 (3.01)**
Standard retirement age		1.27 (3.40)**	1.27 (6.22)**
Country-fixed effects	Yes	Yes	Yes
Country-specific time trends	No	No	No
Time-fixed effects	Yes	Yes	Yes
Observations	484	471	471
R²			

Notes: Absolute value of t-statistics in brackets; * significant at 5% level (no incidence); ** significant at 1% level. All regressions include country-fixed effects (significantly different from zero in all specifications). Model A: balanced panel dataset and robust standard errors. Model B: unbalanced panel dataset and robust standard errors. Model C: unbalanced panel dataset and generalized least squares used to correct for groupwise (countrywise) heteroskedasticity.

Source: Author's estimates.

Blöndal and Scarpetta (1998). Basic specifications (Table 3.2, Model B) suggest that on average a 10 percentage points decline in the implicit tax rate reduces the fall in participation rates between two consecutive (five-year) age groups of older men by about 1.5 percentage points. However, these participation elasticities with respect to implicit tax rates are almost three times lower than those found in the simple cross-country regressions presented above[42] (Figures 3.6 and 3.7, panels (b)) or in the microeconomic literature. For instance, in Gruber and Wise (2002), simulations using option value models estimated on separate microeconomic panel datasets for France, Belgium and the Netherlands suggest that a three-year delay in eligibility ages to old-age and early retirement schemes would raise the labour force participation of the 55–64 age group by about 20 points in each of these countries. The low elasticities typically found in panel data estimates using macroeconomic data may result from the difficulty of disentangling short and long-run effects and/or from the fact that historical changes in implicit tax rates – on which panel data (within) estimates are based – are measured with more error than current implicit tax rates levels. Therefore, it cannot be ruled out, as suggested by Johnson (2000), that simple cross-country regressions actually better capture the long-run participation elasticities of implicit tax rates.

On the basis of the coefficients estimated in Model B, past changes in implicit tax rates and standard retirement ages are found to explain only a third (31 per cent) of the trend decline in older males' labour force participation in OECD countries over the last three decades.[43] This contribution reaches 40 per cent when the whole model (including the effect of rising unemployment rates in a number of continental European countries) is considered. Though this is more than in Blöndal and Scarpetta (1998) or Johnson (2000), it remains clear that other determinants, such as preferences for leisure or 'demand-side' determinants, may have also played a major role in driving down participation rates.

5.   SUMMARY AND CONCLUSIONS

The analysis presented in this chapter has shown that there is currently wide dispersion across OECD countries in implicit tax rates on continued work embedded in old-age pension systems and other social transfer programmes: they are high in most continental European countries, compared with Japan, Korea, English-speaking and Nordic countries. Simple cross-country correlations suggest that such taxes induce older male workers to anticipate their retirement decision. This finding is confirmed by panel data econometric estimates, for each of the 55–59, 60–64 and 65+ age groups.

For the 55–59 age group there is clear evidence that these effects result from a number of social transfer programmes, which have been used de facto as early retirement schemes, rather than from old-age pension systems themselves. For the 60–64 and 65+ age groups, eligibility ages also appear to have a specific impact on the retirement decision, probably reflecting liquidity and/or customary effects.

Given the magnitude of retirement incentives still embedded in a number of old-age pension schemes and other social transfer programmes, the potential impact of policy reforms on labour force participation appears to be fairly large.[44] However, as in previous studies, the estimated participation effects of implicit tax rates are significantly lower than those found in microeconometric analyses of the retirement decision. In addition, past changes in implicit tax rates and standard retirement ages are found to explain only a third of the trend decline in older males' labour force participation in OECD countries over the last three decades. This suggests that even though retirement incentives embedded in old-age pension and other retirement schemes have a major impact on the retirement decision, future research should pay greater attention to other influences, such as preferences for leisure or 'demand-side' factors.

APPENDIX 3.1

Methodology and Assumptions Underlying the Computation of Replacement Rates

The replacement rate is classically defined as:

$$R_R = P_R / Y$$

where R_R is the replacement rate at age R, P_R is the pension level if retiring at age R and Y is the earnings level just before retirement.

For all possible retirement ages between 55 and 70, theoretical replacement rates in both 'normal' and early retirement schemes are computed for three earnings levels (60 per cent, 100 per cent and 140 per cent of average production workers' (APW) earnings) and two household compositions (single worker and married couple with dependent spouse of same age). Thus, these calculations enable computation of average replacement rates across six different situations. In addition to replacement rates at retirement age R, average replacement rates between ages R and $R + 4$ are also constructed.

In order to make these calculations manageable for a wide range of countries and time periods, the following assumptions are made:

- The worker is assumed to enter the labour market at age 20 and work full-time in the private sector without interruption until retirement.
- The age–earnings profile over the working life is assumed to be flat, that is, earnings are assumed to grow in line with countrywide average earnings. Under this assumption, lifetime earnings at the age of retirement are simply equal to 60 per cent, 100 per cent or 140 per cent of APW earnings, depending upon the earnings level considered. A key implication is that changes in the earnings base used in the pension benefit formula are, in general, not reflected in the calculations reported in this paper.
- The reported replacement rates only cover public schemes and mandatory or quasi-mandatory (as in Finland, the Netherlands,[45] Sweden, Switzerland or the UK) private occupational schemes. Occupational schemes offered by employers on a voluntary basis (as in Canada, Germany, Japan or the USA) are not covered.
- The tax treatment of earnings and pension benefits is omitted. The concept of gross earnings considered in the calculations excludes employers' but includes employees' contributions to social security. In so far as most OECD countries tend to apply a favourable tax treatment of pension benefits compared to gross wage earnings, gross replacement rates reported in this paper are generally lower than net replacement rates.

The main source for past and present pension rules is *Social Security Programs throughout the World*, published every two years by the US Department of Health and Human Services. In the case of European member countries, the modelling also relies heavily on MISSOC, *Social Protection in the Member States of the European Union*, published by the Commission of the European Communities. Supplementary information is obtained from national sources and contacts, and in some cases from background material collected in Blöndal and Scarpetta (1998).

APPENDIX 3.2

Methodology and Assumptions Underlying the Computation of Pension, Social Wealth and Implicit Taxes on Continued Work

The calculation of pension wealth levels is directly derived from the computation of replacement rates presented above. However, unlike the latter, which considers six different situations (three earnings levels and two marital situations), it is applied only to a single individual with APW earnings. As a first step, for each possible retirement age R between 55 and 70, the future stream of expected pension payments is computed from age R to age 105. Pension wealth is then computed as the present value of this stream using the following formula:

$$PWY_R = \sum_{A=R}^{A=105} (S_A \times R_A)/(1+r)^{(A-R)}$$

where PWY_R is the pension wealth (as a proportion of earnings) for a single individual with APW earnings retiring at age R, R_A is the replacement rate (computed as P_A/Y), that this, individual would receive at age A if he or she stops working now, r is the real discount rate, and S_A is the value of the survival function at age A. The latter is the probability of being alive at age A conditional upon being alive at age R, and is derived from country-specific mortality tables published each year by the United Nations and the World Health Organization. The survival function allows heavier discounting of pension flows received late in life, since the probability of receiving them is lower.

Pension wealth levels are computed for all possible retirement ages between 55 and 70. When the retirement age is lower than the earliest age at which a pension is available, the pension flow received before that age is simply zero. Social wealth levels are computed in a similar manner, except that the stream of payments considered is what the individual would receive through early pathways into retirement (unemployment, disability and special early retirement schemes) rather than through the 'regular' old-age pension system.

For the three retirement ages 55, 60 and 65, changes in pension or social wealth from working for five additional years (that is, from R to $R+5$) are then computed as:

$$DPWY_R = [PWY_{R+5}] \times [S_{R+5}/(1+r)^5] - PWY_R$$
$$- \sum_{A=R}^{A=R+4} [(S_A \times C_A/Y)/(1+r)^{A-R}]$$

where C_A/Y is the sum of employees and employers rates of contributions to the old-age pension system.

The choice of five-year rather than annual changes in pension or social wealth is dictated by the fact that historical series of labour force participation statistics for older men are available only for five-year age groups. Indeed, a possible measure of retirement incentives for each of the 55–59, 60–64 and 65–69 age groups is the change in pension or social wealth from remaining in the labour market during each of these life spans, that is, from working between ages 55–60, 60–65 and 65–70 respectively. When this change is negative, continuing to work for five additional years carries an implicit tax whose average over the five-year span is:

Average implicit tax on continued work beyond age $I = -DPWY_R/5$

The calculation of levels and changes in pension wealth relies on the following assumptions:

- All of the assumptions that are made to compute replacement rates (see above).
- The real discount rate is set at 3 per cent. A higher (lower) rate would produce higher (lower) implicit taxes on continued work but would not affect the results qualitatively, in particular with regard to cross-country comparisons.
- Individuals are assumed to bear the cost of employers' contributions to the old-age pension system. An alternative choice, which would have produced lower estimates of implicit taxes on continued work, would have been to consider only the share of contributions directly paid for by employees.
- Pensions are assumed to be indexed to prices. This assumption implies a slight underestimation of implicit taxes on continued work in those countries/years where/when pensions are partially or fully indexed to wages. In addition, historical modifications in pension adjustment methods are not reflected in pension wealth estimates.
- When making his decision to withdraw from the labour market or to work for five additional years, the individual is assumed to expect constant economy-wide real earnings if choosing to work. As a result, his lifetime earnings are expected to remain unchanged. This assumption has no effect on replacement rates, but it can affect the magnitude of calculated implicit tax rates across components of the pension system and more generally across countries. While there is no impact in flat-rate schemes, implicit tax rates can be overestimated in earnings-related schemes, all the more so as the reference period for earnings used in the benefit formula is long (for example in the 'new' pension system in Italy). This is because the calculations do not incorporate at the margin the automatic revaluation of past earnings in line with economy-wide earnings as is the rule in most OECD countries, that is, the potential revaluation of past earnings that could take place as a result of the increase in economy-wide earnings during the additional year of work.

• Strictly speaking, the above formula for changes in pension wealth applies only when full-time work cannot be combined with the receipt of any full or reduced pension. Even though this assumption holds for a worker with APW earnings in most countries and at most ages, this is not always true. For instance, work can be combined with the receipt of a reduced old-age pension in Japan (subject to an income test) between ages 60 and 64, or with the receipt of a full pension in New Zealand. In such instances the computation of the change in pension wealth from working for five additional years incorporates the stream of pension payments that the individual would receive over this five-year period (that is, PWY_{R+5} incorporates not only the stream of pension payments received from age $R+5$ but also those received between ages R and $R+4$). As a result, changes in pension wealth are more positive (or less negative) and implicit taxes on continued work are lower than in the case of a strict income test. In the extreme case where the receipt of a pension is not income-tested and no contributions to the old-age pension system have to be paid (for example in New Zealand from age 65), the implicit tax on continued work is simply zero because the stream of pension payments remains unchanged whether the individual keeps working or not (see for instance Johnson 2000).

APPENDIX 3.3

Theoretical Relationship between Replacement Rates and Implicit Taxes on Continued work

The existence of a direct link between the magnitude of the implicit tax rate on continued work and the level of the replacement rate is rather intuitive: the higher the replacement rate, the higher is the opportunity cost of continuing working, that is, the higher is the implicit tax on continued work, ceteris paribus. The calculations presented below establish this link more formally and show that it is in fact more complex than this simple intuition suggests. For clarity purposes it is assumed by convention that $R=0$. In addition, the survival function is assumed to be computed from R to infinity and the mortality rate at each age is supposed to be constant and equal to $p=p_A$. As shown in Appendix 3.2, these assumptions were not made when computing actual pension wealth levels, but they greatly simplify the demonstration. The level of pension wealth of an individual currently eligible for a pension can thus be written as:

$$PWY(0) = \sum_{A=0}^{\infty} (S_A \times R_A)/(1+r)^A$$

where R_A is the replacement rate and S_A is the value of the survival function at age A.

Given the assumption of a constant mortality rate at each age, the survival function is:

$$S_A = \prod_{i=1}^{i=A} (1-p) \approx \prod_{i=1}^{i=A} 1/(1+p) \approx 1/(1+p)^A$$

Combining these two equations, and incorporating the fact that R_A is constant ($R_A = R$) because pensions are assumed to be indexed on prices, we obtain:

$$PWY_0 \approx \sum_{A=0}^{\infty} R_A/(1+r+p)^A \approx R \times [1 + 1/(r+p)]$$

Let us assume that pension rights accrue at rate a, so that $P_{R+1} = (1+a)P_R$, and that no pension can be received before full retirement (that is, there is a strict income test). The present value (that is, at age $R = 0$) of the pension wealth of the individual if he defers the receipt of his pension by one year is:

$$PWY_1/(1+r+p) \approx \sum_{A=1}^{\infty} [R_A \times (1+a)/(1+r+p)^{A-1}]/(1+r+p)$$
$$\approx R \times (1+a)/(r+p)$$

The implicit tax on continuing working for one year is:

$$\text{Implicit tax} = -[(1+r+p) \times PWY_1 - PWY_0 - c]$$
$$= R \times [(r+p)(1+c) - a]/(r+p)$$

This equation states that when $a < (r+p)(1+c)$, that is, when the accrual rate is below the 'actuarially neutral' level, there is an implicit tax on continued work whose magnitude is positively related to the level of the replacement rate.

NOTES

1. Reprinted with permission from Duval, R., *The Retirement Effects of Old-Age Pension and Early Retirement Schemes in OECD Countries*, Economics Department Working Papers No. 370, ECO/WKP(2003)24, © OECD 2004. Slightly re-edited and revised.
2. The views expressed in this chapter are those of the author and should not be construed as those of the OECD. I would like to thank Jean-Marc Burniaux, Florence Jaumotte, Willi Leibfritz, Svenbjörn Blöndal, Jorgen Elmeskov, Mike Feiner and other colleagues in the OECD Economics Department for their valuable comments. I also thank

Christophe Albert and Junichi Izumi for helping me collect detailed information on the history of the French and Japanese pension systems. Invaluable statistical assistance was provided by Catherine Chapuis-Grabiner. E-mail address: romain.duval@oecd.org.

3. In principle, there is no straightforward relationship between the effective retirement age and the labour force participation of older workers. For instance, even if participation is higher in one country than in another, the effective retirement age may still be lower if labour market participants withdraw earlier. However, there is actually a very strong cross-country relationship between both variables: countries with lower participation rates of older workers tend to have lower effective retirement ages. Therefore, increasing the effective retirement age and raising the labour force participation of older workers appear to go hand in hand in practice.

4. For instance, despite being ranked among the highest OECD countries in terms of GDP per capita, Japan and the USA have significantly above-average participation rates for older workers. Similarly, demand for leisure is unlikely to differ drastically across OECD countries given their economic and socio-cultural integration. However, these factors may have contributed to a common trend decline in participation rates of older workers within OECD countries over the past decades, at least to the extent that they have dominated the opposite effects of higher life expectancy and improved health status. For instance, Johnson (2000) provides evidence of negative participation effects of rising living standards for a panel of developed countries, while Costa (1997) suggests similar effects from rising demands for leisure – associated with declining relative prices and improving quality of leisure goods. Nevertheless, these explanations for declining effective retirement ages in the OECD area are not fully convincing. Indeed, they would imply a concomitant trend increase in leisure time during working life. Yet, over the last three decades declines in working time have been modest compared with those in effective retirement ages.

5. Lifetime retirement models also rely on the assumption that individuals have a long planning horizon in making their labour supply decisions and fully recognize the value of accumulating entitlements to future benefits associated with contributions paid.

6. Even if the amount of contributions is so high that it exceeds desired saving, such a PAYGO scheme would still not affect labour supply behaviour so long as individuals can borrow at the same rate used to compute pension benefits.

7. Expected increases in the generosity of pension benefits yield smaller labour supply effects than unexpected ones. The further in advance changes in scheme provisions are announced, the more workers increase their consumption and reduce their savings in anticipation of future pension wealth gains (Feldstein 1974), and the smaller the increase in their total wealth and the corresponding impact on their retirement decision.

8. The more workers care about the welfare of their descendants and realize that the cost of higher benefits will have to be borne by them, the more changes in the generosity of benefits are offset by changes in bequests, and the smaller the 'wealth effect' on labour supply.

9. Anderson et al. (1997) suggest that the large unanticipated increase in the level of social benefits that took place in the USA during the 1970s created windfall gains in the value of retirement assets of those nearing retirement, thus inducing some of them to anticipate their retirement decision. Unlike older workers, younger cohorts were less affected because they had time to adjust their savings patterns to reflect these windfalls.

10. Earnings just prior to retirement are assumed to be a reasonable proxy for expected earnings from work, which in theory should be used in the calculation.

11. For instance, in flat-rate pension systems, these factors may include earnings history, household composition and the amount of other income and/or assets. In earnings-related pension schemes they usually include, inter alia, the length of the working life and other periods to be credited for pension purposes (education, child care, unemployment and so on), as well as the age–earnings profile over the worker's career. Furthermore, these schemes may differ across sectors and/or types of jobs.

12. Replacement rates are computed for, and averaged across, six different situations (three earnings levels and two marital situations), under the main assumption that the

illustrative worker enters the labour market at age 20 and has an uninterrupted full-time career in the private sector until retirement.

13.   Unlike expected replacement rates, simple replacement rates at specific retirement ages could have been misleading. For instance, if in two countries the minimum eligibility age is 65, a worker retiring at age 64 receives no benefit and his/her replacement rate is zero in both cases. Yet, after waiting for a year, he/she may receive a significantly higher pension in one country than in the other. Therefore, considering simple replacement rates at specific ages would incorrectly suggest that both schemes are equally unattractive. In comparison, average expected replacement rates over a five-year period provide a more accurate picture.

14.   These figures refer to the 'steady state' of current pension systems. As a consequence, they incorporate all future effects of recently enacted reforms (for example Austria, France, Italy, Sweden). In addition, in those countries where old-age pension systems are not yet mature (for example Korea, or Norway to a lesser extent), or where new components of the system will mature only gradually (for example the Superannuation Guarantee scheme in Australia, in which participation became mandatory only in 1992), the figures reported in Figure 3.1 are the replacement rates provided by these systems once they reach maturity. However, some planned reforms and changes in pension systems are not incorporated in the calculations because it remains unclear at this stage to what extent they will be implemented in practice (indexation of the basic pension amount against prices instead of wages in the future in Canada and the UK) or what their impact on implicit tax rates will be (planned changes in Japan over the period 2013–25 are not modelled). Also not included are the projected rise in the standard retirement age from 60 to 65 in Korea (as part of the 1998 reform), as well as the future increase in the minimum retirement age (that is, at which superannuation savings can be drawn) from 55 to 60 over the period 2015–25 in Australia.

15.   This does not incorporate early retirement due to long insurance years, which can be accessed from age 61.5 with a 69.5 per cent replacement rate for the theoretical worker considered.

16.   This does not incorporate the early retirement (AFP) scheme, which can be accessed from age 62 with a 34.5 per cent replacement rate for the theoretical worker considered.

17.   In the case of the Netherlands, the modelling at age 60 refers to a 'typical' early retirement (VUT) scheme. However, since the early 1990s these PAYGO schemes have been progressively transformed into less generous, fully-funded systems. As a result of these transformations, the expected replacement rate at age 60 may be overstated.

18.   Australia and Korea are two exceptions (Figure 3.2). However, in both countries, higher replacement rates in current pension systems (at their steady state) compared with the late 1980s reflect their maturation (the Superannuation Guarantee Scheme in Australia, the National Pension Scheme in Korea), rather than an increased generosity in benefit payments.

19.   Three countries for which Figure 3.2 also shows an increase in replacement rates at age 60 are Australia, Korea and Portugal. However, this increase did not affect participation patterns over the past decades, either because it is too recent (Portugal, following the 2002 pension reform which lowered the minimum retirement age from age 65 to 55) or has not yet occurred (Australia and Korea, where pension systems are not yet mature: see above).

20.   Implicit tax rates at age 65 are actually higher than at age 60 in the majority of OECD countries. Nevertheless they are very low in those countries where it is possible to combine work with the receipt of a full or reduced pension (for example Canada, Germany, Luxembourg, the Netherlands, New Zealand), which lowers the OECD average.

21.   Excluding France and Luxembourg – where high implicit subsidies on continued work tend to inflate variance across countries at age 55 – the cross-country dispersion of implicit tax rates is almost four times as high at age 60 as at age 55, and is about 50 per cent higher at age 65 than at age 60.

22. The correlation coefficient between average expected replacement rates and implicit taxes on continued work is about -0.8 at age 60 and -0.5 at age 65.

23. The identification of social transfer programmes that can be used de facto as early retirement devices is based on Blöndal and Scarpetta (1998). Basically, unemployment benefit schemes fall into this category when they include special dispositions for older workers, such as no obligation to search for a job. Similarly, disability schemes are classified as early retirement schemes when disability pensions can be granted not only on the basis of health but labour market criteria.

24. Belgium, Finland, France, Germany, the Netherlands, Portugal, Spain and the UK.

25. Austria and Luxembourg (where disability benefits were considered given their widespread incidence among pensioners) as well as Ireland and Norway (where the modelling refers to the pre-retirement allowance and the special early retirement programme, respectively).

26. Australia, Canada, Iceland, Italy, Japan, Korea, New Zealand, Switzerland and the USA.

27. To see this, one can consider a hypothetical country in which the pensionable age would be 100. Whatever the generosity of future benefits and the pension accrual rate between 60 and 65, pension wealth would be very low at both ages because pension flows to be received far into the future would be heavily discounted. Therefore, the change in pension wealth from continuing working between 60 and 65 would also be very small.

28. For instance, the cross-country correlation coefficient between both variables in 1999 is about 0.8 for the 60–64 age group.

29. Strictly speaking, people in the 50–54 and 55–59 age groups in 1999 belong to different birth cohorts. As a consequence, as computed in Figure 3.6, the difference in participation between these two age groups reflects not only a participation effect but also a cohort effect. However, in practice the latter is very small compared with the former. Therefore, using the difference in participation within a given cohort (that is, the participation rate of the 55–59 age group in 1999 less the participation rate of the 50–54 age group in 1994) would leave Figure 3.6 unaffected. The same applies to Figure 3.7 (55–59 and 60–64 age groups).

30. To see how considering large age bands tends to bias the analysis of participation trends, one can think about a hypothetical country where (different) participation rates of both the 55–59 and 60–64 age groups would have remained constant over past decades. A priori one would expect the participation rate of the aggregate 55–64 age group also to have been stable. Yet it would actually show a decline, because population ageing increases the weight of older age groups with lower participation rates. In this hypothetical example, considering the 55–59 and 60–64 age groups separately would remove this demographic bias.

31. For instance, despite no implicit tax on continued work beyond age 65, the participation rate of the 65–69 age group in Luxembourg ranks among the lowest in the OECD area, partly because high implicit taxes at earlier ages induce massive retirement before age 65.

32. Earnings over the past and potential future years of work, as well as the marginal utility of leisure, would be required to estimate the full model.

33. Unsurprisingly, the standard as well as the early retirement age proved to be insignificant for the 55–59 age group.

34. To a certain extent such shocks reflect business cycles and are therefore already captured by the unemployment rate. However, time-fixed effects were found to be significantly different from zero at the 5 per cent level in all regressions below.

35. For instance no account is taken of the fact that retiring often results from a joint decision made in a household context (see, for example, Coile 2003). Another omitted variable affecting the retirement decision is the presence of voluntary private pension schemes, especially in those countries where such plans are prominent, for example Australia, Canada or the USA. There is indeed ample empirical evidence that large disincentives to work are embedded in some of these schemes (Kotlikoff and Wise 1987; Stock and Wise 1990). However, they may affect the age of departure from a particular firm

rather than labour force withdrawal per se, especially when prior knowledge of their characteristics enables workers to smooth consumption and labour supply over the life cycle.

36. For instance, theoretical replacement rates computed for Spain are significantly higher than actual average replacement rates. One reason for this gap is the assumption of an uninterrupted career used in the modelling, which does not hold in practice in Spain due to persistently high unemployment until very recently. In addition, the calculation of implicit tax rates implicitly assumes that all workers are covered by the old-age pension system. As a result, it does not capture the trend increase in pension coverage experienced in a number of OECD countries over the past three decades.

37. There could also be a problem of reverse causality on two grounds: (i) (older) voters with a strong preference for retirement may push towards lower eligibility ages and higher implicit tax rates; (ii) the deterioration of employment opportunities of older workers may force them out of the labour market, thereby inducing governments to improve the generosity of pension systems and other social transfer programmes. However, Johnson (2000) suggests that the latter bias may be small in practice. Looking at major past changes in scheme provisions in a number of OECD countries, he finds that they have preceded, not followed, declines in older males' participation.

38. In eight out of these 22 countries, time series for participation rates and explanatory variables are significantly shorter.

39. In order to obtain meaningful coefficients for country-specific time trends, Model A is estimated on a balanced (14 countries over the period 1967–99) rather than an unbalanced panel dataset.

40. This variable takes the values 0, 1 and 2 for those countries where retirement incentives embedded in old-age pension and early retirement schemes are classified respectively as low (Australia, Canada, Ireland, Norway, Sweden, the USA), moderate (Germany, Portugal, Spain, the UK) and large (Finland, France, Italy, the Netherlands) on the basis of their implicit tax rates.

41. In order to assess the potential impact of demographic trends on the labour force attachment of older men, specifications including the share of prime-age workers (aged 25–54) in the total working-age population (aged 15–64) as an explanatory variable were also estimated. A priori, usual cohort-crowding effects would suggest a positive effect: the larger the number of prime-age workers compared to older ones, the higher the relative wage rate of the latter and the higher their labour force participation rate – to the extent that the substitution effect dominates the income effect. However, this demographic variable had a significantly negative effect for both the 55–59 and 60–64 age groups. The rationale behind this result remains unclear. One possibility is that the increase in the share of prime-age, better educated workers which occurred throughout the 1970s and the 1980s diminished the employment opportunities of less well-educated older workers. In any event, the coefficients of all other variables (implicit taxes, the standard retirement age and the unemployment rate) were insensitive to the introduction of this demographic variable.

42. At first glance, the latter should be inflated by an omitted variable bias, but this intuition does not appear to be confirmed by the data. In particular, the unemployment rate variable is barely significant at the 5 per cent level and does not reduce the implicit tax rate coefficient in a cross-country regression.

43. This figure is a simple arithmetical average of contributions found for the 14 OECD countries (using the coefficients in Model B) for which lengthy time series of participation rates are available.

44. For quantitative policy simulations (based on the econometric estimates presented in Section 4) see Burniaux et al. (2003).

45. In the case of the Netherlands, a 'typical' early retirement (VUT) scheme is considered between ages 60 and 65. However, since the early 1990s these PAYGO schemes have been progressively transformed into funded systems. Because of these transformations, the modelling adopted here is less relevant now than it was in the 1970s and 1980s.

REFERENCES

Aaron, H. (1982), 'Economic effects of social security', *Studies of Government Finance*, Washington, DC: The Brookings Institution.

Anderson, P., A. Gustman and T. Steinmeier (1997), 'Trends in male labor force participation and retirement: some evidence on the role of pensions and social security in the 1970s and 1980s', NBER Working Paper 6208, October.

Blöndal, S. and S. Scarpetta (1998), 'The retirement decision in OECD countries', OECD Economics Department Working Paper 98.

Burniaux, J.-M., R. Duval and F. Jaumotte (2003), 'Coping with ageing: a dynamic approach to quantify the impact of alternative policy options on future labour supply', OECD Economics Department Working Paper 371.

Casey, B., W. Leibfritz, H. Oxley, E. Whitehouse, P. Antolin and R. Duval (2003), 'Policies for an ageing society: recent measures and areas for further reform', OECD Economics Department Working Paper 369.

Coile, C. (2003), 'Retirement incentives and couples' retirement decisions', NBER Working Paper 9496, February.

Costa, D. (1997), 'Less of a luxury: the rise of recreation since 1888', NBER Working Paper 6054, June.

Disney, R. (1996), *Can We Afford to Grow Older: A Perspective on the Economics of Aging*, Cambridge, MA: MIT Press.

Feldstein, M. (1974), 'Social security, induced retirement and aggregate capital accumulation', *Journal of Political Economy*, **82** (5), 905–26.

Gruber, D. and D. Wise (1999a), 'Social security programs and retirement around the world: introduction and summary', in D. Gruber and D. Wise (eds), *Social Security Programs and Retirement around the World*, Chicago: University of Chicago Press.

Gruber, D. and D. Wise (1999b), *Social Security Programs and Retirement around the World*, Chicago: University of Chicago Press.

Gruber, D. and D. Wise (2002), 'Social security programs and retirement around the world: micro estimation', NBER Working Paper 9407, December.

Johnson, R. (2000), 'The effect of old-age insurance on male retirement: evidence from historical cross-country data', Federal Reserve Bank of Kansas City Working Paper 00–09, December.

Kotlikoff, L. and D. Wise (1987), 'The incentive effects of private pension plans', in Z. Bodie, J.B. Shoven and D.A. Wise (eds), *Issues in Pension Economics*, Chicago: University of Chicago Press, pp. 283–336.

Lazear, E. (1986), 'Retirement from the labor force', in O. Ashenfelter and R. Layard (eds), *Handbook of Labor Economics*, Vol. 1, Amsterdam: North Holland, pp. 305–55.

Lee, C. (2003), 'Labor market status of older males in the United States, 1880–1940', NBER Working Paper 9550, March.

Lumsdaine, R. and O. Mitchell (1999), 'New developments in the economic analysis of retirement', in O. Ashenfelter and D. Card (eds), *Handbook of Labor Economics*, Vol. 3, Amsterdam: North Holland, pp. 3261–308.

Lumsdaine, R., J. Stock and D. Wise (1996), 'Why are retirement rates so high at age 65?', in D. Wise (ed.), *Advances in the Economics of Aging*, Chicago: University of Chicago Press, pp. 61–82.

Mitchell, O. and G. Fields (1984), 'The economics of retirement behaviour', *Journal of Labour Economics*, **2** (1), 84–105.

OECD (2003), *Transforming Disability into Ability: Policies to Promote Work and Income Security for Disabled People*, Paris: OECD.

Peracchi, F. and F. Welch (1994), 'Trends in labor force transitions of older men and women', *Journal of Labor Economics*, **12** (2), 210–42.

Stock, J. and D. Wise (1990), 'Pensions, the option value of work, and retirement', *Econometrica*, **58** (5), 1151–80.

DISCUSSION

Hector Sala

Population ageing implies a risk for the fiscal sustainability of social expenditures, especially if aggregate participation and employment rates decline and old-age dependency ratios rise. In this context, higher labour force participation, in particular of older workers, would be welfare-enhancing. It is thus relevant to know the determinants of the retirement incentives embedded in pension systems and other social transfer programmes (such as unemployment, disability or special early retirement benefits).

The chapter distinguishes four main sets of factors that can affect the retirement decision: (i) standard and early ages of entitlement to pension benefits, (ii) generosity of pension benefits, (iii) the implicit marginal tax attached to pension benefits and (iv) the implicit marginal tax attached to other social transfer programmes.

The first one is the standard and early ages of entitlement to pension benefits, even though retirement elegibility does not induce per se effective retirement due to 'liquidity constraints', 'customary ages', and myopia or imperfect information. The main feature of this variable (the age of entitlement to pension benefits) is a wide variation across OECD countries (especially in early eligibility ages). To better disentangle the factors affecting the retirement decision, country-specific time trends are included to capture secular retirement trends (Model A) and prime-age workers' unemployment rate to control for discouragement effects linked to low employment opportunities, even though this also evolves with the business cycle. In this context, the long-run unemployment rate would allow a clearer distinction between the discouragement effect and the business cycle, while housing prices could play a role in several countries in making explicit a liquidity constraint that in the chapter is indirectly captured by the variable 'standard retirement age'. For example, it could prevent early age retirements below 60 and could be relevant to Model A.

The second one is the generosity of pension benefits. Despite the fact that under a certain set of conditions labour force participation should be independent from replacement rate levels, a number of factors actually imply that public pension systems affect the distribution of income and wealth, both across and within generations, and create wealth effects on the retirement decision. The crucial variable here is the replacement ratio, which is the most straightforward indicator of the generosity of the pension system. The chapter outlines the wide variation across OECD countries of expected replacement ratios in current old-age pension systems, as well as in the recent historical trends of expected replacement ratios.

The third one is the implicit marginal tax (or subsidy) on continued work attached to pension benefits, which at each age consists of the changes in pension wealth from continuing working for an additional year. Given that the substitution effect dominates, high implicit tax rates on continued work tend to bias the retirement decision towards early labour market withdrawal. The data show that the average tax rate across the OECD countries is below 5 per cent at age 55, while it is above 30 per cent at ages 60 and 65. Furthermore, dispersion across OECD countries is very large and there is also a wide variation in the historical changes.

The fourth one is the implicit marginal tax attached to other social transfer programmes, which is controlled via the modelling of a typical 'early retirement route' and displays a similar pattern to the implicit marginal tax rate.

Since it captures some of the effects of elegibility ages and the generosity of benefits, the implicit tax on continued work is the key summary indicator of early retirement incentives embedded in pension schemes.

There are two features worth mentioning related to these variables. First, there are large participation effects of early retirement programmes in the 55–59 age group. Second, there is a significant correlation between the fall in male labour force participation over the age span 60–64 and the implicit tax rate on continued work in 'regular' pension systems.

The econometric analysis employs the above-mentioned variables to explain the change in the participation rates of the age groups 55–59, 60–64 and over 65, so that what it is implicitly being modelled is withdrawal from the labour market. The main findings of the chapter are, first, that a 10 percentage points decline in the implicit tax rate reduces the fall in participation rates by 1.5 percentage points, an elasticity that is about a third of those found in simple cross-country regressions or in the microeconomic literature, and second, that changes in implicit tax rates and standard retirement ages explain about 31 per cent of the declining trend in older males' labour force participation in OECD countries over the past three decades. This leads the author to conclude that the potential impact of policy reforms on labour force participation appears to be fairly large, even though future research should pay attention to other influences, such as preferences for leisure or 'demand-side' factors.

The chapter draws explicit attention to some explanatory factors mentioned, but not taken into account in the analysis as exogenous variables. For example, no account is taken of the fact that retiring often results from a joint decision made in a household context. Voluntary private pension schemes are also omitted from the analysis, and in some countries are especially prominent. There is also a very clear and honest definition of the variables. In particular, the way the steady state replacement rate, pension and social wealth, and implicit taxes on continued work are computed is clearly stated, and both the strengths and limitations of these definitions are very well spelled out. Nevertheless, they incorporate a great deal of assumption. For example, the tax treatment of earnings and pension benefits is omitted, which implies a zero tax rate: an equally arbitrary but positive tax rate could be assumed; the real interest rate is assumed to be 3 per cent, but a substantially lower one may be taken as a discount factor; finally, individuals are assumed to bear all the cost of employer's contributions to the old-age pension system, an assumption that could be relaxed. In other words, there is a lot of work in constructing the variables, but the econometric analysis does not explore all the potential issues that could be studied and, in particular, does not check for the robustness of the results.

The chapter raises interesting points that clearly deserve further attention. For example, it is stated that 'the strong correlation between the replacement rate and the implicit tax rate raises a multi-collinearity issue, thereby excluding the possibility of identifying separately the participation effects of both variables within the same regression' (pages 85–6). Further research could extend exploration of this issue, for example by replicating the estimated results using the replacement ratio, instead of the implicit tax rate, as a explanatory variable. This would further outline the contribution of computing and giving central attention to a concept such as the implicit tax rate.

Second, in Model A, country-specific time trends are included to capture secular retirement trends, such as the increasing demand for leisure. Since the larger the incentive to retire early in a country, the larger the estimated coefficient on the time trend, common-time fixed effects replace country-specific time trends in Model B. This enlarges the coefficients on the implicit tax rates due to 'the fact that changes in participation rates induced by abrupt changes in implicit taxes are usually gradual, and may thus be better captured by simple time trends' (page 87). If the changes in participation rates are gradual, and given that there are sufficient degrees of freedom, it would be desirable to push this investigation further and estimate a dynamic panel. Such dynamic modelling would also help to disentangle short and long-run effects. As pointed out by Duval 'The low elasticities typically found in panel data estimates using macroeconomic data may result from the difficulty of disentangling short and long-run effects' (page 90).

Furthermore, given the heterogeneity displayed by the OECD countries with respect to standard and early ages of eligibility for retirement, the generosity of pension systems (that is, the expected replacement rate) and the implicit tax rates associated with the pension benefits and other social tranfer programmes, it may be possible to group these economies. In particular, for 14 countries (the ones used in Model A) data runs from 1967 to

1999. This sample of countries allows this line of research to be pushed further, towards individual regressions that may provide useful information to group them and to estimate small panel data models so that the imposition of common coefficients becomes less restrictive. In this way, a more detailed perspective on the potential impact of policy reforms on labour force participation will be obtained.

4. The effects of employment protection and product market regulations on the Italian labour market

Adriana D. Kugler and Giovanni Pica[1]

1. INTRODUCTION

Labour market regulations have often been blamed for the poor performance of European labour markets. However, lack of sharp changes in labour market regulations has made it difficult to identify the impact of these regulations on employment. Evidence on the impact of labour market regulations remains mixed (see for example Nickell and Layard 1999). Moreover, even when it is possible to identify the impact of regulations, they appear to have moderate effects (see for example Kugler et al. 2003). For this reason attention has turned to other causes for high and persistent unemployment in Europe.

Recently, attention has focused on the impact of restricted competition in the product market on employment.[2] On the one hand product market regulations may reduce the number of firms and provide firms with market power, thus reducing employment levels due to scale effects. On the other hand product market regulations may introduce barriers to entrepreneurship making it difficult to set up new firms and create new jobs. Bertrand and Kramarz (2002) use a unique panel for the French retail trade industry and find that stronger deterrence of entry by regional zoning boards slowed down employment growth in those regions. Boeri et al. (2000) instead use cross-sectional indicators of product market regulations generated by the OECD for 27 countries and find a negative correlation between their indicator of barriers to entrepreneurship and employment-to-population ratios. Also, Djankov et al. (2002) present new data on the regulation of entry of start-up firms in 85 countries and find that countries with heavier regulation of entry have larger underground economies.

In this chapter we present new evidence on the impact of employment protection legislation exploiting the differential change in severance pay for unfair dismissals in Italy in large and small firms after 1990, and then ask whether the effects of employment protection vary with the strictness of product market regulations. Krueger and Pischke (1998) have argued for example that besides labour market rigidities, restrictions on start-up companies or product market regulations may depress employment by reducing the responsiveness of labour demand with respect to labour costs. We formalize a similar idea using a simple matching model with entry and dismissal costs to illustrate the interaction between regulations of entry and employment protection legislation and then present evidence of the separate and joint effects of regulations in labour and product markets using social security data for Italy.

Italy is an interesting country to study because it is one of the more heavily regulated OECD economies both in terms of barriers to entrepreneurship and in terms of employment protection. Djankov et al. (2002) report that an entrepreneur in Italy has to follow 16 different procedures, pay US$3946 in fees and wait at least 62 business days to acquire the necessary permits to be able to start a business. Also, according to Nicoletti et al. (2000) Italy ranks third, after Turkey and Korea, in terms of the strictness of regulations that generate barriers to entrepreneurship, but they also find that the strictness of these regulations varies across sectors within Italy. Moreover, according to the same study Italy ranks third in terms of the strictness of regulations on permanent contracts. More importantly for our analysis, Italy introduced a labour market reform after 1990 which increased employment protection for workers employed under permanent contracts in firms with less than 15 employees relative to those in firms with more than 15 employees. This reform, together with variation in the regulations of entry across sectors, allows us to identify the interaction between product and labour market regulations in Italy.

The theoretical section of the chapter presents a simple matching model with entry and dismissal costs. Entry costs reflect barriers to entry generated by the costly administrative burdens documented by Nicoletti et al. (2000) and Djankov et al. (2002). Dismissal costs capture the strict employment protection regulation in the form of indemnities for unjust dismissals, advance notice requirements and other procedural inconveniences. In the model, higher entry costs reduce job creation, because the higher entry costs are the more sensitive is job creation to the probability of filling vacancies. However, entry costs have no effect on job destruction because these costs are sunk. Moreover, while a reduction in dismissal costs increases job creation and job destruction, the increase in job creation as a result of lower dismissal costs is smaller the higher the entry costs are. Consequently, an important implication of the model is that stricter regulation of entry reduces the effectiveness of labour market reforms in generating new jobs.

The empirical analysis uses an employer–employee panel from the Italian Social Security Institute (INPS) to examine how the 1990 Italian labour market reform affected worker flows in sectors subject to heavy regulations of entry and those subject to lighter regulations. Our results suggest that the 1990 reform reduced accessions to permanent contracts, especially for women. Moreover, consistent with the predictions of the theory, the results suggest that the effect of the reform in terms of reduced accessions for women was smaller in sectors with heavy regulations of entry. The results also suggest the reform reduced separations from permanent contracts and that the reduction in separations was greatest in regulated sectors. An important implication of our findings is that for labour market deregulation to be effective in terms of generating new jobs, countries also have to reduce administrative burdens and eliminate other regulations that create barriers to entrepreneurship.

The chapter is organized as follows. Section 2 describes regulations in product and labour markets in Italy as well as recent reforms. Section 3 presents a theoretical framework to analyse the impact of entry and dismissal costs on turnover and employment. Section 4 explains the identification strategy used to evaluate the impact of product and labour market regulations in Italy. Section 5 describes the Social Security data and presents estimates of the impact of increased strictness of employment protection in small firms in Italy after 1990 and its interaction with entry regulations on turnover and employment.

2.   REGULATIONS IN ITALY

2.1   Employment Protection Regulations

Italy, together with the other Southern European countries, is considered one of the strictest countries in terms of employment protection legislation (EPL). For example, a study by Lazear (1990) for the period 1956–84 and a study by Bertola (1990) for the late 1980s rank Italy as the strictest country in terms of EPL. A study by the OECD's *Employment Outlook* for the late 1980s ranks Portugal as the strictest country followed by Italy, Spain and Greece. A similar study by the OECD's *Employment Outlook* for the late 1990s, which includes Turkey, North America and transition economies as well, continues to rank Portugal as the strictest, followed by Turkey, Greece, Italy and Spain. The study by Nicoletti et al. (2000), which does not include some of the countries in the OECD's *Employment Outlook* study, also ranks Italy third, after Portugal and the Netherlands, in terms of the strictness of regulations on permanent contracts.

Dismissals were first regulated in Italy in 1966 through Law No. 604, which established that, in case of unfair dismissals, employers had to either hire back workers or pay severance, which depended on tenure and firm size. Severance pay for unfair dismissals ranged between five and eight months for workers with less than two-and-a-half years of tenure, between five and 12 months for those between two-and-a-half and 20 years of tenure, and between five and 14 months for workers with more than 20 years of tenure in firms with more than 60 employees.[3] Firms with fewer than 60 employees had to pay half the severance paid by firms with more than 60 employees. In 1970 the Statuto dei Lavoratori (Law No. 300) established that all firms with more than 15 employees had to hire back workers and pay their forgone wages in case of unfair dismissals, but exempted firms with fewer than 15 employees.[4] A number of recent studies show evidence of the binding effect of this law for firms at the 15-employee threshold. For example, the 2002 annual report by the Italian Statistical Office ISTAT (2002) shows a larger fraction transiting to a smaller size category for firms around the 15 employee threshold than for firms at any other sizes. Similarly, Borgarello et al. (2004) find a higher probability of inaction and a higher probability of reducing firm size than of increasing it for firms at the 15 employee threshold.

Given the high costs of unfair dismissals for larger firms, in 1987 the Italian government liberalized the use of temporary contracts in an attempt to provide more flexibility to employers. Prior to 1987, temporary contracts could be used for specific projects, seasonal work, or for replacement of temporarily absent permanent workers. After 1987, temporary contracts could be used more widely, subject to collective agreements specifying certain target groups. While the extended use of temporary contracts allowed for more flexibility in the labour market, these contracts could only be renewed up to two times and could only have a maximum length of 15 months. Consequently, even though temporary contracts were liberalized after this reform, the use of temporary contracts remained heavily regulated in Italy compared to other countries.[5]

Moreover, soon after the 1987 reform, in 1990 Law No. 108 was introduced, further restricting dismissals for permanent contracts. In particular, this law introduced severance payments of between two-and-a-half and six months pay for unfair dismissals in firms with fewer than 15 employees. In contrast, firms with more than 15 employees still had to hire back workers and pay forgone wages in case of unfair dismissals. This means that the cost of unfair dismissals for firms with fewer than 15 employees increased relative to the cost for firms with more than 15 employees after 1990.[6]

In 1997 Italy moved again in the direction of trying to provide firms with a margin of flexibility by legalizing the use of temporary help agencies.

However, as with the 1987 reform, the legalization of temporary help agencies was limited in that it imposed restrictions on the maximum number of possible renewals of temporary help workers.[7]

While the 1990 reform increased the costs of unfair dismissals for permanent contracts in firms with fewer than 15 employees relative to firms with more than 15 employees, the 1987 and 1997 reforms introduced flexibility at the margin by deregulating the use of temporary contracts and temporary lay-offs. Since our data is for the period of 1986 to 1995, in this chapter we exploit the temporal change in dismissal costs generated by the 1990 reform for permanent workers, which applied differently for small and large firms.[8]

2.2   Entry Regulations

Italy is not only one of the strictest countries in terms of regulation of the labour market, but also in terms of regulations in product markets. In their data set of regulations of entry of start-up firms, Djankov et al. (2002) find that Italy is one of the most restrictive countries in terms of the number of procedures required to set up a business. An entrepreneur in Italy has to follow 16 different procedures to acquire the necessary permits to start a business, which is the same number required in Senegal, Ecuador, Romania and Vietnam, and well above the worldwide average number of 6.04 procedures. This study also finds that, without taking into account bribes, time and out-of-pocket expenses involved in setting up a business in Italy rise to 45 per cent of per capita GDP.

Nicoletti et al. (2000) construct broader measures of product market regulations which capture: (1) barriers to entrepreneurship (for example administrative burdens on start-ups and corporate firms, licensing and permit systems, existence of antitrust exceptions for public enterprises), and (2) state control over business enterprises (for example size of public enterprise sector, price controls in competitive industries).[9] According to their measure of capturing barriers to entrepreneurship, Italy ranks third after Turkey and Korea in terms of strictness among 27 OECD countries, followed by France and Belgium. Disaggregating this measure into what is due to administrative burdens to start-ups, regulatory opacity and barriers to competition, Italy ranks first in terms of administrative burdens to start-ups. Italy also appears heavily regulated in terms of state involvement. According to Nicoletti et al.'s (2000) measure of state control, Italy ranks second after Poland. Separating this measure into a measure of public ownership and involvement in business operations (for example price controls), Italy ranks second after Poland in terms of public ownership and fourth in terms of state involvement after Spain, Greece and Belgium.

While Italy is clearly heavily regulated compared to other countries, within Italy some industries are less heavily regulated than others because many regulations are industry-specific. For example, administrative burdens on start-ups are particularly heavy in Italy, as in France (see Bertrand and Kramarz 2002) for retail distribution companies. Using the OECD international regulation database, Nicoletti (2001) constructs measures of industry-level regulation for seven sectors: retail distribution, road freight, mobile telephony, air passenger transport, fixed telephony, electricity and railways.[10] Using these measures, he ranks industries as very restrictive, restrictive, liberal or very liberal, according to whether the summary indicator of regulation in the industry exceeds by more or less than one standard deviation the average value for the industry in the 28 OECD countries included in the sample.[11] Using these indicators of strictness of regulation in the service sector, retail distribution, road freight, mobile telephony, electricity and railways are ranked as restrictive, while air passenger transport and fixed telephony are ranked as liberal.[12] We also focus on the textile sector as another sector with low entry restrictions in Italy, which has been dominated by small firms.

We use the fact that some industries within Italy are subject to strict regulation of entry while others are faced with lighter entry barriers to study the differential impact of changes in dismissal costs when product markets are more or less regulated. The next section presents a model to illustrate how employment protection and entry regulations, such as those present in Italy, interact in terms of their effects on turnover and employment.

3. THEORETICAL EFFECTS OF EPL AND ENTRY COST

A simple matching model illustrates the individual and joint effects of employment protection legislation and regulations on start-ups. The model is similar to Mortensen and Pissarides's (1994) but adds dismissal costs and fixed set-up costs for opening vacancies. Our theoretical model shows the standard effects of dismissal costs in terms of reducing job creation and job destruction, but in addition it illustrates how barriers to entry mitigate the effects of dismissal costs. This means that there are economic complementarities between labour and product market policies in our model, in the sense that the effectiveness of one policy depends on the implementation of the other policy.[13] Thus, an important implication of the model is that labour market deregulation will be less effective in the presence of heavier regulations of entry.

Firms have a discount factor r. There is a fixed set-up cost K of opening a vacancy and a cost c of holding the vacancy open. There is free entry so that the value of a vacancy is equal to the fixed set-up cost in equilibrium. The number of matches in the economy is given by $m(u, v)$, which depends on the unemployment and vacancy rates u and v since the labour force is normalized to one. The matching function is assumed to increase in both u and v and to be homogeneous of degree one. Accordingly, the arrival rate of applicants is $[m(u, v)]/v = m(1/\theta, 1) = q(\theta)$ with $q'(\theta) < 0$. As in Mortensen and Pissarides (1994) jobs are assumed to start at the highest possible level of productivity ε_m, but jobs are subject to productivity shocks with instantaneous probability λ where the new match-specific productivity ε' is drawn from a distribution function $G(.)$ on the support $[\varepsilon_0, \varepsilon_m]$. Jobs hit by shocks are either terminated or continued, and if they are terminated they have to pay a dismissal cost F, which is assumed to be pure waste. Every period, firms pay a wage $w(\varepsilon)$,

$$w(\varepsilon) = \phi\varepsilon + (1 - \phi)b$$

where b is the reservation wage of the worker and where the wage is a weighted sum of the productivity of the match and the reservation wage.[14]

The values of filled and vacant jobs are

$$rJ(\varepsilon) = \varepsilon - w(\varepsilon) + \lambda \int_{\varepsilon_0}^{\bar{\varepsilon}} [-F - J(\varepsilon)] dG(\varepsilon') + \lambda \int_{\bar{\varepsilon}}^{\varepsilon_m} [J(\varepsilon') - J(\varepsilon)] dG(\varepsilon')$$

$$(4.1)$$

$$rV = -c + q(\theta) [J(\varepsilon_m) - V] \qquad (4.2)$$

where $\bar{\varepsilon}$ is the threshold match-specific productivity at which firms are indifferent between dismissing and retaining the worker. It is straightforward to show that $J(\varepsilon)$ is increasing in ε and there exists a threshold match-specific productivity $\bar{\varepsilon} \in [\varepsilon_0, \varepsilon_m]$ given by the condition $J(\bar{\varepsilon}) = -F$, such that workers are dismissed whenever $\varepsilon \leq \bar{\varepsilon}$ and they are retained whenever $\varepsilon > \bar{\varepsilon}$.

Imposing this condition on Equation (4.2) and integrating by parts, the job destruction schedule is given by the following equation:

$$0 = rF + (1 - \phi)(\bar{\varepsilon} - b) + \lambda\frac{1 - \phi}{r + \lambda}\int_{\bar{\varepsilon}}^{\varepsilon_m}[1 - G(\varepsilon')] d\varepsilon' \qquad (4.3)$$

Consequently, the job destruction schedule is flat and it decreases as dismissal costs F increase, but does not shift with changes in entry costs K. The latter occurs because entry costs are sunk, so they do not affect dismissal decisions.

Free entry implies that the number of vacancies is determined by zero net profits so that the value of a vacancy equals the entry cost $V = K$. Substituting the free entry condition into the value of a vacancy in Equation (4.2) yields:

Labour market adjustments in Europe

$$J(\varepsilon_m) = \frac{rK + c}{q(\theta)} + K$$

where the first term captures the expected flow opportunity cost of opening a vacancy and the second term the cost to be paid up front upon opening. Combining this condition and the job destruction condition and using the fact that $J'(\varepsilon) = (1 - \phi)/(r + \lambda)$, we get the job creation schedule:

$$\frac{1 - \phi}{r + \lambda}(\varepsilon_m - \bar{\varepsilon}) - \left(\frac{rK + c}{q(\theta)} + K + F\right) = 0 \qquad (4.4)$$

The job creation schedule slopes downward. The higher is the threshold that induces dismissals, the lower is the value of a job and the smaller the incentives to open new vacancies. In addition, increases in both dismissal and entry costs reduce the incentives to open new vacancies, shifting down the job creation schedule, that is,

$$\frac{d\bar{\varepsilon}}{dF} = -\frac{r + \lambda}{1 - \phi} < 0 \quad \text{and} \quad \frac{d\bar{\varepsilon}}{dK} = -\frac{r + \lambda}{1 - \phi}\left(1 + \frac{r}{q(\theta)}\right) < 0^{15}$$

In addition, note that the entry cost K affects the slope of the job creation schedule. As K increases, the job creation schedule becomes steeper because firms are more careful about creating new jobs, so that a lower probability of filling the vacancy reduces job creation further.

Given the job creation and job destruction schedules, the equilibrium values of the dismissal threshold and the labour market tightness parameter $\bar{\varepsilon}*$ and $\theta*$ are given by Equations (4.3) and (4.4) (see Figure 4.1). An increase in dismissal costs reduces the dismissal threshold and labour market tightness. The effects on the equilibrium value of $\bar{\varepsilon}*$ are determined by the job destruction equation, which is independent of $\theta*$, so an increase in dismissal costs reduces the dismissals, that is,

$$\frac{d\bar{\varepsilon}*}{dF} = -\frac{(r + \lambda)}{(1 - \phi)} \frac{r}{[r + \lambda G(\bar{\varepsilon}*)]} < 0$$

On the other hand entry costs have no effect on dismissals. The effects on the equilibrium level of $\theta*$ are determined by the job creation schedule, so both dismissal costs and entry costs reduce hiring, that is,

$$\frac{d\theta*}{dK} = \frac{r + q(\theta*)}{rK + c} \frac{q(\theta*)}{q'(\theta*)} < 0$$

$$\frac{d\theta*}{dF} = \frac{\lambda G(\bar{\varepsilon}*)}{[r + \lambda G(\bar{\varepsilon}*)]} \frac{(q(\theta*))^2}{q'(\theta*)(rK + c)} < 0$$

The negative effect of K on θ^* is clear. The entry cost reduces job creation while not affecting job destruction, hence the ratio of vacancies to unemployment decreases (see Figure 4.2). The negative effect of F on θ^* is due to the fact that an increase in F reduces job creation more than job destruction. The reason is that firing costs affect entry due to the lower profits realized at *any* realization of the shock, while they have an effect on destruction only in bad states of the world (see Figure 4.3).

In addition, the effect of an increase in dismissal costs on hiring will be smaller, the higher are entry costs, that is, $(d^2\theta^*)/(dFdK) > 0$. This is because the higher are entry costs, the more sensitive is job creation to the probability of filling vacancies, so higher dismissal costs generate a smaller reduction in hiring or, vice versa, lower dismissal costs generate a smaller increase in hiring. Figure 4.4 shows the effects of an increase in firing costs at different levels of entry costs. The figure shows that higher entry costs shift the job creation down and also increase the slope of the job creation schedule. Consequently, the higher the entry costs, the smaller the effect of an increase in dismissal costs on labour market tightness.[16]

4.   IDENTIFICATION STRATEGY

The goals of this chapter are first, to identify the impact of dismissal costs on permanent employment, and second, to identify how the impact of dismissal costs varies with the strictness of entry regulations. To identify the impact of increases in dismissal costs we compare firms with fewer than 15 employees to firms with more than 15 employees before and after the 1990 reform. One may argue that firm size may be affected by the reform itself. In order to deal with this possibility we define as *small* only firms that have *fewer* than 15 employees in *all* years before the reform and as *large* only firms that have *more* than 15 employees in *all* years before the reform. In other words, we eliminate from the sample the firms whose size crosses the 15-employee threshold before the reform. We do so in order to focus on the firms whose size is already at some 'steady state level' before the reform. The reason is that the theory suggests that *in steady state* EPL should not affect the average employment *levels* but only *deviations* from the average.[17] Moreover, to identify how the impact of dismissal costs varies with the strictness of entry regulations, we compare firms with fewer than 15 employees relative to firms with more than 15 employees in sectors subject to heavier and lighter regulations of entry, before and after the 1990 reform.

The strategy for identifying the impact of the change in dismissal costs is illustrated in Figures 4.5 and 4.6. Figures 4.5 and 4.6 show accession and separation probabilities in firms with fewer than 15 employees relative

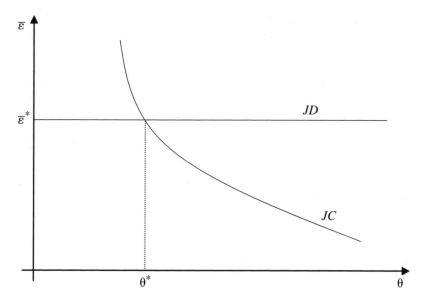

Figure 4.1   Equilibrium values of ε̄* and θ*

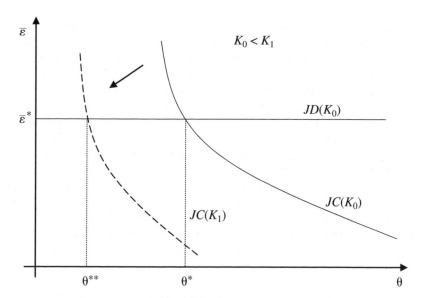

Figure 4.2   Effects of entry costs on JC

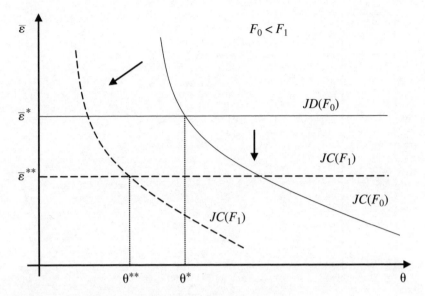

Figure 4.3   Effects of dismissal costs on JC *and* JD

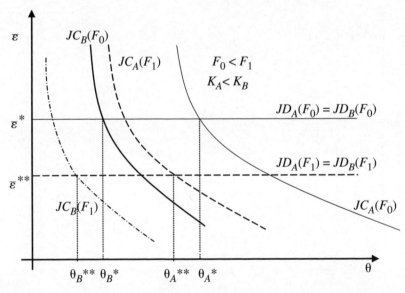

Figure 4.4   Effects of dismissal costs at different levels of entry costs

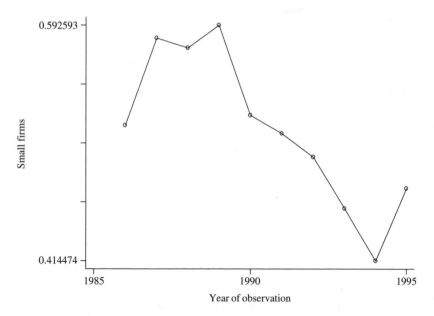

Figure 4.5   Number of yearly accessions in small firms over the total number of yearly accessions

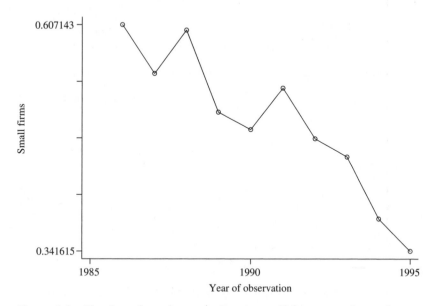

Figure 4.6   Number of yearly separations in small firms over the total number of yearly separations

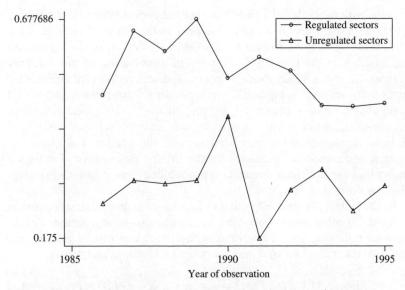

Figure 4.7   Number of yearly accessions in small firms over the total number of yearly accessions in regulated and unregulated sectors

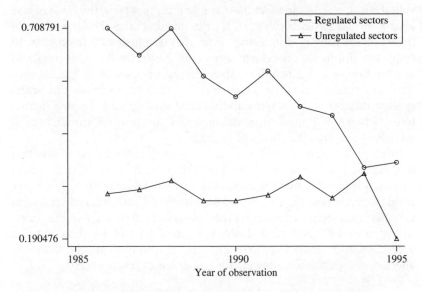

Figure 4.8   Number of yearly separations in small firms over the total number of yearly separations in regulated and unregulated sectors

to firms with more than 15 employees for the period 1986 to 1995. Figure 4.5 shows a sharp decline in accession probabilities in small relative to big firms starting in 1990. Figure 4.6 also shows a decline in the separation probabilities starting in 1989, possibly in anticipation of the reforms. Figures 4.7 and 4.8 also show accession and separation probabilities for small firms relative to big firms, but separating firms into regulated and unregulated sectors according to the Nicoletti (2001) classification. Figure 4.7 shows that while accession probabilities decreased after 1990 in both regulated and unregulated sectors, the decline was greater in unregulated sectors as predicted by the theory. By contrast, Figure 4.8 shows that the decline in separation probabilities was greatest in the regulated sectors.[18]

To control for the possibility that reduced accessions and separations are the result of other shocks occurring during the post-reform period, we estimate the following linear probability model which controls for worker, year and firm effects and for observable worker and firm characteristics:

$$E[m_{ijt} = 1 \mid X_{ijt}, D_j^S, Post_t] = \alpha_i + \tau_t + \beta' X_{ijt} + \delta(D_j^S \times Post_t) \quad (4.5)$$

where $m_{ijt} = 1$ if a match was created or destroyed, that is, if there was either an accession or a separation, for person i in firm j at time t; α_i is an individual effect; τ_t is a year effect; $Post_t$ is a dummy that takes the value of one after 1990 and zero otherwise; D_j^S is a dummy that takes the value of one if the worker is employed in a small firm, that is, a firm with fewer than 15 employees during the pre-reform period, and zero if the worker is employed in a big firm; and X_{ijt} includes worker characteristics such as age, occupation and gender, and firm characteristics such as location, the yearly average number of employees and sectoral productivity. The interaction term between the small firm dummy and the post-reform dummy is included to capture the effects of interest.

While inclusion of time effects allows controlling for the possibility that the change in turnover after the post-reform period was due to macro shocks, it is possible that the cycle affects small and large firms differently. If this were the case, then we should have observed both reduced accessions and increased separations during the post-reform period due to the strong recession of 1992 and 1993. Instead, Figures 4.5 and 4.6 show reduced accessions and separations. Nonetheless, we also estimate the following alternative specification allowing for size-specific cyclical effects:

$$E[m_{ijt} = 1 \mid X_{ijt}, D_j^S, Post_t, E_t] = \alpha_i + \tau_t + \beta' X_{ijt} + \phi E_t$$
$$+ \rho(D_j^S \times E_t) + \delta(D_j^S \times Post_t \times E_t) \quad (4.6)$$

where E_t is an expansion variable which is either an expansion dummy taking the value of zero during the recession years of 1992 and 1993 and one otherwise, or GDP growth. Here the impact of the reform is captured by δ, the coefficient on the interaction of the small firm dummy, the post-1990 dummy and the expansion variable. δ measures the impact of the reform during the post-reform expansion relative to the pre-reform expansion. The size-specific cyclical effect is captured by the coefficient on the interaction term between the small dummy and the expansion variable. Since we are also interested in how the effects of dismissal costs vary with the strictness of regulations of entry, we estimate the effects of interest both for the regulated and unregulated sectors.

5. ESTIMATES OF THE EFFECTS OF EPL AND ENTRY COST

5.1 Data Description

The dataset is drawn from the Italian Social Security Administration (INPS) archives for the years 1986–95. The original dataset collects social security forms from a 1/90 random sample of employees every year, with employees born on 10 March, June, September and December of every year being sampled. The original archives only include information on private sector firms in the manufacturing and service sectors, so it excludes all workers in the public sector and agriculture. We use a 10 per cent random sample from this original dataset.

The dataset includes individual longitudinal records generated using social security numbers. However, since the INPS collects information on private sector employees for the purpose of computing retirement benefits, employees are only followed through their employment spells. The data thus stops following individuals who move into self-employment, the underground economy, unemployment and retirement. The dataset also includes longitudinal records for firms employing the randomly selected workers in the sample using the firms' name, address and social security and fiscal codes.[19] The dataset is thus an employer–employee panel with information on workers and firm characteristics. In particular, the data include information on employees' age, gender, occupation, dates of accession and separation with each firm, type of contract, information on firms' location, sector of employment, number of employees and firms' dates of incorporation and termination. The advantage of this administrative data for the purpose of studying worker transitions is that, contrary to survey data which measures transitions by matching quarterly data and using tenure information to identify job changes, it identifies exact dates of accessions and separations according to when social security contributions began and ended.

Table 4.1 presents descriptive statistics by firm size, before and after the 1990 reform. The table shows lower accession rates for men and women after the reform in small and large firms. However, the table shows a larger drop in accession rates after the reform in small than in large firms. Similarly, separation rates are lower for men and women after the reform in small and large firms, but the drop in separation rates was much more pronounced in small firms. These simple comparisons of means illustrate

Table 4.1   Descriptive statistics by firm size: before and after the reform (full sample)

Variables	Pre-reform	Post-reform	Pre-reform	Post-reform
	Small firms		Large firms	
A. MEN				
Age	35.79	36.99	39.70	40.73
	(11.32)	(10.75)	(10.56)	(10.04)
% Blue collar	0.8052	0.8085	0.6268	0.5959
workers	(0.3961)	(0.3935)	(0.4837)	(0.4907)
Yearly average	6.485	6.897	6725.32	7289.11
size of the firm	(3.9765)	(4.155)	(22087.87)	(22621.88)
Accession rate	0.2337	0.1877	0.1251	0.1115
	(0.4232)	(0.3905)	(0.3308)	(0.3148)
Separation rate	0.3247	0.2555	0.1740	0.1648
	(0.4683)	(0.4361)	(0.3791)	(0.3710)
N	12321	12640	27599	32729
B. WOMEN				
Age	32.18	34.05	35.38	37.10
	(9.721)	(9.4)	(9.7)	(9.445)
% Blue collar	0.4170	0.4254	0.4754	0.4427
workers	(0.4931)	(0.4944)	(0.4994)	(0.4967)
Yearly average	6.3218	6.584	2521.73	3023.13
size of the firm	(3.9831)	(4.1623)	(12125.36)	(13063.76)
Accession rate	0.2212	0.1692	0.1318	0.1192
	(0.4151)	(0.3750)	(0.3383)	(0.3241)
Separation rate	0.3218	0.2415	0.1924	0.1780
	(0.4672)	(0.4280)	(0.3942)	(0.3825)
N	7228	6796	11812	13748

Notes: Only permanent workers are included. The pre-reform period goes from 1986 to 1990, the post-reform period from 1991 to 1995. Standard deviations in parentheses.

the impact of increased dismissal costs on accessions and separations in small relative to big firms.

Tables 4.2 and 4.3 present descriptive statistics for men and women, respectively, by firm size in regulated and less regulated sectors, before and after the 1990 reform. The sample in this table includes only those in sectors

Table 4.2   Descriptive statistics for men by firm size: before and after the reform (regulation sample)

Variables	Pre-reform	Post-reform	Pre-reform	Post-reform
	Small firms		Large firms	
A. REGULATED SECTORS				
Age	36.09	38.17	40.77	41.85
	(11.31)	(10.60)	(10.11)	(9.857)
% Blue collar	0.7240	0.7286	0.6332	0.5481
workers	(0.4471)	(0.4448)	(0.4820)	(0.4977)
Yearly average	5.658	6.0139	36243.54	36483.39
size of the firm	(4.102)	(4.275)	(47379.08)	(47024.12)
Accession rate	0.1929	0.1621	0.0796	0.0675933
	(0.3947)	(0.3687)	(0.2707)	(0.251081)
Separation rate	0.2652	0.2157	0.0970	0.1142
	(0.4416)	(0.4115)	(0.2960)	(0.3181)
N	1493	1437	2639	3669
B. UNREGULATED SECTORS				
Age	34.99	38.60	40.48	39.69
	(9.766)	(10.51)	(11.23)	(10.32)
% Blue collar	0.7746	0.7744	0.7396	0.7494
workers	(0.4193)	(0.4193)	(0.4391)	(0.4336)
Yearly average	8.704	9.049	953.3	1413.34
size of the firm	(3.486)	(3.603)	(3194.91)	(3902.25)
Accession rate	0.1549	0.1098	0.0917	0.0726
	(0.3631)	(0.3135)	(0.2888)	(0.2596)
Separation rate	0.2183	0.1707	0.1748	0.1145
	(0.4146)	(0.3774)	(0.3800)	(0.3186)
N	142	164	818	882

Notes: Only permanent workers and males are included. The pre-reform period goes from 1986 to 1990, the post-reform period from 1991 to 1995. The regulation sample includes workers and firms in the retail, road transportation, electricity, telecommunications, air transportation and textile sectors. Retail, road transportation, electricity and telecommunications are classified as regulated, while the air transportation and textile sectors are classified as unregulated. Standard deviations are in parentheses.

Table 4.3   Descriptive statistics for women by firm size: before and after the reform (regulation sample)

Variables	Pre-reform	Post-reform	Pre-reform	Post-reform
	Small firms		Large firms	
A. REGULATED SECTORS				
Age	32.10	34.52	36.64	38.34
	(9.864)	(9.568)	(8.780)	(9.759)
% Blue collar	0.2490	0.2668	0.1485	0.1571
workers	(0.4326)	(0.4426)	(0.3559)	(0.3641)
Yearly average	4.739	5.277	14675.81	18831.17
size of the firm	(3.520)	(3.8)	(32121.72)	(36654.68)
Accession rate	0.1255	0.1261	0.1072	0.0761
	(0.3315)	(0.3321)	(0.3096)	(0.2653)
Separation rate	0.2238	0.1812	0.1378	0.1264
	(0.4170)	(0.3854)	(0.3450)	(0.3325)
N	956	817	653	815
B. UNREGULATED SECTORS				
Age	32.16	35.18	34.72	36.66
	(10.89)	(10.77)	(10.28)	(9.910)
% Blue collar	0.8698	0.8358	0.7977	0.7669
workers	(0.3370)	(0.3710)	(0.4019)	(0.4231)
Yearly average	7.175	7.381	310.94	784.57
size of the firm	(3.610)	(3.850)	(1102.11)	(2694.88)
Accession rate	0.1154	0.1026	0.0691	0.0949
	(0.320)	(0.3039)	(0.2538)	(0.2932)
Separation rate	0.2456	0.1935	0.1508	0.1474
	(0.4311)	(0.3957)	(0.3580)	(0.3547)
N	338	341	796	875

Notes: Only permanent workers and women are included. The pre-reform period goes from 1986 to 1990, the post-reform period from 1991 to 1995. The regulation sample includes workers and firms in the retail, road transportation, electricity, telecommunications, air transportation and textile sectors. Retail, road transportation, electricity and telecommunications are classified as regulated, while the air transportation and textile sectors are classified as unregulated. Standard deviations are in parentheses.

which can be classified as more or less restrictive in terms of product market regulations. In particular, this sample includes workers and firms in the retail, road transportation, electricity, telecommunications, air transportation and textile sectors. Following Nicoletti's (2001) ranking of industries, we classify retail, road transportation, electricity and telecommunications as regulated and air transportation and textiles as less regulated. As does Table 4.1, these tables show that accession and separation rates fell after the reform in small relative to large firms. In addition, these tables show that reduced accession rates after the reform were smaller in regulated sectors. This is consistent with the idea that higher entry costs mitigate the turnover effects of dismissal costs. The next section presents equivalent regression results which control for covariates.

5.1.1   Effect on accessions

Table 4.4 reports marginal effects of a linear probability model for accessions estimated using Equations (4.5) and (4.6). The dependent variable is a variable that takes the value of one if the person joined a firm in a given year and zero otherwise. The basic specification controls for age, occupation dummies, and firm and year effects. The effect of interest is captured by the interaction between the post-reform dummy and a dummy for firms under 15 employees during the pre-reform period. The reported standard errors allow for clustering by period-size group to control for common random effects within these cells.

Panels A and B of Table 4.4 show the results for men and women, respectively. The results show a large and statistically significant decline in permanent accessions in small relative to large firms after the 1990 reform was introduced. Column (1) shows that accession probabilities decreased by 0.0306 or 15.4 per cent for men and by 0.0359 or 16.2 per cent for women in small relative to big firms during the reform years. Including sector-specific trends and sector productivity in columns (2) and (3) reduces the effects on accession probabilities to between 0.0246 and 0.0251 for men and to between 0.0335 and 0.0339 for women.

Columns (4) and (5) of Table 4.4 report the results controlling for size-specific cyclical effects as in Equation (4.6). The results for men in panel A show a smaller effect of between 0.0232 and 0.0171 using the expansion dummy and GDP growth, respectively, to control for size-specific cyclical effects. By contrast, the results for women now show bigger effects of between 0.0468 and 0.0507 when the size-specific cyclical effect is controlled with the expansion dummy and GDP growth, respectively. Finally, since we are using panel data we also include worker effects to account for the possibility that less-employable individuals may look for employment in smaller firms. The results with size-specific cyclical effects as well as individual fixed effects in column (6) show a smaller but still significant effect for men of 0.0154 or 6.6 per cent and a bigger effect for women of 0.0508 or 23 per cent. The much larger reduction in hiring as a result of increased dismissal costs for women than for men is consistent with the view that dismissal costs have a much larger effect on outsiders than insiders.

Table 4.5 shows the marginal effects of models which include interactions with a regulated sector dummy, which allow a contrast to be made between how the effect differs in regulated and unregulated sectors. The third level interaction on the small dummy, the post-90 dummy and the regulated dummy captures the differential effect of the increase in unfair dismissal costs in the regulated sector relative to the unregulated sector.

Table 4.4   Effects of the 1990 reform on accessions (full sample)

Regressors	(1)	(2)	(3)	(4)	(5)	(6)
	A. MEN ($N = 85222$)					
Post-1990	0.01227	0.0066	0.0073	0.0095	−0.0016	0.0004
	(0.0125)	(0.0079)	(0.0081)	(0.0090)	(0.0096)	(0.0057)
Small firms	0.0674**	0.0647**	0.0648**	0.0647**	0.0513*	0.0356**
	(0.0027)	(0.0025)	(0.0026)	(0.0026)	(0.0131)	(0.0095)
Post-1990 ×	−0.0306**	–	–	−0.0232**	−0.0171	−0.0154
small firms	(0.0011)	0.0251**	0.0246**	(0.0031)	(0.0066)	(0.0075)
		(0.0030)	(0.0030)			
	B. WOMEN ($N = 39548$)					
Post-1990	0.0110	−0.0025	0.0006	0.0096	0.0051	0.0150*
	(0.0315)	(0.0118)	(0.0106)	(0.0113)	(0.0077)	(0.0088)
small firms	0.0710**	0.0703**	0.0697**	0.0698**	0.1002*	0.0609**
	(0.0029)	(0.0020)	(0.0021)	(0.0021)	(0.0196)	(0.0137)
Post-1990 x	−0.0359**	–	–	−0.0468**	−0.0507*	−0.0508**
small firms	(0.0012)	0.0339**	0.0335**	(0.0009)	(0.0102)	(0.0107)
		(0.0008)	(0.0008)			
Sector and region fixed effects	Yes	Yes	Yes	Yes	Yes	Yes
Trend	Yes	No	No	No	No	No
Productivity	No	No	Yes	Yes	Yes	No
Sector specific trends	No	Yes	Yes	Yes	Yes	Yes
Workers fixed effects	No	No	No	No	No	Yes
Recession dummy	No	No	No	Yes	No	No
GDP growth rate	No	No	No	No	Yes	Yes

Notes: Robust standard errors in parentheses allow for clustering by period/size. All specifications control for year, sector and region effects, age, a gender dummy, a white-collar dummy and total number of employees in the firm. Some specifications include sectoral productivity which is calculated as value added deflated using a sector-level PPI over the number of workers using 1995 as the base year. Columns (4)–(6) control for size-specific cyclical effects. Column (4) interacts the small dummy with an expansion dummy, which takes the value of one for 1992–93 and zero otherwise, while columns (5) and (6) interact the small dummy with GDP growth. Column (6) controls for worker effects. ** denotes significance at the 1% level and * denotes significance at the 5% level.

Table 4.5   Effects of the 1990 reform on accessions (regulation sample)

Regressors	(1)	(2)	(3)	(4)	(5)	(6)
			A. MEN ($N = 11232$)			
Regulated sector	−0.0207	−33.67	−33.84	−33.26	−34.85	2.655
	(0.0313)	(38.29)	(37.02)	(38.10)	(35.91)	(11.56)
Post-1990	0.0016	0.0077	0.0082	0.011	0.0137	0.0264
	(0.0210)	(0.0398)	(0.0381)	(0.0430)	(0.0332)	(0.0308)
Small firms	0.0404**	0.0418**	0.0419**	0.0418**	0.0547**	0.0423
	(0.0030)	(0.0030)	(0.0030)	(0.0030)	(0.0134)	(0.0723)
Post-1990 ×	−0.0064	−0.0089*	−0.0089*	−0.0331**	−0.0162*	−0.0637
small firms	(0.0029)	(0.0039)	(0.0039)	(0.0040)	(0.0064)	(0.0494)
Post-1990 ×	0.0178**	0.0125	0.0176	0.0175	0.0102	0.0181
regulated sector	(0.0024)	(0.0458)	(0.0445)	(0.0495)	(0.0423)	(0.0342)
Small firms ×	0.0362**	0.0383*	0.0389*	0.0386*	0.0046	0.0106
regulated sector	(0.0093)	(0.0118)	(0.0117)	(0.0118)	(0.0173)	(0.0781)
Post-1990 ×	−0.0120*	−0.0148	−0.0161	0.0143	0.0031	0.0259
small firms ×	(0.0042)	(0.0114)	(0.0110)	(0.0116)	(0.0092)	(0.0533)
regulated sector						
			B. WOMEN ($N = 5581$)			
Regulated sector	−	−	−	−	−	−
Post-1990	0.0472*	0.0366	0.0372	0.0562	0.0409	0.0342
	(0.0141)	(0.0215)	(0.0212)	(0.0252)	(0.0279)	(0.0300)
Small firms	0.0360**	0.0378**	0.0378**	0.0378**	0.0684	0.0789
	(0.0012)	(0.0017)	(0.0017)	(0.0017)	(0.0345)	(0.0563)
Post-1990 ×	−0.0349**	−0.0389**	−0.0388**	−0.0487**	−0.0557**	−0.0311
small firms	(0.0017)	(0.0014)	(0.0013)	(0.0011)	(0.0187)	(0.0384)
Post-1990 ×	−0.0575**	−0.0355	−0.0318	−0.0594	−0.0618	−0.0449
regulated sector	(0.0017)	(0.0294)	(0.0292)	(0.0347)	(0.0390)	(0.0422)
Small firms ×	−0.0424**	−0.0414**	−0.0412**	−0.0409**	−0.0719	−0.0362
regulated sector	(0.0016)	(0.0030)	(0.0028)	(0.0026)	(0.0442)	(0.0733)
Post-1990 ×	0.0685**	0.0679**	0.0675**	0.0748**	0.0830**	0.0402
small firms ×	(0.0025)	(0.0059)	(0.0054)	(0.0057)	(0.0218)	(0.0501)
regulated sector						
Sector and region fixed effects	Yes	Yes	Yes	Yes	Yes	Yes
Trend	Yes	No	No	No	No	No
Productivity	No	No	Yes	Yes	Yes	No
Sector specific trends	No	Yes	Yes	Yes	Yes	Yes
Workers fixed effects	No	No	No	No	No	Yes
Recession dummy	No	No	No	Yes	No	No
GDP growth rate	No	No	No	No	Yes	Yes

Notes: The regulation sample includes workers and firms in the retail, road transportation, electricity, telecommunications, air transportation and textile sectors. The retail, road transportation, electricity and telecommunications are classified as regulated, while the air transportation and textile sectors are classified as unregulated. Robust standard errors in parentheses allow for clustering by period/size. All specifications control for year, sector and region effects, age, a gender dummy, a white-collar dummy and total number of employees in the firm. Some specifications include sectoral productivity which is calculated as value added deflated using a sector-level PPI over the number of workers using 1995 as the base year. Columns (4)–(6) control for size-specific cyclical effects. Column (4) interacts the small dummy with an expansion dummy, which takes the value of one for 1992–93 and zero otherwise, while columns (5) and (6) interact the small dummy with GDP growth. Column (6) controls for worker effects. ** denotes significance at the 1% level and * denotes significance at the 5% level.

As in Table 4.4 the results show reduced accessions for men and women in small relative to big firms during the reform years. The results for men show no differential effects of the reform in regulated and unregulated sectors. By contrast, the results for women generally show a smaller reduction in accessions in regulated sectors relative to unregulated sectors. The results for women are consistent with the idea that the effect of the reforms in terms of reduced hiring should be smaller in sectors faced with higher entry costs.

5.1.2 Effect on separations

Table 4.6 reports marginal effects of a linear probability model for separations. The dependent variable is now a variable that takes the value of one if the person separated from the firm in a given year and zero otherwise.[20] As before, panel A reports the results for men and panel B for women. The results show that separation probabilities decreased for both men and women. For example, the results from the basic specification show a decrease in separation probabilities of 0.0615 or 18.9 per cent for men and of 0.0637 or 19.8 per cent for women. Controlling for sector-specific trends and sector productivity the effects drop to 0.0607 and 0.0623 for men and women, respectively.

The results controlling for size-specific cyclical effects in columns (4) and (5) of Table 4.6 show smaller effects of between 0.0551 and 0.0579 for men and larger effects of between 0.0861 and 0.0899 for women. Moreover, the results controlling for worker effects are smaller but continue to show significant reductions in separations in small relative to big firms during the reform period. The results with both size-specific cyclical effects and worker effects now show a reduction in separations of 0.0237 or 7.3 per cent for men and of 0.034 or 10.6 per cent for women in small relative to big firms after 1990.

Table 4.6　Effect of the 1990 reform on separations (full sample)

Regressors	(1)	(2)	(3)	(4)	(5)	(6)
			A. MEN ($N = 85222$)			
Post-1990	−0.0258	−0.0262*	−0.0284**	−0.0254*	−0.0176	−0.0505**
	(0.0150)	(0.0050)	(0.0047)	(0.0062)	(0.0093)	(0.0065)
Small firms	0.1161**	0.1153**	0.1155**	0.1154**	0.1104**	0.0858**
	(0.0044)	(0.0044)	(0.0041)	(0.0041)	(0.0095)	(0.0108)
Post-1990 ×	−0.0615**	−0.0607**	−0.0609**	−0.0551**	−0.0579**	−0.0237**
small firms	(0.0015)	(0.0022)	(0.0018)	(0.0018)	(0.0044)	(0.0084)
			B. WOMEN ($N = 39548$)			
Post-1990	0.0027	−0.0113	−0.0063	0.0074	0.0140	−0.0222*
	(0.0416)	(0.0132)	(0.0010)	(0.0104)	(0.0102)	(0.0100)
Small firms	0.1210**	0.1206	0.1210**	0.1211**	0.1708**	0.1103**
	(0.0028)	(0.0025)	(0.0027)	(0.0026)	(0.0234)	(0.0157)
Post-1990 ×	−0.0637**	−0.0623	−0.0624**	−0.0861**	−0.0899**	−0.034**
small firms	(0.0012)	(0.0028)	(0.0030)	(0.0032)	(0.0136)	(0.0123)
Sector and region fixed effects	Yes	Yes	Yes	Yes	Yes	Yes
Trend	Yes	No	No	No	No	No
Productivity	No	No	Yes	Yes	Yes	No
Sector specific trends	No	Yes	Yes	Yes	Yes	Yes
Workers fixed effects	No	No	No	No	No	Yes
Recession dummy	No	No	No	Yes	No	No
GDP growth rate	No	No	No	No	Yes	Yes

Notes:　Robust standard errors in parentheses allow for clustering by period/size. All specifications control for year, sector and region effects, age, a gender dummy, a white-collar dummy and total number of employees in the firm. Some specifications include sectoral productivity which is calculated as value added deflated using a sector-level PPI over the number of workers using 1995 as the base year. Columns (4)–(6) control for size-specific cyclical effects. Column (4) interacts the small dummy with an expansion dummy, which takes the value of one for 1992–93 and zero otherwise, while columns (5) and (6) interact the small dummy with GDP growth. Column (6) controls for worker effects. ** denotes significance at the 1% level and * denotes significance at the 5% level.

Table 4.7 shows the marginal effects of models which include interactions with a regulated sector dummy. The effects of the reform become insignificant for men, but, as in Table 4.6, the results for women show reduced separations in small relative to big firms after the reform. Moreover,

Table 4.7   Effects of the 1990 reform on separations (regulation sample)

Regressors	(1)	(2)	(3)	(4)	(5)	(6)
			A. MEN ($N = 11232$)			
Regulated sector	−0.0132	−0.9932	−1.337	−0.1253	1.71	−
	(0.0363)	(10.02)	(8.213)	(8.478)	(10.24)	−
Post-1990	−0.1059**	−0.0855**	−0.0844**	−0.0821**	−0.0805**	−0.0822*
	(0.0203)	(0.0177)	(0.0149)	(0.0158)	(0.0115)	(0.0359)
Small firms	0.0426**	0.0420**	0.0421**	0.0421**	0.0388	0.0444
	(0.0088)	(0.0090)	(0.0089)	(0.0089)	(0.0446)	(0.0843)
Post-1990 ×	0.0070	0.0075	0.0076	0.0272**	0.0098	−0.0587
small firms	(0.0052)	(0.0057)	(0.0057)	(0.0052)	(0.026)	(0.0575)
Post-1990 ×	0.0795**	0.0516	0.0618*	0.0672*	0.0765*	0.0485
regulated sector	(0.0022)	(0.0280)	(0.0250)	(0.0271)	(0.0239)	(0.0399)
Small firms ×	0.0955**	0.0907**	0.0920**	0.0913**	0.0898	0.0632
regulated sector	(0.0118)	(0.0130)	(0.0144)	(0.0142)	(0.0467)	(0.0910)
Post-1990 ×	−0.0777**	−0.0696**	−0.0720**	−0.0833**	−0.0699*	0.0682
small firms ×	(0.0037)	(0.0086)	(0.0101)	(0.0102)	(0.0284)	(0.0621)
regulated sector						
			B. WOMEN ($N = 5581$)			
Regulated sector	−	−	−	−	−	−
Post-1990	−0.0077	−0.0219	−	−0.0218	−0.0113	−0.0642
	(0.0189)	(0.0203)	−0.0218	(0.0188)	(0.0329)	(0.0365)
			(0.0205)			
Small firms	0.0930**	0.0928**	0.0928**	0.0929**	0.0986*	0.1259
	(0.0027)	(0.0027)	(0.0027)	(0.0027)	(0.0393)	(0.0685)
Post-1990 ×	−0.0499**	−0.0489**	−0.0489**	−0.076**	−0.0522*	0.0232
small firms	(0.0017)	(0.0008)	(0.0008)	(0.0009)	(0.0211)	(0.0467)
Post-1990 ×	−0.0108	0.0065	0.0073	0.0329	0.0171	−0.0005
regulated sector	(0.0013)	(0.0285)	(0.0262)	(0.0234)	(0.0463)	(0.0514)
Small firms ×	−0.0293**	−0.0369**	−0.0368**	−0.0366**	0.0004	−0.0049
regulated sector	(0.0053)	(0.0038)	(0.0039)	(0.0032)	(0.0658)	(0.0891)
Post-1990 ×	0.0184**	0.0299**	0.0298**	0.0151*	0.0098	0.0213
small firms ×	(0.0018)	(0.0058)	(0.0061)	(0.0054)	(0.0357)	(0.0610)
regulated sector						
Sector and region fixed effects	Yes	Yes	Yes	Yes	Yes	Yes
Trend	Yes	No	No	No	No	No
Productivity	No	No	Yes	Yes	Yes	No
Sector specific trends	No	Yes	Yes	Yes	Yes	Yes
Workers fixed effects	No	No	No	No	No	Yes
Recession dummy	No	No	No	Yes	No	No
GDP growth rate	No	No	No	No	Yes	Yes

Notes: The regulation sample includes workers and firms in the retail, road transportation, electricity, telecommunications, air transportation and textile sectors. Retail, road transportation, electricity and telecommunications are classified as regulated, while the air transportation and textile sectors are classified as unregulated. Robust standard errors in parentheses allow for clustering by period/size. All specifications control for year, sector and region effects, age, a gender dummy, a white-collar dummy and total number of employees in the firm. Some specifications include sectoral productivity which is calculated as value added deflated using a sector-level PPI over the number of workers using 1995 as the base year. Columns (4)–(6) control for size-specific cyclical effects. Column (4) interacts the small dummy with an expansion dummy, which takes the value of one for 1992–93 and zero otherwise, while columns (5) and (6) interact the small dummy with GDP growth. Column (6) controls for worker effects. ** denotes significance at the 1% level and * denotes significance at the 5% level.

the results for men show bigger effects of the reform on separations in regulated sectors, while the results for women show bigger effects in the less regulated sectors.[21]

5.1.3 Net employment effect

The effects of the reform on net employment can be determined using the following steady state conditions,

$$\lambda_S e_S = \theta_S u$$
$$\lambda_L e_L = \theta_L u$$

where $\lambda_S = \lambda G(\bar{\varepsilon}_S^*)$, $\theta_S = \theta_S^* q(\theta_S^*)$, $\lambda_L = \lambda G(\bar{\varepsilon}_L^*)$, and $\theta_L = \theta_L^* q(\theta_L^*)$. The first steady-state condition requires the flow into unemployment out of small firms to be equal to the flow out of unemployment into small firms, and the second condition requires the flow into unemployment out of large firms to be equal to the flow out of unemployment into large firms. In addition, the following identity must hold:

$$u = 1 - e$$

where

$$e = [p_S \times e_S + (1 - p_S) \times e_L]$$

where p_S is the share of employment in small firms. Using the two steady-state conditions and the identity to solve for employment yields:

$$e = \left[\frac{p_S \lambda_L \theta_S + (1 - p_S) \lambda_S \theta_L}{\lambda_S \lambda_L + p_S \lambda_L \theta_S + (1 - p_S) \lambda_S \theta_L} \right]$$

The results above suggest accessions and separations decreased by 6.6 per cent and 7.3 per cent for men. Using these results together with average accessions and separation rates in small and large firms and the share of employment in small firms before the reform in the top panel of Table 4.1, suggests an increase in men's employment of less than a tenth of a percentage point due to the reform. In contrast, the results for women suggest greater decreases in accessions and separations of 23 per cent and 10.6 per cent, respectively. Combining these results with the average accession and separation rates in small and large firms and the share of employment in small firms for women before the reform in panel B of Table 4.1, suggests a decline in women's employment of about 1 per cent as a result of the reform. The results for men and women suggest no net employment effects due to increased dismissal costs for insiders but negative employment effects for workers likely to be outsiders. Moreover, the results above show greater effects of the reform in unregulated sectors, especially in terms of accessions, suggesting that most of the losses in employment after the increase in dismissal costs occurred in less regulated sectors.

6.   CONCLUSIONS

Labour and product market regulations have often been blamed for the high unemployment in Europe. Yet the empirical evidence on the impact of these regulations is mixed. In this chapter we present new evidence on the impact of dismissal costs on turnover and employment and ask how the employment consequences of dismissal costs vary with the strictness of entry regulations.

We first present a model which shows that while dismissal costs reduce both accessions and separations, the impact of dismissal costs on hiring is mitigated when entry costs are higher. This is because the higher the entry costs, the more careful are firms in creating new jobs. This result thus suggests that barriers to entry reduce the effectiveness of labour market deregulation.

We use an employer–employee panel from the Italian Social Security Administration archives to examine the impact of labour and product market regulations empirically. We exploit the fact that dismissal costs increased after 1990 in Italy for firms with fewer than 15 employees relative to larger firms. Our estimates suggest the 1990 reform reduced accessions by 6.6 per cent and 23 per cent for men and women, respectively. In addition our estimates suggest a reduction in separations of 7.3 per cent and 10.6 per cent for men and women, respectively, as a result of the reform. These results are robust to the inclusion of sectoral productivity, size-specific cyclical effects and firm and worker effects. Combining these results with the steady-state equations from the model suggests no disemployment effects of dismissal costs for men, who are more likely to be insiders, but a decline of about 1 per cent in the employment of women, who are more likely to be outsiders.

We then look at the impact of the 1990 reform on turnover in sectors subject to more and less restrictive entry regulations. While several authors have documented very costly administrative burdens in Italy, these authors also document the variability in entry regulation across sectors within Italy. We exploit this variability together with the changes in dismissal costs after 1990 for small relative to large firms to examine how labour and product market regulations interact. Our results suggest a smaller impact of the 1990 reform on accessions in regulated than in less regulated sectors, especially for women. An important implication of our theoretical and empirical findings is that for labour market deregulation to be effective in terms of generating new jobs, countries also have to eliminate administrative burdens that generate barriers to entrepreneurship.

NOTES

1. We are grateful to Joshua Angrist, Giuseppe Bertola, Juan J. Dolado, Monique Ebell, Jordi Galí, Pietro Garibaldi, Christian Haefke, Andrea Ichino, Paloma López-García, Julián Messina and Steve Pischke for useful suggestions. We thank Bruno Contini of the LABORatorio Riccardo Revelli for kindly providing us with the INPS data and Federico Cingano and Alfonso Rosolia for providing us with data on sector-level productivity and GDP growth. Adriana Kugler acknowledges financial support from CREI at Universitat Pompeu Fabra and from the Spanish Ministry of Science and Technology through grant No. SEC–2000–1034. E-mail addresses: adkugler@uh.edu; gio.pica@gmail.com.
2. See for example Bertrand and Kramarz (2002), Blanchard and Giavazzi (2003), Boeri et al. (2000), Fonseca et al. (2001), Gersbach and Schniewind (2001), Messina (2003) and Nickell (1999).
3. By contrast, severance pay for fair dismissals is paid from workers' retained earnings, so they entail no cost to employers.
4. Boeri and Jimeno (2005) present a theoretical explanation of why these exemptions may be in place to begin with. They argue that exempting small firms reduces the disemployment effect of EPL, because small firms subject to EPL have to pay much higher efficiency wages to discourage shirking than large firms.
5. Note that according to the OECD's *Employment Outlook* (1999) Italy ranked first in terms of strictness of the regulation of fixed-term contracts during the 1980s and it continued to rank first during the 1990s.
6. In 1991 the Italian government also introduced other reforms. In one, it aimed at providing fiscal incentives by reducing payroll taxes (that is, social security contributions) for firms with more than 15 employees. As shown in Kugler et al. (2003), while an increase in dismissal costs should reduce both hiring and dismissals, a reduction in payroll taxes should increase hiring but have no effect on dismissals. Consequently this reform should have increased hiring but should not have affected dismissals. Another reform implemented in 1991 deals with collective dismissals taking place in firms with more than 15 employees. It introduces a special procedure in the case where at least five workers are dismissed (in a range of 110 days). In order to deal with this (potentially) confounding

factor, we have also limited our sample to firms below 35 employees (less subject to be hit by shocks forcing them to fire as many as five employees or more) and the results are unchanged. Finally, in 1992 the government also eliminated a wage indexation mechanism (Scala Mobile) which had been adopted in 1945 and which applied to firms of all sizes.

7.   OECD measures of the strictness of regulations on temporary help agencies ranked Italy first in the late 1980s, but ranked Italy sixth in the late 1990s after Turkey, Greece, Spain, Portugal and Belgium (OECD *Employment Outlook* 1999).

8.   In our empirical analysis we also tried limiting the sample to the period from 1987 to 1996 to eliminate any possible effect of the liberalization of temporary contracts in 1987. In any case though, we concentrate on permanent workers in our analysis.

9.   A number of studies have analysed the impact of product market regulations on employment, the employment consequences of immigration, productivity and investment using these indicators (Boeri et al. 2000; Angrist and Kugler 2003; Nicoletti and Scarpetta 2003; Alesina et al. 2005).

10.   See Boylaud (2000) for a detailed study of the road freight and retail sectors, Boylaud and Nicoletti (2000) for a detailed study of the telecommunications sector, Gönenc and Nicoletti (2000) for a detailed study of the air passenger transportation sector, and Gönenc et al. (2000) for a detailed study of each of these sectors.

11.   The reason for ranking the industry strictness by comparing the industry in a country to the industry's average in all countries in the sample is that some industries may be subject to market failures so that regulation may be justified. This means that it makes sense to compare Italy's electricity sector to the electricity sector in other countries rather than to Italy's retail distribution sector which is unlikely to face the same market failures as the electricity sector.

12.   While some of these sectors have been affected by regulatory reform, the most important changes in the regulatory environment occurred after the period we study (see Goglio 2001 for a detailed description of these reforms). For example, Telecom Italia was privatized in 1997 and telecommunications services were fully liberalized also in 1997. In electricity, ENEL (the public legal monopoly until then) became a joint stock company in 1991. However, it was not until 1999 that the sector was fully liberalized by introducing functional unbundling of the industry and limiting the generation and import of ENEL to 50 per cent. Similarly in railways, Ferrovie dello Stato (the integrated public monopolist until then) was transformed into a joint stock company in 1992. However, it was not until 1999 that the law required legal separation between the network operators and the service company and that international operators were allowed to access this market.

13.   Orszag and Snower (1999) discuss economic and political complementarities between unemployment benefits and taxes, where political complementarities arise when the ability to gain political consent for one policy depends on the implementation of the other policies. Blanchard and Giavazzi (2003) instead discuss political complementarities between labour market regulations that determine the bargaining power of workers and entry regulations.

14.   This is equivalent to Nash bargaining with zero bargaining power to workers. Although by continuity the results extend to the case of positive bargaining power (provided it is not too high), we keep this wage setting rule for simplicity.

15.   Note that the reduction in job creation as a result of an increase in entry costs is greater than the reduction due to an increase in dismissal costs. This is because the entry cost generates both an up front cost and a flow cost $rK/q(\theta)$, while the firing cost only generates an up front cost.

16.   This is similar to the reduction in the labour demand elasticity generated by the constraint on entrepreneurship in Krueger and Pischke's (1998) model.

17.   Firm size during the pre-reform period is highly correlated with current firm size but not affected by the reform. The correlation between the average firm size during the pre- and post-reform periods is 0.95.

18.   The results below show that this is driven by the results for men, as the impact of the reform on women's separations was smaller in the regulated sector. Note that our theory

does not make any predictions on the relative impact of increased dismissal costs on separations in regulated and unregulated sectors.
19. While the dataset includes a random sample of workers, the probability that a firm is selected increases with size.
20. The controls in these specifications are as in the linear probability models for accessions.
21. Our theoretical analysis in Section 3 does not predict anything about the differential impact of dismissal costs in regulated or unregulated sectors.

REFERENCES

Alesina, A., S. Ardagna, G. Nicoletti and F. Schiantarelli (2005), 'Regulation and investment', *Journal of the European Economic Association*, 3 (4), 791–825.

Angrist, J. and A. Kugler (2003), 'Protective or counter-productive? Labour market institutions and the effect of immigration on EU natives', *Economic Journal*, 113, 302–31.

Bertola, G. (1990), 'Job security, employment, and wages', *European Economic Review*, 54 (4), 851–79.

Bertrand, M. and F. Kramarz (2002), 'Does product market regulation hinder job creation? Commercial zoning and retailing employment in France', *Quarterly Journal of Economics*, 117 (4), 1369–414.

Blanchard, O.J. and F. Giavazzi (2003), 'The macroeconomic effects of regulation and deregulation in goods and labor markets', *Quarterly Journal of Economics*, 118 (3), 879–909.

Boeri, T. and J.F. Jimeno (2005), 'The effects of employment protection: learning from variable enforcement', *European Economic Review*, 49 (8), 2057–77.

Boeri, T., S. Scarpetta and G. Nicoletti (2000), 'Regulation and labor market performance', CEPR Discussion Paper 2420.

Borgarello, A., P. Garibaldi and L. Pacelli (2004), 'Employment protection legislation and the size of firms', *Il Giornale degli Economisti*, 1.

Boylaud, O. (2000), 'Regulatory reform in road freight and retail distribution', OECD Economics Department Working Paper 255.

Boylaud, O. and G. Nicoletti (2000), 'Regulation, market structure and performance in telecommunications', OECD Economics Department Working Paper 237.

Djankov, S., R. La Porta, F. López-de-Silanes and A. Shleifer (2002), 'The regulation of entry', *Quarterly Journal of Economics*, 117 (1), 1–37.

Fonseca, R., P. López-García and C. Pissarides (2001), 'Entrepreneurship, start-up costs and employment', *European Economic Review*, 45, 692–705.

Gersbach, H. and A. Schniewind (2001), 'Product market reforms and unemployment in Europe', IZA Discussion Paper 255.

Goglio, A. (2001), 'Sectoral regulatory reforms in Italy: framework and implications', OECD Economics Department Working Paper 294.

Gönenc, R. and G. Nicoletti (2000), 'Regulation, market structure and performance in air passenger transportation', OECD Economics Department Working Paper 254.

Gönenc, R., M. Maher and G. Nicoletti (2000), 'The implementation and the effects of regulatory reform: past experience and current issues', OECD Economics Department Working Paper 251.

ISTAT (2002), *Annual Report*, Rome: ISTAT Publications.

Krueger, A. and J.-S. Pischke (1998), 'Observations and conjectures on the US employment miracle', presented at Third Public German-American Academic Council Symposium, Bonn.

Kugler, A. (1999), 'The impact of firing costs on turnover and unemployment: evidence from the Colombian labour market reform', *International Tax and Public Finance*, **6** (3), 389–410.

Kugler, A., J.F. Jimeno and V. Hernanz (2003), 'Employment consequences of restrictive permanent contracts: evidence from Spanish labor market reforms', CEPR Working Paper 3724.

Lazear, E. (1990), 'Job security provisions and employment', *Quarterly Journal of Economics*, **105** (3), 699–726.

Messina, J. (2003), 'Sectoral structure and entry regulations', IZA Discussion Paper 747.

Mortensen, D.T. and C.A. Pissarides (1994), 'Job creation and job destruction in the theory of unemployment', *Review of Economic Studies*, **61** (3), July, 397–415.

Nickell, S. (1999), 'Product markets and labor markets', *Labor Economics*, **6**, 1–20.

Nickell, S. and R. Layard (1999), 'Labor market institutions and economic performance', in D. Card and O. Ashenfelter (eds), *Handbook of Labor Economics*, Vol. 3C, Amsterdam: NorthHolland, pp. 3029–84.

Nicoletti, G. (2001), 'Regulation in services: OECD patterns and economic implications', OECD Economics Department Working Paper 287.

Nicoletti, G. and S. Scarpetta (2003), 'Regulation, productivity and growth: OECD evidence', *Economic Policy*, **18** (36), 9–72.

Nicoletti, G., S. Scarpetta and O. Boylaud (2000), 'Summary indicators of product market regulation with an extension to employment protection legislation', OECD Economics Department Working Paper 226.

OECD (1999), *Employment Outlook*, Paris: OECD.

Orszag, M. and D. Snower (1999), 'Anatomy of policy complementarities', IZA Discussion Paper 41.

DISCUSSION

Monique Ebell

I would like to begin my discussion by emphasizing how much I enjoyed reading this paper. Kugler and Pica is one of very few papers to examine the interactions between labour and product market regulations empirically, which is indeed a valuable contribution. In particular, the authors set up a very simple, stylized model of labour and product market regulation interactions. They then use a nice natural experiment – a tightening of firing restrictions for small Italian firms subject to differing degrees of regulation – to try to identify these interactions empirically.

Of course, my job as a discussant is to be critical of the paper. I will first make some comments on the model, before moving on to discuss the empirics. I hope that these comments are understood as being constructive, aiming to point out where and how the arguments brought forth in the paper could be made even stronger.

Kugler and Pica's Model

Kugler and Pica present a very stylized model of the interactions between labour and product market regulations. In their model, entry costs work exclusively on the job creation margin. Entry costs make it more costly to create jobs, shifting the job creation schedule downward. In addition, entry costs and tightness interact along the job creation schedule. When the labour market is very tight, firms are more sensitive to entry costs.

The main question posed in this section will be: how robust are these model findings to loosening the restrictive simplifying assumptions made? I will focus on three such assumptions:

1. workers have zero bargaining power;
2. firms are short-lived, that is, the firm's entry cost is paid every time a vacancy is opened;
3. perfect competition exists in product markets despite the presence of explicit barriers to entry.

The gist of this section is that relaxing each of the above assumptions would forge links between entry costs and the job destruction margin, allowing for a richer set of theoretical results to take to the data.

Workers have zero bargaining power

The authors assume that the wage is given by: $w(\varepsilon) = \phi\varepsilon = (1 - \phi)b$. The authors claim that this wage would also result from Nash bargaining when the workers' bargaining power is zero. The zero-bargaining power wage leads to a job destruction condition which is unrelated to entry costs K:

$$0 = rF + (1 - \phi)(\bar{\varepsilon} - b) + \lambda\,\frac{1 - \phi}{r + \lambda}\int_{\bar{\varepsilon}}^{\varepsilon_m}[1 - G(\varepsilon')]dG(\varepsilon')$$

If workers' bargaining power is given by $\beta > 0$, however, it is straightforward to derive the wage as:

$$w(\varepsilon) = (1 - \beta)b + \beta\{\varepsilon + c\theta - K[r(1 - \theta) + \lambda G(\bar{\varepsilon})]\}$$

The presence of the entry/vacancy cost K in the wage is important since it creates a link between the entry/vacancy cost and job destruction. In particular, now K would show up in the job destruction condition. When K increases, the wage decreases at each level of productivity ε. This implies that jobs remain valuable to the firm at lower levels of productivity, lowering the job destruction threshold $\bar{\varepsilon}$. A lower job destruction threshold should shift the job destruction schedule (4.3) downwards. In addition, the fact that K is multiplied by labour market tightness θ in the wage also introduces a slope effect. When tightness is high, the impact of K on the wage is greater, also increasing the impact on the job destruction threshold, making the job destruction schedule steeper.

To sum up this point: allowing for non-zero worker bargaining power would allow Kugler and Pica to derive a richer set of effects of entry costs on the labour market. It would be nice to see whether they could get any mileage out of these richer effects in their empirical section.

Short-lived firms

In Kugler and Pica's set-up, firms are short-lived in the sense that firms have the same lifespan as a single vacancy and job. This is illustrated in the

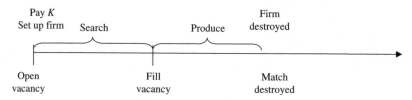

Figure 4D.1   Kugler and Pica's short-lived firms

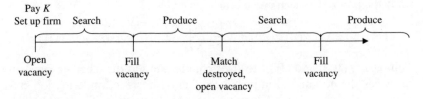

Figure 4D.2   Long-lived firms

timeline in Figure 4D.1. The top half describes the product market, while the bottom half describes the labour market.

Clearly, firms and vacancies live and die in perfect synchronization. The conceptual difficulty with this setup is that K could be both interpreted as a hiring cost, incurred whenever a vacancy is opened, or as an entry cost, incurred whenever a firm is created. This is rather puzzling, especially in light of the view that a firm's historical *raison d'être* is precisely to outlive individual workers.

One could easily imagine an alternative set-up, in which firms do indeed outlive their workers. This 'long-lived firm' set-up is illustrated in Figure 4D.2.

Now vacancies remain short-lived, while firms live indefinitely. This has two main effects. First, firms' longer lives imply that entry costs K can be amortized over a longer period of time, making them less important in hindering job creation. Second, when a firm destroys a job it now receives the value of a new vacancy in return, rather than the value zero associated with destruction of both the firm and the vacancy. This makes destroying jobs somewhat more attractive to firms, creating a further channel by which entry costs affect the job destruction margin.

Formally, under long-lived firms the value of a job becomes:

$$rJ(\varepsilon) = \varepsilon - w(\varepsilon) + \lambda \int_{\varepsilon_0}^{\bar{\varepsilon}} [-F + V - J(\varepsilon)]dG(\varepsilon')$$

$$+ \lambda \int_{\bar{\varepsilon}}^{\varepsilon_m} [J(\varepsilon') - J(\varepsilon)]dG(\varepsilon')$$

and the job destruction threshold satisfies $J(\bar{\varepsilon}) = -F + V$. Hence, making firms long-lived amounts to reducing firing costs by the value of a vacancy V. By free entry $V = K$ and the job creation schedule becomes:

$$\frac{1 - \phi}{r + \lambda}(\varepsilon_m - \bar{\varepsilon}) - \left(\frac{rK + c}{q(\theta)} + F\right) = 0 \quad \text{(JC)'}$$

while the job destruction curve is now given by:

$$r(F - K) + (1 - \phi)(\bar{\varepsilon} - b) + \lambda \frac{1 - \phi}{r + \lambda} \int_{\bar{\varepsilon}}^{\varepsilon_m} [1 - G(\varepsilon')]d\varepsilon' = 0 \quad \text{(JD)}'$$

Comparing (JC)' and (JD)' to their counterparts in the Chapter, one can easily see the diminished importance of entry costs in hindering job creation and the new role for K in promoting job destruction. The fact that the term $(rK + c)/q(\theta)$ remains in the job creation curve implies that the interaction between entry costs and job creation, the subject of the chapter's empirical experiment, is preserved. Hence, accounting for long-lived firms would preserve the main conclusions of the paper, while providing a richer set of empirical implications to test.

Perfect competition and barriers to entry
Kugler and Pica assume:

(a)   entry costs, that is, barriers to entry;
(b)   perfect competition;
(c)   one-worker firms.

That is, firms face barriers to entry, but as soon as they have 'jumped over' those barriers, they find themselves in a pool of firms which compete perfectly. Since barriers to entry are prime sources of imperfect competition, it would be more consistent to allow for imperfect competition among the firms in this model.[1]

In turn, imperfect competition calls into question the validity of assuming one-worker firms. Under perfect competition firm size is indeterminate anyway, so assuming that all firms have the same size and normalizing this size to one is harmless. Under imperfect competition, however, firm size is determinate, and normalizing the size to one may not be harmless at all (see Cahuc and Wasmer 2001).

Hence, a preferable set of assumptions would be:

(a)   entry costs, that is, barriers to entry;
(b)   monopolistic competition;
(c)   multi-worker firms.

The latter trio of assumptions would open up further channels by which entry costs might affect the labour market. Entry costs K affect the degree of competition which firms face, which would in turn affect their output and pricing decisions, firm profits and so on. This would allow entry costs to affect both the job creation and job destruction decisions.

Empirics

This section will focus on two aspects of the empirical exercise which might hold room for improvement.

Unregulated versus regulated industries

Kugler and Pica wish to examine the differential effects of increasing firing costs on regulated and unregulated firms. To separate firms into 'regulated' and 'unregulated' groups, Kugler and Pica use an index developed by Nicoletti (2001). Using the Nicoletti index for the purposes of testing Kugler and Pica's model is somewhat problematic however.

Kugler and Pica's model defines 'unregulated' to be 'low entry cost'. Hence, to test their model, Kugler and Pica would need an index which separates Italian industries into two groups: 'high entry cost' and 'low entry cost'. As a proxy, they could also use an index which compares the degree of regulation faced by different industries within one country.

Unfortunately the Nicoletti index is not suitable for such a classification of industries within one country since Nicoletti (2001) compares the degree of regulation of each industry across countries. That is, the Nicoletti index compares the air transportation industry in Italy (calling it 'unregulated') with the air transportation industry in Germany (calling it 'regulated'). This index does *not* make any direct statements about the degree of regulation in Italian air transport as compared to Italian telecommunications.

In practical terms the question becomes whether the classification that results from Nicoletti's index provides a reasonable grouping of industries. The 'less regulated' industries for Italy become air transportation and textiles, while the 'regulated' group includes retailing, road transportation, electricity and telecommunications. Still, it may well be the case that Italian textile firms face lower barriers to entry than their counterparts in the telecommunications sector. It is difficult to imagine, however, that entry costs (including the costs of fulfilling safety standards) in air transport are lower than those in retailing.

Women versus men

Kugler and Pica note that their regression coefficients are in general larger for women, as well as being more significant. They conjecture that this may be due to the fact that women are more likely to be outsiders to the labour market. Although this is plausible, it would be nice to be reassured that no female-specific policy changes (for example, changes in statutory maternity leave or in laws pertaining to sexual harassment) coincided with the change in entry regulations. It would also be nice to check for similar effects among other insider/outsider pairs, like younger versus prime-age workers or union versus non-union members.

Note

1. Examples of models which combine barriers to entry with explicit monopolistic competition among firms are Blanchard and Giavazzi (2003) and Ebell and Haefke (2003, 2004).

References

Blanchard, O. and F. Giavazzi (2003), 'The macroeconomic effects of regulation and deregulation in goods and labor markets', *Quarterly Journal of Economics*, **118** (3), 879–909.

Cahuc, P. and E. Wasmer (2001), 'Does intrafirm bargaining matter in the large firm's matching model?', *Macroeconomic Dynamics*, **5**, 742–47.

Ebell, M. and C. Haefke (2003), 'Product market deregulation and labor market outcomes', IZA Discussion Paper 957.

Ebell, M. and C. Haefke (2004), 'The missing link: product market regulation, collective bargaining and the European unemployment puzzle', mimeo, Universitat Pompeu Fabra.

Nicoletti, G. (2001), 'Regulation in services: OECD patterns and economic implications', OECD Economics Department Working Paper 226.

5. On the determinants of job flows in Europe: sectoral factors and institutions

Ramón Gómez-Salvador, Julián Messina and Giovanna Vallanti[1]

1. INTRODUCTION

The access to longitudinal firm databases has allowed the development of an empirical literature that examines the process of job creation, job destruction and, more generally, job reallocation at the firm level. This literature has allowed a better understanding of the behaviour of gross flows that are behind net employment changes. Indeed, we have learnt that two economies with broadly similar employment growth patterns can be characterized by significantly different underlying flows, that is, firms' behaviour. Moreover, gross job flows may be considered a proxy for labour market flexibility to the extent that they provide a measure of the responsiveness of the labour market to changes in economic conditions. On the theoretical side, differences in the stylized facts of job flows across countries have led to the development of theories that try to link these differences with the institutional framework of labour markets.

Available studies show that job creation and destruction coexist independently of the cyclical position of the economy, that is, when overall employment is both expanding or decreasing, showing that the adjustment process in the labour market is complex and the behaviour of firms is heterogeneous. Figure 5.1 illustrates the process of job reallocation. One limitation of most of the studies presenting international comparisons of job flows is the lack of comparability (OECD 1994). This is related to the fact that different sources could refer to different concepts, such as firm or establishment, different time intervals or periodicity, and, more importantly, different sectoral coverage. All these factors should be taken into account to get reliable conclusions.

In this chapter we examine cross-sectional patterns of job flows for 16 European countries using a unique homogeneous dataset of continuing

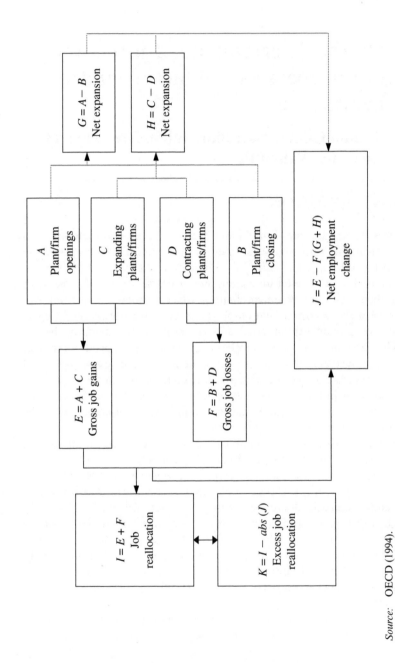

Source: OECD (1994).

Figure 5.1 Components of job reallocation

firms, that is, excluding start-ups and shutdowns, that covers the whole spectrum of productive sectors. First, we provide a characterization of job flows and examine cross-country differences and regularities. The magnitude and persistence of job flows in relation to firm characteristics (for example size, relevant sector and capital intensity) is reported in order to identify patterns among different groups of firms within and across the countries studied. Next, we study the impact that institutional differences among countries may have on job reallocation. While in Gómez-Salvador et al. (2004) we focused on the time and cross-country variation of job flows, here we analyse sectoral differences. Theory suggests that job turnover is partly determined by labour market policies such as employment protection legislation, unemployment benefits and wage-setting institutions. Differences in technology across sectors require different patterns of employment adjustment. Thus, if the institutional framework matters in explaining job creation and job destruction, sectoral patterns should differ across countries with different labour market institutions. We consider the effects of a number of policy measures on job turnover by distinguishing job flows across 29 productive sectors for a selected sample of EU countries.

We show that even if technological characteristics seem to be the main driving factor in explaining the dynamics of the labour market, country-idiosyncratic factors cannot be ruled out. However, each institution or regulation may act in different directions, some tightening and some facilitating the adjustment of employment. We find that policies aiming to protect employees' jobs have a negative effect on the dynamics of job reallocation. This is consistent with an ample theoretical literature. In particular, the negative effect of employment protection legislation appears more concentrated in industrial than in service sectors, although these effects are partially counter-balanced by the use of temporary contracts. The tax wedge and the generosity of the duration of unemployment benefits have similar effects across all sectors, reducing the extent of job reallocation.

The remainder of the chapter is organized as follows. In Section 2 we present the theoretical motivations of our study and the most recent empirical evidence. Section 3 describes the dataset used in our analysis and defines concepts and measures of gross job flows that have been extensively used in the empirical analysis. Section 4 evaluates gross and net job flows at both aggregate and sectoral level. Moreover, persistence rates of job flows across countries are considered. Section 5 assesses whether institutional differences matter in explaining job flows. Section 6 concludes.

2. EMPIRICAL EVIDENCE AND THE LINK WITH LABOUR MARKET INSTITUTIONS

2.1 Stylized Facts

There exists a large literature that has characterized the stylized facts – including size and cyclical properties – of the job reallocation process either for specific countries or showing country comparisons. Empirical studies on job flows include papers by Davis and Haltiwanger (1992, 1999), Davis et al. (1996) and Haltiwanger and Schuh (1999) for US manufacturing industry, Blanchflower and Burgess (1996) for the UK, Broersma and Gautier (1997) for the Netherlands, Albæk and Sørensen (1995) for Denmark, Lagarde et al. (1994) for France, Dolado and Gómez-Salvador (1995) for Spain, Contini et al. (1991) for Italy and Contini et al. (1995) for countries of the European Union. In addition, OECD (1994) and OECD (1996) report results on job flows for ten OECD countries for a period between the late 1980s and early 1990s, and Gómez-Salvador et al. (2004) examine job flows in the 1990s for 13 EU countries.

A common result in these studies is the fact that jobs are simultaneously created and destroyed in all the countries independently of the cyclical position of the economy. Another stylized fact is that job creation and destruction are negatively correlated, although their volatility tends to differ. It appears that in Anglo-Saxon countries job destruction is more volatile than job creation, leading to counter-cyclical job reallocation, while in Continental Europe the volatility is more similar and job reallocation is mostly acyclical. Finally, job reallocation varies across sectors, being higher in services than in manufacturing, depends on firms' characteristics, such as size, age and capital intensity, and is found to be a persistent phenomenon.

2.2 Job Flows and Labour Market Institutions

From a theoretical perspective, there are several reasons to believe that labour market institutions and policies may affect firms' employment decisions. In a partial equilibrium framework, Bertola (1990) shows how firing costs affect firm employment decisions by reducing both job creation and job destruction rates and therefore total job turnover. The cyclical implications are therefore clear: since firing costs make firing more costly during downturns and hiring more costly during upturns, employment will be less volatile over the cycle. However, the effect on the level of employment remains unclear. The role of firing restrictions in search equilibrium models is analysed in Garibaldi (1998) and Mortensen and Pissarides (1999a). All these studies predict a negative association between job turnover and firing restrictions.

Mortensen and Pissarides (1999b) and Pissarides (2000) incorporate the effects of both passive and active labour policies in a quite generalized framework of search-equilibrium. According to their model, both unemployment benefits and employment taxes decrease job creation and increase job destruction through an increase in the costs of labour. In equilibrium, the economy will settle at a higher unemployment rate while the effect on the overall job reallocation remains ambiguous. A job subsidy reduces the cost of the matching, inducing higher job creation. But job destruction increases as well because of the increase in market tightness, which improves the worker's option in the labour market. This time the effect on equilibrium unemployment is undetermined. A firing tax has an opposite effect on both job creation and job destruction, implying lower job reallocation.

The role of unions on employment and unemployment dynamics has been emphasized in a number of studies. It has been argued that unions may influence worker exit behaviour through wages kept above the market clearing level and through other 'non-wage' aspects (Farber 1986; Freeman 1980). In both cases the presence of unions contributes to improving the employee–employer relationship, making job separation more costly for the worker and then reducing job turnover. On the other hand, Bertola and Rogerson (1997) show how wage compression induced by either a centralized bargaining system or by the presence of wage floors, may be conducive to higher job turnover through an increase in job creation by the more productive firms and job destruction by the less productive ones because they cannot adjust wages.

From an empirical point of view, a preliminary attempt to relate facts with theory is that of Garibaldi et al. (1997). They present cross-country bivariate relationships between job turnover and several measures of labour market institutions and policies for selected OECD countries. As suggested by the theory, the cross-country comparison reveals a negative correlation between job reallocation and the strictness of employment protection. As regards unemployment benefits, they also appear to be negatively correlated with job reallocation, but the correlation changes sign when unemployment benefits are measured through the replacement rate rather than by their duration. The correlation between active policies and job turnover turns out to be slightly positive. However, the result is driven by the presence in the sample of Sweden, characterized by both high job turnover and an expenditure in active labour policies much higher than in the remaining EU countries. Garibaldi et al. (1997) also address the issue raised by Leonard and Van Audenrode (1993) on the effect of industry subsidies on job reallocation. Arguing that a subsidy to declining firms supported by a tax on growing firms reduces job creation and job destruction and under certain conditions also labour demand, Leonard and Van Audenrode predict a negative correlation between job reallocation and industry subsidies. Garibaldi et al. find a negative, though not significant, relationship and claim that the result in such a small sample is mainly driven by the two countries in Leonard and Van Audenrode, namely Belgium and the USA. Using new available indexes for employment protection legislation for a number of OECD countries, OECD (1999) reassesses the link between employment protection legislation and labour market flexibility. Simple bivariate associations seem to suggest a negative correlation between the strictness of employment protection legislation and job turnover rates even if such correlation tends to disappear when multivariate techniques are used to control for other factors influencing job turnover.

Regarding the role of unions, in contrast with the argument made in Bertola and Rogerson (1997), Lucifora (1998) for Italy and Blanchflower and Burgess (1996) for the UK find a negative correlation between unions and the rate of turnover. More recently, Heyman (2001) tests for the presence of a positive relationship between job reallocation and the degree of wage compression using a panel of Swedish establishment-level data. The Bertola–Rogerson hypothesis is supported somewhat by the analysis, the effect of wage dispersion on job reallocation is found to be negative and significant in the manufacturing sector.

Multivariate analysis on the effects of product and labour rigidities on labour market dynamics is presented in Salvanes (1997) and Gómez-Salvador et al. (2004). Salvanes uses 2-digit level data for seven OECD countries characterized by different degrees of regulation, and tests the effect of employment protection, wage bargaining centralization and industry subsidies on job flows. The findings on employment protection are in line with previous studies, with stricter dismissal costs having a negative impact on job creation and job destruction rates. Interestingly, centralized wage bargaining also has a negative impact on labour market flexibility by reducing job creation, contradicting the theoretical insights and empirical evidence reported by Bertola and Rogerson (1997). With regard to industrial subsidies, they have a positive impact on job reallocation in contrast with the evidence presented in Leonard and Van Audenrode (1993). In Gómez-Salvador et al. (2004) we control for differences across countries related to compositional effects due to differences in the age, size and capital intensity distribution of the firms. Our findings on a sample of 13 EU countries regarding EPL and the degree of centralization are in line with those of Salvanes, but we do not find a significant role of sectoral subsidies in the determination of job flows. In contrast, the generosity of unemployment benefits consistently reduces job turnover in our sample (Gómez-Salvador et al. 2004).

3. DATA AND JOB FLOWS DEFINITIONS

3.1 Data Sources

The 'Amadeus' database produced by Bureau van Dijk (BvD) contains comparable firm-level data for most EU countries since 1990, covering the non-financial private sector. In total it includes more than 3 million different firms. Apart from employment data, data at firm level include a wide range of financial information (for example profit and loss account, balance sheet and so on) and descriptive information (industry and activity codes, incorporation year and so on). Information in Amadeus permits the classification of firms by details of industries, size, age and average wage. In order to be included in Amadeus, a company should satisfy the following size criteria (figures for the UK, Germany, France and Italy; figures in parentheses for all other countries): operating revenues equal to at least 1.5 (1) million euro, total assets equal to at least 3 (2) million euro and number of employees equal to at least 15 (10).

The main advantage of this database is that the information is reasonably homogeneous across countries, allowing meaningful cross-country comparisons. In addition, information is provided on narrowly defined sectors and data on both manufacturing and non-manufacturing sectors are reasonably representative. The availability of data on services is quite an interesting feature of our dataset, given that most of the previous studies mainly rely on data for the manufacturing sector. The restriction of the analysis on job reallocation to a single sector can lead to misleading generalizations when the sector is not representative of other industries. Moreover, the fact that the manufacturing sector has experienced a stable contraction in employment in the last decade may have affected the dynamics of job flows (Foote 1998).

The main limitation is the fact that it is not possible to distinguish in our database between continuing firms, start-ups or shut-downs. Therefore the strategy followed to avoid the risk of 'false' flows is to restrict our analysis to continuing firms, for example firms that are in the sample for at least two consecutive periods. Although this is quite standard in the literature, it introduces a downward bias in the estimates of job flows, given that, according to previous studies, births and deaths of firms account for at least one quarter of the estimated job flows. However, job turnover at continuing firms is precisely the component of overall turnover that is more likely to be affected by some of the labour market institutions considered in this chapter (for example EPL). Another limitation is related to the definition used which refers to firms rather than to establishments. There are several reasons why establishment data may be preferred to firm-level data.

Measuring job flows at firm level may understate the actual magnitude of total gross flows among plants.[2] The use of firm-level data may lead to longitudinal linkage problems (and to spurious flows) if ownership and organizational changes (that is, mergers, acquisitions and so on) are not accounted for.[3] This may be less of a problem with plant-level data – plant being defined in terms of physical location of production. However, cross-country comparisons of establishment data pose serious difficulties as there is important heterogeneity in the definition of establishment across datasets (OECD 1994). This is less of a problem with firm data. Finally, the inclusion criteria in Amadeus introduce a bias against very small firms. The representativeness of the data is assessed in Section 3.3.

3.2　Job Flows Definitions

The conventions of Davis and Haltiwanger (1992 and 1999) are followed in defining job flows statistics. They denote the level of employment at firm level in period t with n_{ft} and let Δn_{ft} denote the change in employment between period t and $t-1$. Moreover let S^+ be the set of firms in sector S with $\Delta n_{ft} > 0$ and S^- be the set of firms in sector S with $\Delta n_{ft} < 0$. We calculate job creation by summing employment changes in S^+. Correspondingly job destruction is calculated by summing all the (absolute) changes in S^-. Rates of job creation (JC) and job destruction (JD) are obtained by dividing by the size of sector. Firm size at time t is calculated as the average employment between period t and $t-1$, that is, $x_{ft} = 0.5(n_{ft} + n_{ft-1})$. Accordingly, the sector size is defined as $X_{st} = \Sigma_{f \in S} x_{ft}$.

Job flow rates can equivalently be expressed as the size-weighted average over firms' growth rates as follows

$$JC_{st} = \sum_{f \in S_t^+} |g_{ft}| \frac{x_{ft}}{X_{st}} \qquad \text{Job creation rate}$$

$$JD_{st} = \sum_{f \in S_t^-} |g_{ft}| \frac{x_{ft}}{X_{st}} \qquad \text{Job destruction rate}$$

$$\text{where } g_{ft} = \frac{\Delta n_{ft}}{x_{ft}}$$

The sum of job creation rate and job destruction rate is the job reallocation (JR).[4] It gives the total number of employment positions reallocated in the economy. The difference between job creation and job destruction is the net employment growth (NET). The amount of job reallocation over and above what is needed to accommodate the aggregate net change in employment is the excess job reallocation (*EJR*), defined as $JR_{st} - |NET_{st}|$. *EJR* is bounded between zero and *JR* and gives a measure of overall heterogeneity of the firm-level outcome of employment changes. *EJR* is equal to zero if all firms change employment in the same direction. Finally, the minimum worker reallocation (*minWR*) that is required to accommodate the reallocation of jobs is defined as $max[JC_{st}, JD_{st}]$.[5]

3.3 Sample Description

The analysis focuses on the EU countries, except Italy, plus Norway and Switzerland. Initial exploration of Italian data showed important inconsistencies between annual employment growth rates computed from Amadeus and from other sources, which do not seem to be related to specific outliers. A potential explanation is the over-representation of small firms in Italy. Since Amadeus excludes small firms from the sample, this might give a more distorted representation of aggregate flows in Italy than in the other countries considered.[6] Table 5.1 shows the final sample composition and the sample period for each country, after filtering the observations from possible outliers and missing values.[7]

Table 5.1 Final sample composition

	Total number of firm observations per year	Sample period
Austria	9486	1995–2000
Belgium	27185	1992–2000
Denmark	13083	1996–2001
Finland	7471	1997–2000
France	50437	1993–2000
Germany	89459	1994–2000
Greece	10264	1996–2000
Ireland	484	1994–2000
Luxembourg	113	1992–2000
Netherlands	15384	1994–2000
Norway	17117	1996–2000
Portugal	1262	1995–2000
Spain	44189	1994–2000
Sweden	29334	1998–2001
Switzerland	1151	1996–2000
UK	31332	1992–2000

Notes: Series are available in Amadeus. The series considered are from unconsolidated statements.

Table 5.2 reports the sample breakdown of firms by size measured in terms of number of employees. The average shares of firms and employees over the sample period are considered for each country and class size. OECD estimates are also reported. Though the size criteria according to which the dataset has been constructed tends to penalize small and

Table 5.2   Distribution of firms and employment by firm size

		Data source	Firm size (number of employees)		
			Small 1–99	Medium 100–499	Large 500+
Austria	empl	Amadeus	0.404	0.279	0.317
		OECD	–	–	–
	firms	Amadeus	0.906	0.082	0.013
Belgium	empl	Amadeus	0.381	0.224	0.395
		OECD	0.460	0.191	0.349
	firms	Amadeus	0.939	0.051	0.010
Denmark	empl	Amadeus	0.410	0.247	0.343
		OECD	0.614	0.176	0.210
	firms	Amadeus	0.926	0.063	0.011
Finland	empl	Amadeus	0.313	0.269	0.418
		OECD	0.443	0.171	0.386
	firms	Amadeus	0.897	0.084	0.019
France	empl	Amadeus	0.301	0.246	0.452
		OECD	0.501	0.162	0.337
	firms	Amadeus	0.887	0.094	0.019
Germany	empl	Amadeus	0.211	0.215	0.574
		OECD	0.446	0.182	0.372
	firms	Amadeus	0.849	0.124	0.027
Greece	empl	Amadeus	0.378	0.263	0.360
		OECD	0.534	0.293	0.173
	firms	Amadeus	0.911	0.077	0.012
Ireland	empl	Amadeus	0.266	0.452	0.282
		OECD	–	–	–
	firms	Amadeus	0.683	0.286	0.032
Luxembourg	empl	Amadeus	0.073	0.476	0.451
		OECD	0.500	0.266	0.234
	firms	Amadeus	0.349	0.547	0.104
Netherlands	empl	Amadeus	0.570	0.250	0.180
		OECD	–	–	–
	firms	Amadeus	0.945	0.050	0.005
Norway	empl	Amadeus	0.498	0.252	0.250
		OECD	–	–	–
	firms	Amadeus	0.951	0.043	0.006

Table 5.2 (continued)

		Data source	Firm size (number of employees)		
			Small 1–99	Medium 100–499	Large 500+
Portugal	empl	Amadeus	0.217	0.343	0.440
		OECD	0.595	0.195	0.210
	firms	Amadeus	0.770	0.195	0.036
Spain	empl	Amadeus	0.406	0.236	0.358
		OECD	0.654	0.145	0.200
	firms	Amadeus	0.935	0.055	0.010
Sweden	empl	Amadeus	0.391	0.195	0.414
		OECD	–	–	–
	firms	Amadeus	0.952	0.039	0.009
Switzerland	empl	Amadeus	0.045	0.262	0.693
		OECD	0.545	0.201	0.254
	firms	Amadeus	0.398	0.447	0.155
UK	empl	Amadeus	0.154	0.254	0.592
		OECD	0.491	0.172	0.338
	firms	Amadeus	0.728	0.219	0.053

Notes: The figures in the table are average values over the sample period. Data for the OECD are from the OECD (1994) (based on 'Enterprises in Europe').

newly-established firms, small firms account for the majority of the sampled firms in almost all the countries. Comparing the distribution of our sample with the distribution calculated using the OECD employment data, it seems that the bias towards large firms is more significant for Luxembourg where small firms account for less than 10 per cent of total employment against 50 per cent reported by the OECD, and the UK with 16 per cent of employment in small firms against 50 per cent in the OECD figures. With regard to the other countries, the sample appears to cover the size distribution of firms relatively well.

Table 5.3 shows the distribution of firms and employment by sector. The sample appears to be representative of both manufacturing and non-manufacturing sectors. Moreover, the sectoral coverage is rather homogeneous across countries and stable over time.

Finally, Table 5.4 compares employment information derived from Amadeus with the information derived from the EU Labour Force Survey (LFS). The first column of the table reports for each country the ratio between the total employment from Amadeus and the corresponding LFS series. The coverage ranges from 49 per cent for Belgium to 5 per cent for

Table 5.3 *Distribution of firms and employment by sector (NACE code, rev. 1)*

		Data source	Sectors								
			01–05	10–14	15–37	40–41	45	50–55	60–64	70–74	75–99
Austria	empl	Amadeus	0.002	0.004	0.300	0.014	0.149	0.321	0.066	0.096	0.047
		LFS	0.014	0.004	0.315	0.015	0.121	0.289	0.100	0.086	0.056
	firms	Amadeus	0.003	0.007	0.216	0.002	0.182	0.418	0.071	0.084	0.017
Belgium	empl	Amadeus	0.004	0.004	0.394	0.021	0.083	0.205	0.142	0.125	0.023
		LFS	0.008	0.005	0.367	0.015	0.097	0.227	0.135	0.090	0.055
	firms	Amadeus	0.011	0.003	0.228	0.002	0.122	0.381	0.080	0.141	0.032
Denmark	empl	Amadeus	0.011	0.002	0.372	0.002	0.078	0.238	0.115	0.159	0.023
		LFS	0.031	0.001	0.314	0.011	0.094	0.254	0.111	0.105	0.079
	firms	Amadeus	0.022	0.002	0.254	0.001	0.137	0.306	0.060	0.189	0.029
Finland	empl	Amadeus	0.004	0.004	0.433	0.019	0.066	0.209	0.113	0.123	0.028
		LFS	0.029	0.003	0.333	0.020	0.081	0.215	0.114	0.133	0.073
	firms	Amadeus	0.008	0.003	0.281	0.016	0.103	0.329	0.071	0.158	0.031
France	empl	Amadeus	0.005	0.006	0.408	0.020	0.073	0.204	0.098	0.151	0.036
		LFS	0.023	0.004	0.316	0.016	0.095	0.250	0.108	0.124	0.064
	firms	Amadeus	0.010	0.006	0.270	0.002	0.103	0.354	0.060	0.154	0.041
Germany	empl	Amadeus	0.004	0.007	0.395	0.019	0.068	0.194	0.111	0.153	0.050
		LFS	0.023	0.010	0.372	0.015	0.120	0.251	0.082	0.063	0.064
	firms	Amadeus	0.011	0.005	0.281	0.005	0.136	0.336	0.052	0.140	0.035
Greece	empl	Amadeus	0.024	0.018	0.432	0.067	0.047	0.242	0.092	0.042	0.035
		LFS	0.021	0.012	0.291	0.028	0.119	0.285	0.130	0.054	0.061
	firms	Amadeus	0.019	0.015	0.377	0.001	0.051	0.389	0.045	0.072	0.031
Ireland	empl	Amadeus	0.004	0.009	0.445	–	0.040	0.216	0.149	0.109	0.029
		LFS	0.032	0.007	0.306	0.016	0.110	0.289	0.078	0.094	0.068
	firms	Amadeus	0.007	0.021	0.416	–	0.049	0.301	0.072	0.107	0.027

Country		Source	01–05	10–14	15–37	40–41	45	50–55	60–64	70–74	75–99
Luxembourg	empl	Amadeus	–	0.001	0.586	0.025	0.070	0.138	0.128	0.043	0.009
		LFS	0.017	0.001	0.239	0.012	0.171	0.298	0.127	0.089	0.047
	firms	Amadeus	–	0.009	0.497	0.027	0.070	0.253	0.052	0.079	0.013
Netherlands	empl	Amadeus	0.013	0.006	0.310	0.009	0.142	0.244	0.080	0.153	0.042
		LFS	0.025	0.004	0.260	0.010	0.091	0.305	0.101	0.144	0.061
	firms	Amadeus	0.022	0.002	0.192	0.001	0.138	0.294	0.064	0.261	0.026
Norway	empl	Amadeus	0.021	0.042	0.378	0.011	0.090	0.281	0.080	0.075	0.023
		LFS	0.029	0.025	0.236	0.016	0.091	0.296	0.123	0.128	0.058
	firms	Amadeus	0.030	0.013	0.246	0.007	0.113	0.400	0.057	0.110	0.024
Portugal	empl	Amadeus	0.003	0.006	0.402	0.009	0.140	0.189	0.170	0.063	0.016
		LFS	0.037	0.007	0.386	0.014	0.138	0.242	0.072	0.054	0.051
	firms	Amadeus	0.006	0.003	0.382	0.005	0.119	0.391	0.030	0.053	0.011
Spain	empl	Amadeus	0.012	0.011	0.364	0.014	0.093	0.248	0.092	0.119	0.047
		LFS	0.053	0.009	0.307	0.012	0.143	0.266	0.081	0.080	0.048
	firms	Amadeus	0.015	0.007	0.307	0.004	0.118	0.366	0.053	0.100	0.031
Sweden	empl	Amadeus	0.007	0.004	0.366	0.013	0.070	0.206	0.109	0.179	0.046
		LFS	0.017	0.004	0.322	0.014	0.077	0.224	0.109	0.159	0.074
	firms	Amadeus	0.014	0.003	0.207	0.007	0.095	0.378	0.072	0.185	0.039
Switzerland	empl	Amadeus	0.000	0.001	0.369	0.016	0.019	0.240	0.056	0.264	0.034
		LFS	0.013	0.002	0.281	0.013	0.103	0.291	0.104	0.126	0.067
	firms	Amadeus	0.001	0.002	0.340	0.039	0.023	0.243	0.060	0.259	0.032
UK	empl	Amadeus	0.011	0.009	0.341	0.008	0.045	0.274	0.068	0.157	0.087
		LFS	0.013	0.007	0.299	0.014	0.073	0.302	0.097	0.123	0.072
	firms	Amadeus	0.011	0.005	0.287	0.002	0.072	0.252	0.053	0.193	0.124

Notes: LFS is the EU Labour Force Survey (Eurostat) Sectors. 01–05 Agriculture, forestry and fishing; 10–14 Mining and quarrying; 15–37 Manufacturing; 40–41 Energy and water supply; 45 Construction; 50–55 Trade, restaurants and hotels; 60–64 Transportation and communication; 70–74 Business services; 75–99 Community, social and personal services. The figures in the table are average values over the sample period.

Table 5.4   Coverage and net employment growth

	Coverage (%)	Employment growth (%)		Correlation
		LFS	Amadeus	
Austria	18.9	0.31	1.19	0.80
Belgium	48.6	1.08	1.34	0.73
Denmark	29.9	0.94	2.84	0.68
Finland	27.5	4.65	4.02	−0.25
France	23.4	1.15	1.84	0.96
Germany	36.2	0.36	0.68	0.41
Greece	32.6	2.44	2.60	0.64
Ireland	5.9	6.51	5.36	0.50
Luxembourg	23.6	1.11	0.67	0.18
Netherlands	9.8	2.68	2.25	0.76
Norway	30.3	2.69	4.16	0.60
Portugal	5.3	2.24	1.48	0.20
Spain	24.2	4.25	5.26	0.83
Sweden	33.2	1.71	4.54	−0.86
Switzerland	19.2	0.61	1.80	−0.76
UK	27.2	1.37	2.26	0.80
Euro area (average)*	30.4	1.24	1.66	0.59

Notes: LFS is the EU Labour Force Survey (Eurostat). The figures in the table are average values over the sample period. * The values for the euro area are simple averages of the corresponding values calculated at country level.

Portugal. The average coverage for the euro area is around 30 per cent of the LFS estimates. The next two columns show the employment growth rate derived from Amadeus and the corresponding percentage changes in the LFS employment series, on average. The correlation is positive for almost all countries in the sample with the exception of Finland, Sweden and Switzerland. Figure 5.2 compares the evolution of employment growth from our sample with the LFS. Overall, the employment figures in our sample follow quite closely those obtained from the survey (the average correlation is 0.6).

4.   SOME FACTS ABOUT JOB CREATION AND JOB DESTRUCTION

This section presents the results of the estimated job flows from different perspectives. The first part shows aggregate flows, such as job creation and destruction and job reallocation. The second and third parts concentrate

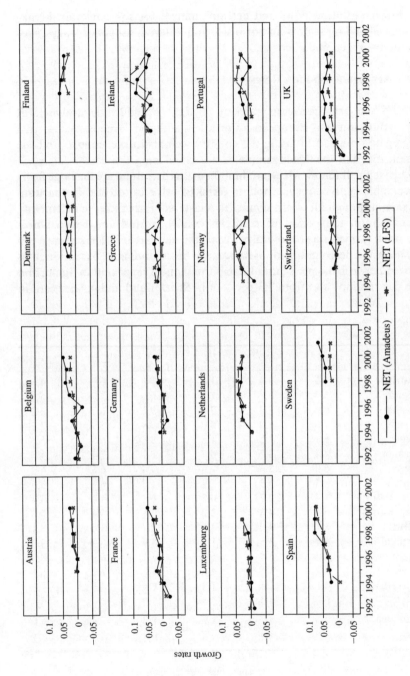

Figure 5.2 Net employment changes by country: Amadeus and EU Labour Force Survey (Eurostat)

157

on job reallocation flows and net job changes for some relevant break-downs, including sectors and firm size and different ranges of wages, productivity and capital intensity.

4.1   Aggregate Job Flow Rates

Table 5.5 reports the average rates of *JC*, *JD*, *JR*, *NET*, *EJR* and *minWR* for all our sample of European countries. In addition, it reports a euro area aggregate obtained by using the country weights in the sample[8] and the simple mean of the whole sample.

   A first result found, which is common in this literature, are the large flows observable in all countries, both in terms of job creation and destruction. In fact, although all of the countries registered a net increase of employment/jobs in the period of study, especially Ireland and Spain which recorded growth rates above 5 per cent, the coexistence of significant job creation and destruction flows is a broadly-based finding. Job creation rates moved between 3.4 per cent in Luxembourg and 8.6 per cent in Spain, and job destruction rates from 2.3 per cent in Switzerland and 4.4 per cent in

Table 5.5   Average job flow rates

	JC	JD	NET	JR	EJR	MinWR
Austria	4.6	3.4	1.2	7.9	6.7	4.6
Belgium	5.2	3.8	1.3	9.0	7.7	5.5
Denmark	6.2	3.3	2.8	9.5	6.7	6.2
Finland	7.0	3.0	4.0	9.9	5.9	7.0
France	5.1	3.2	1.8	8.3	6.5	5.3
Germany	4.4	3.7	0.7	8.1	7.4	4.7
Greece	6.0	3.4	2.6	9.4	6.8	6.0
Ireland	8.5	3.2	5.4	11.5	6.1	8.5
Luxembourg	3.4	2.7	0.7	6.1	5.4	3.4
Netherlands	6.5	4.3	2.2	10.8	8.4	6.6
Norway	8.1	4.0	4.1	12.1	8.0	8.1
Portugal	4.9	3.5	1.5	8.4	6.9	5.0
Spain	8.6	3.4	5.2	12.1	6.9	8.6
Sweden	8.1	3.6	4.5	11.7	7.2	8.1
Switzerland	4.1	2.3	1.8	6.4	4.6	4.1
UK	6.6	4.4	2.3	11.0	8.7	6.9
Euro area	5.6	3.7	1.9	9.3	7.4	5.6
Mean	6.1	3.4	2.6	9.5	6.7	6.2

Note: The figures in the table are average values over the sample period.

the UK. Two interesting examples which illustrate that flows occur in spite of stagnant net employment growth are Germany and Luxembourg, where there was almost no gain in employment during the sample period and job creation and destruction flows were around or above 3 per cent.

These developments led to job reallocation rates around 10 per cent on average. That means that around one-tenth of jobs were either created or destroyed per year on average. Country developments varied between 6.1 per cent in Luxembourg and 12.1 per cent in Norway and Spain. This high turnover is also captured by excess job reallocation, which was around 7 per cent for most countries. Moreover, this reallocation of jobs had an important effect on workers' movements, as measured by the minimum worker reallocation, which was around or above 5 per cent in most countries.

How do these estimates compare with those for other economic areas and with previous estimates? Three main aspects should be considered when doing country comparisons: (i) the period covered – as results may depend on whether the period is a recession or an expansion, (ii) the unit of definition – as mentioned before, flows are expected to be higher if the unit is an establishment/plant compared with a firm, and (iii) the sectors included – as flows are expected to be higher in services than in manufacturing. Having this in mind, Davis et al. (1996) estimate an average job reallocation of 19.4 per cent between 1973 and 1988 for the US manufacturing sector, which is much higher than our estimate for European countries. However, the comparison entails some problems as the US data refer to establishments instead of firms and include start-ups and shut-downs, which can account for around 20 per cent of flows in the USA. Previous estimates for Germany, France and Finland (see OECD 1994) are slightly higher than those presented here, although not only do they refer to a different period but also the unit of observation is the establishment instead of the firm.

More interesting is the comparison between countries within our sample. Taking the UK as a benchmark for comparison, labour markets appear less flexible in the euro area as a whole. Thus, job reallocation was 11.0 per cent in the UK and 9.3 per cent in the euro area, and excess job reallocation 8.7 per cent and 7.4 per cent respectively. However, there are remarkable differences across countries within the euro area aggregate.

For a better understanding of firm-level job dynamics it is also useful to measure the persistence of decisions to create or to destroy jobs. Job reallocation may not be a persistent phenomenon if it is related to temporary lay-offs and recalls. To the extent that job flows are persistent, they must be associated with long-term joblessness or worker reallocation across firms. Following Davis et al. (1996), we define the N-period persistence of job creation as the fraction of newly-created jobs at time t that survives through the period $t + N$. Analogously, the N-period persistence of job destruction

Table 5.6   Average persistence rate for job creation and job destruction

	Job creation		Job destruction	
	One year	Two years	One year	Two years
Austria	0.92	0.86	0.86	0.79
Belgium	0.80	0.71	0.75	0.63
Denmark	0.81	0.72	0.68	0.54
Finland	0.86	0.80	0.70	0.62
France	0.82	0.74	0.70	0.56
Germany	0.91	0.85	0.87	0.77
Greece	0.77	0.69	0.66	0.56
Ireland	0.87	0.83	0.67	0.53
Luxembourg	0.79	0.68	0.78	0.67
Netherlands	0.80	0.72	0.64	0.56
Norway	0.90	0.79	0.82	0.61
Portugal	0.81	0.73	0.69	0.57
Spain	0.85	0.78	0.64	0.55
Sweden	0.86	0.79	0.71	0.56
Switzerland	0.86	0.76	0.82	0.68
UK	0.83	0.75	0.71	0.57
Euro area	0.85	0.78	0.72	0.61
Mean	0.85	0.77	0.72	0.60

Note: The figures in the table are average values over the sample period.

is defined as the fraction of jobs destroyed at time t that do not reappear through the period $t + N$.

Table 5.6 summarizes the persistence rates of job creation and job destruction over a one and two-year horizon. On average, 85 per cent of newly-created jobs persist at least one year in Europe and 75 per cent of recently destroyed jobs. After two years the persistence rates fall to 77 per cent and below 61 per cent respectively. This indicates that firm-level job decisions are highly persistent. These results also indicate that job creation is more persistent than job destruction. However, this can be partly explained by activity developments, as our results refer mostly to a period of expansion, and persistency rates of *JC* and *JD* tend to show a pro- and counter-cyclical pattern respectively.

Comparing these results with those of Davis et al. (1996) for the USA, it appears that job creation persistence after one year is much higher in European countries, while job destruction persistence is lower. Cyclical developments can partly explain these differences. Within the EU, although

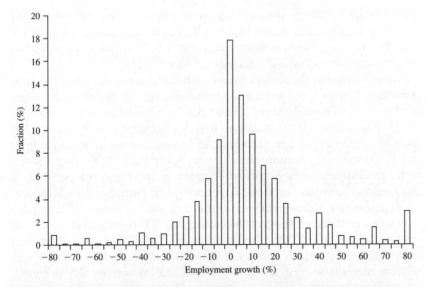

Notes: Distributions of firms by employment growth rate (annual observations) for the panel of European countries in the period 1992–2000. The growth rates are defined as the change in employment divided by the average employment between two consecutive periods. Firms for which employment remains unchanged are not included.

Figure 5.3   *Distribution of continuing firms according to employment growth rates*

the country variation is high, the euro area shows relatively higher persistency rates on average than the UK.

Figure 5.3 shows the distribution of firms by ranges of employment growth rates for our sample of European countries during the 1990s. The height of each bar indicates the share of firms growing at each respective range of growth rate. It appears that both for *JC* and *JD* firms are mainly concentrated in the lowest ranges of growth with 18 per cent of firms experiencing an average change in employment of between −5 and +5 per cent per year and 40 per cent between −10 and +10 per cent. The proportion generally descends as the range of growth increases/decreases. Figure 5.3 also shows that firms are more concentrated at low growth rate ranges in job destruction than in job creation, reflecting a predominantly expansionary period.

4.2   Job Reallocation by Sector and Firm Size

In order to assess to what extent the process of job reallocation affects different activities in the economy and which ones are the most affected, nine sectors are considered (2-digit NACE classification):[9] Agriculture, forestry and fishing (01–05), Mining and quarrying (10–14), Manufacturing (15–37), Energy and water supply (40–41), Construction (45), Trade (50–55), Transport and communication (60–64), Business services (70–74) and Community, social and personal services (75–99).

Table 5.7 reports the average rates of job reallocation and net job change by sector. It shows that job reallocation flows are significant in all sectors and confirms a broadly-based coexistence of job creation and destruction flows. For instance, job reallocation flows in Agriculture range from 0.9 in Switzerland to 23 per cent in Ireland. In Manufacturing, flows range from 5.6 in Luxembourg to more than 10 per cent in Ireland, Norway and the UK. In Business services job reallocation ranges from 6.5 per cent in Switzerland to around or above 17 per cent in Norway, Spain and Sweden.

Regarding the sectors that created more jobs in our sample of European countries, as expected, most of the net increase was registered in the service sector, especially in Trade, Business services and Community, social and personal services which grew on average above 4 per cent. Construction also registered positive net job creation, on average by 3.6 per cent, throughout the period. By contrast, employment gains in the industrial sector were more modest.

Following the previous comparison between the euro area and the UK, job reallocation flows were higher in all sectors in the UK, except in Agriculture, probably reflecting the restructuring still taking place in the agricultural sector in some euro area countries.

Next, we assess the differences in labour market flows across difference class-sizes of firms. The concept used in the analysis refers to the average size of the firm in two consecutive periods. The average size is used instead of the current size as the former is expected to give a better indication of the intended scale of operations. We divide the sample into eight categories: 1–19 employees, 20–49, 50–99, 100–249, 250–499, 500–999, 1000–2499 and 2500 and over. Table 5.8 reports the average rates of job reallocation by firm size. It shows that the process of job reallocation is high in all size groups, but clearly is more significant among smaller firms. In fact, there is an inverse relationship between the size of the firm and the intensity of job reallocation. For the smallest firms, job reallocation varies between countries from 9.6 per cent in Ireland and 17.5 per cent in the Netherlands, for medium-sized firms (250–499) between 6.3 per cent in Luxembourg and Switzerland and 13.5 per cent in Ireland, and for the biggest firms between 2 per cent in Luxembourg and 9.1 per cent in Norway. On average, job reallocation falls from 14.1 per cent for the smallest firms to 5.6 per cent for the biggest ones. Interestingly, this downward pattern in job reallocation is explained by the fact that both job creation and job destruction declined monotonically with the size of the firm.

Table 5.7   *Average job reallocation and net employment growth by sector (NACE 2-digit)*

		01–05	10–14	15–37	40–41	45	50–55	60–64	70–74	75–99
Austria	JR	10.2	9.6	7.1	7.6	7.2	8.4	8.2	11.8	5.5
	NET	−4.9	2.4	0.6	−2.9	1.0	1.2	3.9	2.4	1.7
Belgium	JR	14.0	7.8	7.4	2.1	10.8	10.0	7.3	14.2	10.9
	NET	5.8	−2.1	−0.5	−0.7	2.4	1.5	0.9	6.8	3.2
Denmark	JR	9.9	11.6	9.0	12.5	12.3	9.1	8.1	11.4	10.5
	NET	0.0	4.0	1.5	−3.6	4.7	3.6	2.4	4.6	4.9
Finland	JR	10.7	11.1	8.4	8.3	13.4	10.8	7.6	15.1	9.6
	NET	2.8	−0.3	2.6	−2.7	7.8	4.6	2.8	8.3	6.2
France	JR	9.6	8.5	7.1	2.5	8.7	9.3	7.5	12.4	8.9
	NET	2.4	−2.7	0.3	0.2	0.5	2.8	2.6	5.3	3.8
Germany	JR	9.0	7.8	6.7	6.4	8.6	7.7	9.1	10.4	8.8
	NET	−0.9	−4.3	−0.5	−4.0	0.1	2.4	−1.7	2.0	3.7
Greece	JR	10.1	9.1	8.1	4.4	18.2	12.0	4.9	15.8	10.5
	NET	0.0	1.1	1.4	1.4	6.9	5.2	−0.1	5.6	3.7
Ireland	JR	22.9	9.7	11.5	–	19.9	10.7	9.4	16.3	7.3
	NET	1.1	6.8	3.4	–	10.7	5.8	5.8	11.4	4.4
Luxembourg	JR	–	21.5	5.6	1.2	7.2	8.0	6.1	8.2	10.7
	NET	–	18.1	0.0	0.3	−1.6	1.1	3.6	3.2	9.3
Netherlands	JR	13.4	14.3	8.1	5.4	9.6	11.5	11.5	16.3	11.5
	NET	2.8	−4.6	0.3	−2.3	2.3	3.2	3.6	4.3	3.0
Norway	JR	16.0	11.1	10.7	8.2	13.2	12.6	12.4	16.9	10.9
	NET	8.6	2.0	1.6	−2.3	5.5	6.3	4.7	9.2	6.0
Portugal	JR	10.6	7.1	7.1	12.6	11.0	10.2	6.0	14.8	5.7
	NET	6.0	1.9	0.8	5.8	3.5	5.0	−3.0	5.3	2.4
Spain	JR	15.9	10.1	9.7	7.4	17.9	12.9	9.3	16.7	12.2
	NET	6.9	−1.9	3.4	0.0	7.2	6.7	2.7	9.5	7.2
Sweden	JR	13.7	5.6	9.5	12.8	12.0	11.0	9.9	17.6	14.2
	NET	−0.6	−0.3	2.9	−0.3	6.4	4.9	3.8	7.2	8.6
Switzerland	JR	0.9	7.6	6.7	2.5	11.8	6.6	6.1	6.5	4.5
	NET	0.9	−7.3	1.5	−0.9	−2.3	2.1	2.6	2.7	1.9
UK	JR	6.4	10.1	10.1	7.8	14.7	10.4	10.1	13.5	11.7
	NET	0.0	−1.9	−0.5	−3.6	2.1	4.6	3.6	3.2	4.8
Euro area	JR	10.5	8.5	7.3	5.5	10.2	9.1	8.6	12.3	9.4
	NET	1.2	−3.0	0.3	−2.1	1.6	3.0	0.3	4.1	4.0
Mean	JR	11.6	10.2	8.3	6.7	12.3	10.1	8.4	13.6	9.6
	NET	2.6	0.7	1.2	−0.6	3.6	4.4	2.8	6.1	5.2

Notes: Sectors: 01–05 Agriculture, forestry and fishing; 10–14 Mining and quarrying; 15–37 Manufacturing; 40–41 Energy and water supply; 45 Construction; 50–55 Trade, restaurants and hotels; 60–64 Transportation and communication; 70–74 Business services; 75–99 Community, social and personal services.

Table 5.8   *Average job reallocation and net employment growth by size category*

		\multicolumn{8}{c}{Size of the firm in number of employees}							
		1–19	20–49	50–99	100–249	250–499	500–999	1000–2499	Over 2500
Austria	JR	11.5	8.9	8.6	8.6	7.6	7.6	6.8	3.4
	NET	4.4	1.9	1.0	1.0	−0.5	0.2	1.4	1.0
Belgium	JR	14.7	10.8	11.2	10.1	7.0	6.8	6.7	5.8
	NET	4.5	2.1	2.6	1.6	0.5	0.4	0.2	−0.2
Denmark	JR	12.7	11.2	11.3	10.3	8.5	7.7	8.4	5.2
	NET	5.6	3.9	4.0	3.2	2.6	1.2	2.0	0.5
Finland	JR	13.6	12.7	12.5	12.6	8.7	9.1	9.0	4.2
	NET	7.5	5.7	5.5	3.4	4.2	4.5	4.0	0.0
France	JR	12.9	10.1	10.9	10.0	7.8	7.4	7.5	5.3
	NET	5.5	2.7	3.4	2.9	2.3	1.7	0.9	−0.3
Germany	JR	12.4	9.4	8.9	9.1	7.6	8.1	6.7	7.3
	NET	7.1	3.4	2.2	1.6	1.1	0.8	−0.1	−0.9
Greece	JR	13.6	12.0	12.2	12.4	7.9	10.1	5.1	3.7
	NET	5.0	3.4	3.5	3.4	2.6	4.1	0.2	0.2
Ireland	JR	9.6	11.3	13.0	12.5	13.5	12.5	10.3	2.2
	NET	3.9	5.9	6.7	5.9	8.9	2.7	−3.3	1.3
Luxembourg	JR	13.1	9.8	9.4	8.3	6.3	5.3	6.5	2.0
	NET	3.0	1.6	1.1	1.3	0.5	0.6	3.1	−0.2
Netherlands	JR	17.5	13.6	10.8	10.9	8.3	8.5	7.1	6.9
	NET	4.7	2.1	2.1	2.5	2.6	1.2	0.6	−2.4
Norway	JR	14.4	12.8	12.7	12.5	11.8	10.6	11.1	9.1
	NET	7.5	5.4	4.7	3.5	4.0	1.8	−0.7	4.7
Portugal	JR	14.2	10.9	9.9	8.6	8.3	8.9	7.7	5.8
	NET	7.0	4.4	3.5	1.7	1.9	2.4	2.1	−2.9
Spain	JR	17.0	13.9	13.7	12.5	10.2	10.4	10.0	8.8
	NET	9.2	6.2	6.3	5.7	4.4	4.6	4.1	29.0
Sweden	JR	13.9	13.7	13.5	13.2	11.8	10.8	9.1	6.0
	NET	7.2	6.1	5.3	5.2	6.1	4.4	0.5	0.9
Switzerland	JR	16.8	13.2	9.7	8.2	6.3	5.9	6.9	5.5
	NET	11.3	6.9	3.0	1.8	1.9	0.1	−0.2	3.0
UK	JR	17.0	14.2	12.6	12.9	11.6	11.4	10.8	8.8
	NET	6.5	4.6	3.6	3.1	2.7	2.4	1.4	1.3
Euro area	JR	13.3	10.4	10.2	9.9	8.0	8.2	7.2	6.7
	NET	6.6	3.5	3.0	2.4	1.8	1.6	0.8	−0.3
Mean	JR	14.1	11.8	11.3	10.8	9.0	8.8	8.1	5.6
	NET	6.2	4.1	3.7	3.0	2.9	2.1	1.0	0.6

How does net employment growth relate to the size of the firm? As shown in Table 5.8, although a positive net change in employment was recorded in all sizes of firm on average, there is again a negative relation between net employment growth rates and the size of the firm. For the smallest firms net job creation varies between 3 per cent in Luxembourg and 11.3 per cent in Switzerland, for medium-sized firms between −0.5 per cent in Austria and 8.9 per cent in Ireland and for the biggest firms between −2.9 per cent in Portugal and 4.7 per cent in Norway. For the EU on average, net job creation drops from 6.2 per cent for the smallest firms to 0.6 per cent for the biggest ones.

4.3 Job Reallocation by Ranges of Wages, Productivity and Capital Intensity

In this section, job flows are also considered for three additional characteristics of the firm, that is, with respect to the distribution of firms as regards the level of wages, productivity and capital intensity. They are respectively obtained as the ratio of compensation of employees, value added and fixed capital, to the number of employees. Firms are separated in each country into five groups defined by quintiles of the firm distribution of wages, productivity and capital intensity. This is done for the whole sample in each country, after deflating the variables by means of the GDP deflator. It is worth mentioning that in some countries slight differences can arise compared with the aggregate flows and net changes, due to the fact that compensation, productivity and fixed capital are only available for a sub-sample of firms.[10] These three characteristics are interrelated as wage levels are expected to reflect overall productivity levels, and the latter is partly linked to the amount of capital in the firm. Our interest is in understanding the role that the level of technological progress plays in the process of job reallocation in European firms. In principle, one would expect that more capital-intensive plants should operate with more human capital-intensive workforces and then exhibit lower rates of job reallocation in general and job destruction in particular (Davis et al. 1996).

The first part of Table 5.9 shows job reallocation flows and net employment growth by wage category. Two main types of patterns are found in the relationship between the level of wages and job reallocation. A negative relationship in some countries (including Belgium, Portugal and Spain), that is, the lower the level of wages the higher the turnover, and a U-shaped relationship in some other countries (including France, Germany and the Netherlands), which is mainly due to an increase in the flows in the upper quintile. By contrast, net job flows showed in almost all cases a negative relationship with the level of average wages, that is, net job creation has

Table 5.9 *Average job reallocation and net employment growth by wage, productivity and capital intensity categories (quintiles)*

		Wage					Productivity					Capital intensity				
		1	2	3	4	5	1	2	3	4	5	1	2	3	4	5
Austria	JR	8.8	7.4	7.2	7.6	6.6	9.0	8.2	6.7	6.1	7.9	11.4	8.3	5.8	7.4	9.6
	NET	0.3	1.9	-0.7	-1.0	-4.0	-1.8	2.0	0.2	-1.7	-2.5	1.0	-1.0	1.4	-1.9	-3.9
Belgium	JR	15.7	10.8	9.8	8.5	7.8	10.7	8.0	8.0	7.7	7.5	13.5	10.9	9.1	9.7	7.8
	NET	5.6	3.6	2.3	0.8	-0.7	2.7	0.6	0.5	0.6	-0.4	3.8	2.4	1.0	1.2	-0.2
Denmark	JR	10.5	9.8	9.3	9.4	11.2	–	–	–	–	–	13.2	11.7	9.7	9.4	9.8
	NET	4.1	3.0	2.2	2.7	3.2	–	–	–	–	–	4.9	4.9	3.4	2.6	1.1
Finland	JR	15.9	11.4	9.9	9.0	9.3	–	–	–	–	–	16.9	12.3	11.5	9.7	8.7
	NET	10.3	5.1	3.4	3.5	2.0	–	–	–	–	–	12.2	6.8	5.9	4.4	1.2
France	JR	12.5	10.0	8.6	7.2	8.1	12.6	10.2	8.7	7.6	7.5	12.4	10.8	9.7	8.9	7.2
	NET	6.9	4.1	2.2	0.1	-0.2	5.3	3.1	2.1	1.2	0.2	4.8	3.2	3.0	2.1	0.3
Germany	JR	6.9	6.4	5.6	5.9	6.7	6.7	6.2	5.1	5.6	8.1	8.1	7.2	8.3	6.6	9.9
	NET	0.1	-2.5	-1.5	-1.9	-1.8	-1.1	-2.0	-1.3	-1.5	-0.7	-0.5	-3.5	-0.9	-4.3	-4.8

Greece	JR	—	—	—	—	—	—	—	—	—	—	25.1	25.5	22.2	21.5	24.1
	NET	—	—	—	—	—	—	—	—	—	—	11.8	11.3	8.7	1.6	-0.7
Ireland	JR	13.7	14.3	12.0	10.4	12.4	—	—	—	—	—	13.5	13.7	10.9	12.1	12.5
	NET	7.6	5.3	5.8	4.6	6.1	—	—	—	—	—	6.8	6.6	4.1	5.1	7.5
Luxembourg	JR	7.0	7.4	6.8	6.0	4.5	7.8	6.6	7.5	5.8	5.2	9.0	8.2	6.5	4.4	5.7
	NET	2.4	0.9	0.2	-0.2	0.2	2.4	-0.6	-0.7	0.9	1.0	3.3	-1.5	-0.4	-0.2	1.8
Netherlands	JR	8.9	7.6	7.0	6.8	8.2	9.1	6.9	7.8	6.7	7.3	13.5	12.2	12.1	11.3	11.5
	NET	4.3	2.7	1.5	-0.3	0.6	3.6	1.3	1.3	2.0	0.8	4.1	4.1	4.0	2.3	-1.0
Norway	JR	22.9	19.0	13.6	12.5	14.6	—	—	—	—	—	23.6	18.5	17.1	15.5	14.5
	NET	17.1	11.1	6.7	2.8	-0.4	—	—	—	—	—	14.5	9.8	7.0	5.9	2.0
Portugal	JR	12.3	10.4	9.3	8.3	7.5	9.0	10.1	8.9	9.9	7.9	11.5	10.5	9.9	7.6	7.6
	NET	6.9	1.6	3.8	2.3	-1.1	0.9	3.0	2.1	2.3	1.2	1.9	5.2	2.4	1.0	0.0
Spain	JR	15.6	17.4	14.7	13.2	9.9	20.7	16.2	14.6	12.6	10.5	16.3	16.4	14.2	12.4	12.1
	NET	9.6	10.2	7.0	5.8	1.4	13.3	8.5	7.2	5.1	2.6	8.1	8.3	7.2	5.5	3.3
Sweden	JR	19.6	13.4	11.5	11.0	15.2	—	—	—	—	—	19.9	15.0	13.5	11.8	12.1
	NET	12.1	6.6	5.2	2.6	4.4	—	—	—	—	—	11.8	7.1	6.5	4.7	1.3

Table 5.9 (continued)

		Wage					Productivity					Capital intensity				
		1	2	3	4	5	1	2	3	4	5	1	2	3	4	5
Switzerland	JR	5.6	6.3	4.5	4.8	3.0	5.7	7.0	4.8	6.1	3.5	5.6	6.4	3.6	6.1	3.3
	NET	4.4	-1.2	-0.9	-1.8	-0.8	4.5	-1.9	-1.5	-4.4	-2.5	4.2	1.8	-1.5	-4.7	-0.7
UK	JR	10.8	10.9	12.9	12.1	14.1	10.6	10.8	13.2	11.9	14.2	11.0	10.6	12.9	12.0	12.8
	NET	3.8	0.2	2.5	2.2	2.1	3.0	1.3	3.0	2.7	3.6	3.2	1.3	2.3	2.7	2.0
Euro area	JR	10.0	8.9	7.8	7.4	7.5	10.0	8.4	7.4	7.1	8.2	11.2	10.0	9.8	8.6	9.9
	NET	3.4	1.2	0.8	-0.2	-0.9	2.3	0.8	0.7	0.2	-0.1	2.6	0.5	1.6	-0.9	-2.1
Mean	JR	12.5	10.8	9.5	8.9	9.3	10.2	9.0	8.5	8.0	8.0	14.0	12.4	11.1	10.4	10.6
	NET	6.4	3.5	2.6	1.5	0.7	3.3	1.5	1.3	0.7	0.3	6.0	4.2	3.4	1.7	0.6

Notes: Quintiles are constructed from the distribution of firms' annual remuneration per worker (wage), value added per worker (productivity) and fixed capital per worker (capital intensity). The series are deflated using the GDP deflator (base year 1995).

been concentrated in those firms with lower wages. The main exception to these general patterns is the UK, which shows a clearly positive relationship between job flows and the level of wages and for which net job creation is broadly-based among all wage categories. It should be mentioned, however, that the share of employment is more balanced between all five categories in France and Germany than in the UK, where around 80 per cent of the employment falls in the lowest two groups and only 10 per cent in the highest two. On average, job reallocation moves from the first to the fifth quintile between 12.5 per cent and 9.3 per cent and net job creation between 6.4 per cent and 0.7 per cent.

The pattern of wages is confirmed by that of productivity in most EU countries (see second part of Table 5.9). Job reallocation flows tend to be negatively related to productivity levels, that is, flows are higher in low productive firms. However, following the U-shaped pattern previously mentioned, job flows are also high for the most productive firms in some countries. In general, net job creation tends to be concentrated in low productive firms. On average, job reallocation moves between 10.2 per cent and 8 per cent and net job creation between 3.3 per cent and 0.3 per cent.

As regards capital intensity, again job flows and net job creation in EU countries tend to be concentrated in firms within the lower quintiles. As shown in the third part of Table 5.9, job reallocation was, on average, between 14 per cent in the lowest quintile and 10.6 per cent in the highest quintile, and net job creation between 6 per cent and 0.6 per cent respectively.

One possible explanation for these developments could be the leading role that service activities played in job flows and job creation in the second half of the 1990s in most EU countries. Indeed, most service activities are expected to foster less-productive jobs, and therefore lower paid jobs, and to be less intensive in capital, compared with manufacturing activities, which were shrinking in the period of study. This would not explain, however, the different behaviour between the euro area and the UK.

5. JOB FLOWS, SECTORAL STRUCTURE AND INSTITUTIONS

Previous sections highlighted important differences in job flows according to firm characteristics such as size, average labour productivity and capital intensity. Thus, we now firstly address whether country-idiosyncratic factors are apparent in the patterns of job flows once technological characteristics have been accounted for and, secondly, we assess the role of institutions in the dynamics of the labour market. If technology matters for job flows, there should be a similar pattern of job reallocation between sectors in different countries. Most importantly, if the institutional and regulatory framework is relevant for job creation and job destruction, these sectoral patterns should differ across countries with different labour and product market institutions.

5.1   The Data

We will distinguish job flows across 29 sectors for a restricted sample of 12 countries.[11] The sectors represent the whole spectrum of economic activities and the time period covered ranges from 1992 to 2000. As the focus is on the role of the institutional and regulatory framework after controlling for technological differences (the sector), the analysis is based on country-sectoral averages over time. A more general empirical framework in which time series and cross-sectional patterns of job flows are examined is presented in Gómez-Salvador et al. (2004). In contrast with our companion paper, the focus here on the sectoral dimension will allow us to test for differential effects of institutions in manufacturing and service sectors.

According to our previous discussion (Gómez-Salvador et al. 2004), we concentrate on several institutional and regulatory aspects of the labour markets under study. These can be classified according to the following groups:

- *Wage-setting institutions*   These include an indicator of union density and an indicator of the extent of coordination in the wage bargaining process, which ranges from one to three according to the increasing degree of coordination.
- *Tax and benefits systems*   This group includes two indicators of the size (replacement rate) and the duration of unemployment insurance systems and the tax wedge between the real (monetary) labour cost faced by the firms and the consumption wage received by the employees. The latter is normalized by GDP while the first two increase with the generosity of unemployment benefits.[12]
- *Restriction to the hiring and firing*   Three alternative measures of the relative stringency of hiring and firing rules are considered. These include an index of the overall stringency of employment protection legislation (EPL), and two indices that distinguish between regulations affecting temporary workers and permanent workers. All these indices increase in scale from zero to six with the strictness of EPL. Additionally we include the share of workers holding temporary contracts as a percentage of total employment.[13]
- *Sectoral employment subsidies*   An indicator of the share of sectoral and ad hoc state aids as a percentage of GDP.[14]

5.2 Empirical Results

Next we search for country and sectoral effects in the determination of job flows. Table 5.10 presents the results of OLS regressions of job reallocation and excess job reallocation on country and sectoral dummies. Column (A) provides clear evidence of systematic industry-level patterns in the pace of job reallocation, accounting for more than half of the variation

Table 5.10   *Average job reallocation, job creation and job destruction.*
              Industry and country effects: OLS estimates (t-values in
              parentheses)

Model	(A)	(B)	(C)	(D)	(E)	(F)	(G)	(H)	(I)
Dependent variable	JR	JC	JD	JR	JC	JD	JR	JC	JD
Intercept	11.49	6.71	4.78	10.90	6.29	4.60	12.04	6.44	5.60
	(16.17)	(10.33)	(13.03)	(17.69)	(11.05)	(17.82)	(18.04)	(10.66)	(13.98)
Sector 2	−2.33	−2.64	0.30				−2.33	−2.64	0.30
	(2.32)	(2.87)	−0.59				(2.92)	(3.65)	−0.63
Sector 3	−3.27	−2.17	−1.09				−3.08	−2.16	−0.91
	(3.43)	(2.50)	(2.22)				(4.05)	(3.14)	(2.01)
Sector 4	−2.87	−2.59	−0.28				−2.68	−2.58	−0.10
	(3.01)	(2.97)	(0.57)				(3.53)	(3.74)	(0.22)
Sector 5	−3.14	−1.23	−1.91				−3.07	−1.21	−1.86
	(3.19)	(1.37)	(3.75)				(3.92)	(1.71)	(3.95)
Sector 6	−4.22	−2.71	−1.50				−3.90	−2.53	−1.37
	(4.35)	(3.07)	(3.00)				(5.06)	(3.62)	(2.96)
Sector 7	−4.09	−2.91	−1.18				−3.90	−2.90	−1.00
	(4.29)	(3.34)	(2.40)				(5.13)	(4.21)	(2.20)
Sector 8	−3.22	−1.48	−1.73				−2.90	−1.29	−1.60
	(3.33)	(1.68)	(3.47)				(3.76)	(1.86)	(3.47)
Sector 9	−3.27	−1.91	−1.36				−3.20	−1.88	−1.31
	(3.32)	(2.12)	(2.68)				(4.08)	(2.66)	(2.79)
Sector 10	−2.81	−1.61	−1.20				−2.63	−1.60	−1.02
	(2.95)	(1.85)	(2.44)				(3.45)	(2.33)	(2.25)
Sector 11	−3.06	−1.79	−1.27				−2.75	−1.60	−1.14
	(3.17)	(2.02)	(2.55)				(3.57)	(2.30)	(2.48)
Sector 12	−1.52	−0.51	−1.01				−1.33	−0.50	−0.83
	(1.60)	(0.59)	(2.06)				(1.76)	(0.73)	(1.83)
Sector 13	−2.94	−1.96	−0.97				−2.94	−1.96	−0.97
	(2.92)	(2.14)	(1.88)				(3.68)	(2.71)	(2.04)
Sector 14	−2.22	−0.96	−1.25				−1.90	−0.78	−1.12
	(2.29)	(1.09)	(2.51)				(2.47)	(1.12)	(2.43)
Sector 15	−4.85	−4.18	−0.67				−4.42	−3.92	−0.50
	(4.60)	(4.34)	(1.24)				(5.25)	(5.14)	(1.00)
Sector 16	1.11	1.67	−0.55				1.30	1.68	−0.38
	(1.17)	(1.92)	(1.13)				(1.71)	(2.44)	(0.83)

Table 5.10 (continued)

Model	(A)	(B)	(C)	(D)	(E)	(F)	(G)	(H)	(I)
Dependent variable	JR	JC	JD	JR	JC	JD	JR	JC	JD
Sector 17	−2.35	−0.41	−1.94				−2.17	−0.40	−1.76
	(2.47)	(0.48)	(3.94)				(2.85)	(0.59)	(3.87)
Sector 18	−0.94	0.31	−1.25				−0.43	0.60	−1.03
	(1.00)	(0.36)	(2.58)				(0.57)	(0.87)	(2.27)
Sector 19	−1.31	1.03	−2.34				−1.12	1.04	−2.16
	(1.38)	(1.18)	(4.76)				(1.48)	(1.51)	(4.75)
Sector 20	−0.39	0.95	−1.35				−0.44	0.80	−1.24
	(0.41)	(1.08)	(2.70)				(0.57)	(1.15)	(2.69)
Sector 21	−3.11	−1.38	−1.73				−2.93	−1.37	−1.55
	(3.27)	(1.59)	(3.52)				(3.85)	(1.99)	(3.41)
Sector 22	4.45	3.79	0.65				4.45	3.79	0.65
	(4.43)	(4.13)	(1.26)				(5.57)	(5.24)	(1.36)
Sector 23	3.04	2.53	0.51				3.12	2.56	0.56
	(3.09)	(2.82)	(1.00)				(3.98)	(3.61)	(1.19)
Sector 24	6.83	8.02	−1.19				6.96	8.00	−1.04
	(7.05)	(9.06)	(2.38)				(9.01)	(11.45)	(2.26)
Sector 25	1.60	2.49	−0.89				1.79	2.50	−0.71
	(1.68)	(2.87)	(1.81)				(2.36)	(3.64)	(1.57)
Sector 26	1.21	2.47	−1.26				1.04	2.32	−1.27
	(1.18)	(2.63)	(2.38)				(1.28)	(3.13)	(2.60)
Sector 27	−2.24	0.65	−2.89				−1.97	0.82	−2.80
	(2.27)	(0.72)	(5.68)				(2.51)	(1.17)	(5.95)
Sector 28	−0.63	0.97	−1.60				−0.36	1.14	−1.51
	(0.64)	(1.08)	(3.16)				(0.47)	(1.62)	(3.22)
Austria				−2.45	−1.48	−0.97	−2.37	−1.39	−0.98
				(2.79)	(1.82)	(2.64)	(4.49)	(2.90)	(3.10)
Belgium				−1.63	−0.99	−0.63	−1.63	−0.99	−0.63
				(1.88)	(1.24)	(1.74)	(3.12)	(2.10)	(2.03)
Denmark				−0.77	0.28	−1.05	−0.89	0.14	−1.03
				(0.88)	(0.35)	(2.86)	(1.70)	(0.30)	(3.27)
Finland				−0.35	1.17	−1.53	−0.35	1.17	−1.53
				(0.41)	(1.46)	(4.18)	(0.68)	(2.48)	(4.87)
France				−2.19	−0.91	−1.27	−2.19	−0.91	−1.27
				(2.51)	(1.13)	(3.50)	(4.19)	(1.93)	(4.07)
Germany				−2.45	−1.64	−0.80	−2.45	−1.64	−0.80
				(2.81)	(2.04)	(2.21)	(4.68)	(3.46)	(2.58)
Greece				−0.09	0.85	−0.95	−0.21	0.71	−0.93
				(0.11)	(1.05)	(2.58)	(0.41)	(1.50)	(2.94)
Ireland				1.38	3.11	−1.72	1.07	2.72	−1.65
				(1.27)	(3.08)	(3.76)	(1.61)	(4.52)	(4.14)
Luxembourg				−5.20	−3.50	−1.70	−5.91	−4.25	−1.66
				(1.57)	(1.14)	(1.22)	(2.88)	(2.28)	(1.35)

Table 5.10 (continued)

Model	(A)	(B)	(C)	(D)	(E)	(F)	(G)	(H)	(I)
Dependent variable	JR	JC	JD	JR	JC	JD	JR	JC	JD
Netherlands				0.47	0.40	0.06	0.34	0.26	0.08
				(0.53)	(0.5)	(0.18)	(0.66)	(0.55)	(0.27)
Norway				1.25	1.99	−0.73	1.25	1.99	−0.73
				(1.44)	(2.47)	(2.02)	(2.40)	(4.20)	(2.35)
Portugal				−2.07	−0.51	−1.56	−1.51	−0.04	−1.46
				(2.14)	(0.57)	(3.84)	(2.57)	(0.08)	(4.17)
Spain				1.01	2.22	−1.21	1.01	2.22	−1.21
				(1.16)	(2.76)	(3.31)	(1.94)	(4.69)	(3.86)
Sweden				0.99	1.67	−0.67	0.99	1.67	−0.67
				(1.15)	(2.08)	(1.84)	(1.91)	(3.53)	(2.15)
Switzerland				−4.35	−2.18	−2.17	−3.99	−2.02	−1.97
				(4.49)	(2.44)	(5.34)	(6.81)	(3.80)	(5.61)
No. of observations	384	384	384	384	384	384	384	384	384
Adj. R^2	0.523	0.531	0.231	0.164	0.156	0.112	0.698	0.709	0.345

Notes: Sector definitions: 1 Agriculture, forestry and fishing; 2 Mining and quarrying; 3 Food, beverages and tobacco; 4 Textiles; 5 Wood products; 6 Paper products, publishing and printing; 7 Refined petroleum, nuclear fuel and chemical products; 8 Rubber and plastic products; 9 Other non-metallic products; 10 Basic metals and fabricated metal products; 11 Machinery and equipment; 12 Electrical and optical equipment; 13 Transport equipment; 14 Other manufacturing sectors; 15 Electricity, gas and water supply; 16 Construction; 17 Sale, maintenance and repair of motor vehicles; 18 Wholesale trade, except for motor vehicles; 19 Retail trade, except for motor vehicles; 20 Hotels and restaurants; 21 Transport and communications; 22 Financial intermediation and insurance; 23 Real estate and renting; 24 Computer and related activities; 25 Research and development; 26 Public administration, defence and education; 27 Health and social work; 28 Other community, social and personal services.

according to the adjusted R^2, even for a large and heterogeneous group of countries. However, country-idiosyncratic factors in the determination of the job flows cannot be disregarded. According to column (D), differences across countries explain 16 per cent of the variation in job reallocation. Moreover, country effects are jointly significant when sectoral dummies are included in the regression (column (G)). The importance of between country components in the determination of the job flows can be observed in the increase in explanatory power after the introduction of country dummies. Country and sectoral effects together account for almost 70 per cent of the variance of job reallocation, in contrast with 52 per cent when country effects are not included. Job creation and job destruction present similar patterns. However, country and sectoral fixed characteristics explain a much larger portion of the variance of the former. Similar to the case of *JR*, the adjusted R^2 for *JC* is 0.709, and less than half in the case of *JD*.

Table 5.10 shows that service industries (sectors 17 to 28) typically exhibit larger job flows than manufacturing industries. Accordingly, the strong growth pattern of Computer and related activities is reflected in the dynamic job flows. This sector shows the highest job reallocation and job creation rates, seven and eight points above those observed in the Agriculture, forestry and fishing sector (our reference industry). On the other extreme, Electricity, gas and water supply and Refined petroleum, nuclear fuel and chemical products appear as the industries with the slowest patterns of job reallocation.

The aim of our next set of regressions is to uncover the determinants of the country-idiosyncratic factors in the patterns of job reallocation. Thus, we substitute the country dummies of the previous specification for a set of indicators of labour market institutions and product market policies. Table 5.11 presents OLS regressions of job reallocation, job creation and job destruction on a set of labour market institutions and sectoral dummies. Sectoral characteristics are controlled for by introducing sectoral dummies. The last row shows the Breush-Pagan Lagrange multiplier test for the presence of country random effects. With regard to job creation and job reallocation, the null hypothesis of absence of country random effects is accepted (in column (E) it is rejected at the 1 per cent level), suggesting that most of the cross-country variation is captured by the institutional and regulatory indicators. Supporting this last claim, the Adjusted R^2 in these specifications is very close to that obtained in the previous table when country dummies replaced the institutional variables. However, this is not the case for job destruction where country random effects cannot be rejected. Indeed, for *JD* most of the institutional variables and sectoral dummies are not significant, indicating greater variability in the data that these fixed indicators are not able to capture. Since the institutional variables do not have a sectoral component, there is a potential problem of overestimation of the significance of the institutional indicators due to underestimated standard errors. To take into account this possibility, we report t-statistics computed from standard errors that are robust to country clustering.

As expected, the strictness of employment protection legislation has a negative and significant impact on the extent of job reallocation. This result is robust no matter which indicator of EPL is considered. Interestingly, we find strong (and statistically significant) negative effects of firing restrictions in the creation of employment, suggesting that firms anticipate the

Table 5.11 Whole economy – institutional determinants of average job reallocation, job creation and job destruction: OLS estimates (t-values from cluster robust standard errors in parentheses)

Model	(A)	(B)	(C)	(D)	(E)	(F)	(G)	(H)	(I)
Dependent variable	JR	JR	JR	JC	JC	JC	JD	JD	JD
Intercept	16.42	16.85	14.28	9.51	9.86	7.44	6.90	6.98	6.84
	(12.44)	(12.18)	(11.00)	(7.54)	(7.44)	(4.95)	(6.68)	(6.82)	(7.29)
Tax wedge	-4.74	-6.11	-1.89	-4.22	-5.60	-2.03	-0.51	-0.50	0.13
	(3.42)	(4.12)	(1.22)	(3.91)	(3.11)	(0.88)	(0.27)	(0.28)	(0.07)
Temporary contracts	0.06	0.05	0.10	0.09	0.08	0.13	-0.02	-0.02	-0.02
	(2.56)	(2.01)	(4.13)	(5.51)	(2.80)	(7.23)	(1.22)	(1.42)	(1.48)
Subsidies	-0.53	-1.46	-0.34	0.02	-1.00	-0.36	-0.56	-0.45	0.02
	(1.05)	(3.55)	(0.58)	(0.08)	(1.81)	(0.66)	(2.12)	(1.73)	(0.05)
Replacement rate	2.85	2.54	1.66	3.24	2.72	1.10	-0.39	-0.17	0.55
	(2.30)	(2.01)	(1.46)	(3.55)	(2.38)	(1.11)	(0.28)	(0.16)	(0.56)
Benefit duration	-4.00	-4.33	-2.31	-3.86	-4.08	-1.95	-0.14	-0.24	-0.35
	(4.95)	(4.79)	(3.37)	(6.07)	(3.89)	(2.77)	(0.22)	(0.31)	(0.73)
Union density	1.20	1.57	0.25	1.42	1.88	1.26	-0.21	-0.31	-1.00
	(1.87)	(2.53)	(0.29)	(3.01)	(2.30)	(1.15)	(0.27)	(0.41)	(1.07)
Union coordination	0.22	0.63	-0.32	0.55	0.94	0.01	-0.32	-0.31	-0.33
	(0.83)	(1.89)	(1.25)	(1.88)	(2.04)	(0.04)	(1.13)	(0.7)	(1.39)
EPL	-2.54	–	–	-2.77	–	–	0.23	–	–
	(4.17)			(5.41)			(0.32)		
EPL regular contracts	–	-1.01	–	–	-1.04	–	–	0.02	–
		(3.65)			(3.19)			(0.08)	

175

Table 5.11 (continued)

Model	(A)	(B)	(C)	(D)	(E)	(F)	(G)	(H)	(I)
Dependent variable	JR	JR	JR	JC	JC	JC	JD	JD	JD
EPL temporary contracts	-0.27	–	–	-0.93	–	–	-0.65	–	–
			(3.44)			(2.22)			(1.07)
Sector dummies	Yes	Yes	Yes	Yes	Yes	Yes	Yes	Yes	Yes
No. of observations	309	309	309	309	309	309	309	309	309
Adjusted R^2	0.678	0.672	0.670	0.707	0.698	0.687	0.311	0.310	0.316
Breush-Pagan (p-value)	0.36	0.92	0.94	0.63	0.215	0.034	0.002	0.002	0.014

cost burden of hiring additional workers in countries with tight dismissal restrictions. The role of firing restrictions is partially counterbalanced by the use of temporary contracts which clearly increase the job flows in the economy by boosting employment creation. This result suggests that some countries might be using temporary and atypical forms of employment to overcome the cost burden imposed by restrictions to employment adjustment. With regards to industrial subsidies, the results in column (B) suggest that public subsidies might reduce job reallocation, preventing job destruction in shrinking sectors and presumably reducing job creation in dynamic industries where higher taxes are collected in order to finance such subsidies (Leonard and Van Audenrode 1993). Although negative, this effect is not always statistically significant as suggested by columns (A) and (C). However, the negative effect of job subsidies is noticeable in the *JD* regressions presented in column (G).

Evidence points in the expected direction with regards to the tax wedge which presents a negative (and significant) effect on the dynamics of job reallocation, especially by hindering job creation. The results for passive labour market policies are in line with those obtained by Contini et al. (1995). We find that the replacement rate and duration of benefits have asymmetric effects on the nature of job flows, the former reducing job reallocation and the latter increasing this measure.

Regarding wage-setting institutions the evidence is mixed. We find that higher union density increases job flows by raising job creation. The net density rate has a positive and statistically significant sign at the 5 per cent level in the specifications presented in columns (B) and (C) and at the 10 per cent level in column (A). However, regarding wage-setting coordination it is found to have a positive and significant (at the 10 per cent level) impact on job turnover only in column (B). These results can be interpreted in the light of the theoretical insights discussed by Bertola and Rogerson (1997).

Next, we explore the extent to which labour market institutions have different effects in different sectors of the economy. For instance union bargaining power might not be the same across sectors within the country, being weaker in some service branches where short-term and fixed-term contracts are more important. Similarly, if atypical forms of employment are more important in service industries, EPL restrictions are expected to have a less important role on the determination of the job flows of this sector.

Table 5.12 presents the same specifications for the whole economy but with industrial and service industries considered separately. We will concentrate here on the most salient features of the comparison between these two tables. Note that firing restrictions have a much sharper effect on the dynamics of job flows in industrial than in service sectors. EPL provisions

Table 5.12   Industrial and services sectors – institutional determinants of average job reallocation, job creation and job destruction: OLS estimates (t-values from cluster robust standard errors in parentheses)

Model	Industrial sectors			Services sectors		
	(A)	(B)	(C)	(D)	(E)	(F)
Dependent variable	*JR*	*JR*	*JR*	*JR*	*JR*	*JR*
Intercept	12.31	13.11	9.40	17.68	17.27	16.11
	(8.65)	(8.75)	(6.57)	(9.04)	(8.42)	(8.44)
Tax wedge	−3.94	−6.17	−0.54	−6.41	−6.65	−3.64
	(2.55)	(3.66)	(0.31)	(2.89)	(2.85)	(1.46)
Temporary contracts	0.12	0.10	0.17	−0.01	−0.002	0.01
	(4.27)	(3.31)	(6.05)	(0.28)	(0.04)	(0.33)
Subsidies	−0.97	−2.21	−1.28	−0.03	−0.78	0.78
	(1.72)	(4.82)	(1.83)	(0.04)	(1.18)	(0.84)
Replacement rate	1.12	1.06	−1.37	4.71	3.31	4.97
	(0.81)	(0.75)	(1.02)	(2.4)	(1.64)	(2.8)
Benefit duration	−3.03	−3.78	−0.49	−5.61	−4.99	−4.68
	(3.28)	(3.65)	(0.62)	(4.47)	(3.55)	(4.39)
Union density	1.00	1.43	0.50	1.50	2.11	−0.10
	(1.40)	(2.07)	(0.5)	(1.46)	(2.11)	(0.08)
Union coordination	0.69	1.36	−0.06	−0.33	−0.37	−0.70
	(2.26)	(3.55)	(0.22)	(0.81)	(0.74)	(1.78)
EPL	−3.59	–	–	−1.51	–	–
	(5.21)	–	–	(1.58)	–	–
EPL regular contracts	–	−1.56	–	–	−0.19	–
	–	(5.00)	–	–	(0.45)	–
EPL temporary contracts	–	–	−0.95	–	–	−0.99
	–	–	(3.01)	–	–	(2.33)
	–	–	–	–	–	–
Sector dummies	Yes	Yes	Yes	Yes	Yes	Yes
No. of observations	166	166	166	133	133	133
Adjusted R²	0.552	0.547	0.499	0.689	0.683	0.697
Breush-Pagan (p-value)	0.251	0.475	0.277	0.256	0.561	0.078

show a negative and statistically significant sign for both *JR* and *JC* in the industrial sectors regardless of the indicator of EPL considered, while in the case of services this is only the case in two out of the six specifications. Similarly, the evidence points to a clearer effect of temporary contracts in facilitating the creation of industrial employment. At the same time, the

Table 5.13 Sensitivity analysis: institutional effects after dropping one country

Variable	Min	Max	Number of regressions	Accept. rate[*] (%)
All sectors				
EPL	−3.05	−1.64	12	100.0
Tax wedge	−7.07	−1.73	12	91.7
Temporary contracts	−0.06	0.01	12	91.7
Subsidies	−1.36	0.22	12	33.3
Replacement rate	−1.50	4.65	12	83.3
Benefit duration	−4.70	−1.41	12	83.3
Union density	−0.05	1.87	12	75.0
Union coverage	−0.76	0.54	12	8.3

Note: [*]Number of the regressions with respect to total in which the institution is significant at the 10 per cent level.

significance of the replacement rate variable seems to be driven by the expansion of employment in service industries but not in manufacturing. As regards sectoral subsidies, if they are shifting resources from the growing to the contracting sectors, we should find a more significant negative impact on industrial sectors than in services, possibly counterbalanced by a negative effect in the creation of employment in the service sector. Our results partially support the former.

Table 5.13 presents sensitivity analysis with respect to the number of countries included in the regression specification presented in column (A) of Table 5.11. In line with theoretical predictions, the most relevant institutional factor in shaping job flows is the strictness of employment protection legislation, the only institution that keeps its significance for every combination of 11 countries. Interestingly, the share of temporary contracts becomes non-significant when Spain is excluded from the sample, a finding in line with country evidence that clearly states the significance of the use of these type of contracts in circumventing stringent dismissal laws.

6. CONCLUSIONS

In this chapter we have analysed job flows for a panel of EU countries using a unique homogeneous dataset that covers the whole spectrum of productive sectors. After examining patterns of job flows across countries and some firms' characteristics (for example size, productive sector, capital intensity and so on), we turn to multivariate methods to address the effects of institutional differences among countries on job dynamics. The analysis is based on variation across 29 manufacturing and services sectors in 12 EU countries. We found that differences in job reallocation rates are largely explained by technological features, which are captured by common patterns within sectors across different countries. On average, service industries typically exhibit stronger patterns of job flows than manufacturing sectors. In particular, job flows in Computer and related activities are estimated to be 10 percentage points higher than in Textiles and in Transport equipment, while the gap falls to around 3 percentage points for Wholesale trade and Hotels and restaurants relative to Textiles and Transport equipment. Interestingly, the gap is overall mainly explained by differences in job creation while job destruction is broadly similar.

However, institutional differences are also an important factor, explaining more than 16 per cent of the variation in job reallocation and job creation across countries once sectoral characteristics have been controlled for. We focused on several institutional and regulatory aspects of both labour and product markets as potential explanatory sources of cross-country variation in labour market flows. As expected, we found that the strictness of employment protection legislation (EPL) has a negative and significant effect on job reallocation whatever specification considered, though the role of EPL appears to be less important in the determination of service sector job flows than in manufacturing sectors. Moreover, the impact of firing restrictions is partially mitigated by the presence of temporary contracts, which have a positive effect on job creation and job reallocation, especially in the industrial sector. With regard to the role of wage-setting institutions, we found that union density increases job creation, resulting in higher job reallocation in unionized countries.

NOTES

1. We are grateful to Neale Kennedy, Alfred Stiglbauer, Jarkko Turunen and participants at the ECB/CEPR Labour market workshop 'What helps or hinders labour market adjustments in Europe' for their comments and suggestions. We also thank Jean-Paul Genot for assistance with Amadeus. The views presented in this paper are those of the authors and do not necessarily reflect the views of the European Central Bank. All the errors are our own. Correspondence address: Ramón Gómez-Salvador, European Central Bank, Kaiserstrasse 29, D-60311 Frankfurt am Main; e-mail: ramon.gomezsalvador@ecb.int.
2. Job creation and job destruction resulting from movement between establishments within the same firm offset each other at the firm level. As a result, higher job reallocation rates are expected at the establishment level. Schuh and Triest (2000) estimate for the USA that job flows between firms represent less than 60 per cent of the total job flows between establishments owned by these firms.

3. See Davis et al. (1996) for a detailed discussion on problems arising from the measurement of employment changes at the establishment/firm level.
4. The growth measure as defined above is monotonically correlated with the conventional measure defined as the change in employment divided by the lagged employment, and the two measures are approximately the same for small growth rates. Moreover, unlike the conventional measure, which ranges from -1 and $+\infty$, this measure of growth rate is symmetric around zero, being bounded in the interval $[-2, 2]$, and allows employment expansions and contractions to be treated symmetrically.
5. To relate job flows to worker reallocation, notice that $X_{st} \times JR_{st}$ represents an upper bound for the number of workers who change jobs or employment status (from employed to non-employed and conversely) in response to firm-level employment changes. On the other hand $X_{st} \times max[JC_{st}, JD_{st}]$ represents the lower bound.
6. The main findings of the chapter, presented in Sections 4 and 5, are largely unaffected by the inclusion of Italy.
7. The following exclusion criteria have been used to clean the sample: (1) firms for which only consolidated accounts are available; (2) observations for which employment growth rate is missing value; (3) observations for which the growth rates of compensation per employee is less then -50 per cent or more than 50 per cent; (4) for Austria and Germany there is very little information on wages in Amadeus. Thus, in order to clean possible outliers an additional filter was applied: observations in the 1st and 99th percentile of employment growth for firms with more than 250 employees were deleted.
8. The results do not change significantly from those obtained using the weights from the EU Labour Force Survey.
9. Sectors are defined according to the 2-digit NACE classification (NACE code, rev 1).
10. The shares of employment in comparison with the initial sample are 69 per cent, 55 per cent and 72 per cent respectively.
11. Luxembourg, Greece, Norway and Switzerland are excluded from the analysis due to lack of institutional data. The final panel is slightly unbalanced, since some sectors in the small countries did not meet the requirement for representativeness, which was set to 20 firms per year.
12. Wage-setting coordination, unemployment benefits and the tax wedge are taken from Nickell et al. (2001).
13. EPL indices are described in Nicoletti et al. (1999) and the share of temporary contracts is extracted from the EU Labour Force Survey.
14. Source: New Cronos Database (Eurostat).

REFERENCES

Albæk, K. and B.E. Sørensen (1998), 'Worker flows and job flows in Danish manufacturing, 1980–91', *Economic Journal*, **108** (451), 1750–71.
Bertola, G. (1990), 'Job security, employment and wages', *European Economic Review*, **34**, 851–86.
Bertola, G. and R. Rogerson (1997), 'Institution and labour reallocation', *European Economic Review*, **41**, 1147–71.
Blanchflower, D. and S. Burgess (1996), 'Job creation and job destruction in Great Britain in the 1980s', CEP Discussion Paper 287.
Boeri, T. and U. Cramer (1992), 'Employment growth, incumbents and entrants: evidence from Germany', *International Journal of Industrial Organisation*, **10**, 545–66.
Broersma, L. and P.A. Gautier (1997), 'Job creation and job destruction by small firms: an empirical investigation for the Dutch manufacturing sector', *Small Business Economics*, **8**, 1–14.

Contini, B., A. Gavosto, R. Revelli and P. Sestito (1991), 'Creazione e distruzione di posti-lavoro in Italia, 1984–89', Temi di discussione, Banca d'Italia.

Contini, B., L. Pacelli, M. Filippi, G. Lioni and R. Revelli (1995), 'A study on job creation and job destruction in Europe', study for the Commission of the European Communities, DG V.

Davis, S.J. and J. Haltiwanger (1992), 'Gross job creation, gross job destruction and employment reallocation', *Quarterly Journal of Economics*, **107**, 819–63.

Davis, S.J. and J. Haltiwanger (1999), 'Gross job flows', in O. Ashenfelter and D. Card (eds), *Handbook of Labour Economics*, Vol. 3B, Amsterdam: North-Holland, pp. 2711–805.

Davis, S.J., J. Haltiwanger and S. Schuh (1996), *Job Creation and Job Destruction*, Cambridge, MA: MIT Press.

Dolado, J.J. and R. Gómez-Salvador (1995), 'Creación y destrucción de empleo en el sector privado manufacturero español: un analisis descriptivo', *Investigaciones Económicas*, **XIX** (3), 371–93.

Farber, H.S. (1986), 'The analysis of union behaviour', in O. Ashenfelter and R. Layard (eds), *Handbook of Labour Economics*, Vol. 2, Amsterdam: North-Holland, pp. 1039–89.

Foote, C.L. (1998), 'Trend employment growth and the bunching of job creation and destruction', *Quarterly Journal of Economics*, **113** (3), 809–34.

Freeman, R.B. (1980), 'The exit-voice tradeoff in the labour market: unionism, job tenure, quits and separations', *Quarterly Journal of Economics*, **94**, 643–73.

Garibaldi, P. (1998), 'Job flows dynamics and firing restrictions', *European Economic Review*, **42**, 245–75.

Garibaldi, P., J. Konings and C.A. Pissarides (1997), 'Gross job reallocation and labour market policy', in D.J. Snower and G. la Dehesa (eds), *Unemployment Policy: Government Options for the Labour Market*, Cambridge: Cambridge University Press, pp. 557–87.

Gómez-Salvador, R., J. Messina and G. Vallanti (2004), 'Gross job flows and institutions in Europe', *Labour Economics*, **11**, 469–85.

Haltiwanger, J.C. and S. Schuh (1999), 'Gross job flows between plants and industries', *New England Economic Review*, March/April, 41–64.

Heyman, F. (2001), 'Wage dispersion and job turnover: evidence from Sweden', Trade Union Institute for Economic Research Working Paper 181.

Lagarde S., E. Maurin and C. Torelli (1994), 'Créations et suppressions d'emplois en France: une étude de la période 1984–1992', *Economie et Prévision*, **113–14** (213), 67–88.

Leonard, J. and M. Van Audenrode (1993), 'Corporatism run amok: job stability and industrial policy in Belgium and the United States', *Economic Policy*, **17**, 355–89.

Lucifora, C. (1998), 'The impact of unions on labour turnover in Italy: evidence from establishment level data', *International Journal of Industrial Organization*, **16**, 353–76.

Mortensen, D. and C. Pissarides (1999a), 'New developments in models of search in the labour market', in O. Ashenfelter and D. Card (eds), *Handbook of Labour Economics*, Vol. 3, Amsterdam: North-Holland, pp. 2567–627.

Mortensen, D. and C. Pissarides (1999b), 'Job reallocation, employment fluctuations and unemployment', CEP Discussion Paper 0421.

Mumford, K. and P. Smith (1999), 'Job reallocation and average job tenure: theory and workplace evidence from Australia', University of York Discussion Papers in Economics 96/46.

Nickell, S., L. Nunziata, W. Ochel and G. Quintini (2001), 'The Beveridge curve, unemployment and wages in the OECD from the 1960s to the 1990s', CEP Discussion Paper 0502.

Nicoletti, G., S. Scarpetta and O. Boylaud (1999), 'Summary indicators of product market regulation with an extension to the employment protection legislation', OECD Economic Department Working Paper, 226.

OECD (1994), *Employment Outlook*, Chapter 3, Paris: OECD.

OECD (1996), *Employment Outlook*, Chapter 5, Paris: OECD.

OECD (1999), *Employment Outlook*, Chapter 2, Paris: OECD.

Pissarides, C.A. (2000), *Equilibrium Unemployment Theory*, Cambridge, MA: MIT Press.

Salvanes, K.G. (1997), 'Market rigidities and labour market flexibility: an international comparison', *Scandinavian Journal of Economics*, **99**, 315–33.

Schuh, S. and R.K. Triest (2000), 'The role of firms in job creation and destruction in US manufacturing', *New England Economic Review*, **6** (2), 29–44.

DISCUSSION

Sascha O. Becker

The analysis of job flows is of paramount importance for understanding the capability of labour markets to adjust to shocks. Gross job flows may therefore be considered a proxy for labour market flexibility. Two strands of literature, one theoretical and one empirical, have sharpened our understanding of reallocations in the labour market.

Job search and matching models have introduced trade in the labour market as a decentralized economic activity which is uncoordinated, time-consuming and costly for both firms and workers. Policies such as firing costs may put restrictions on job flows and therefore inhibit adjustments in the labour market.

The seminal empirical work of Davis and Haltiwanger (1992) for the USA has directed attention to gross job flows as a more adequate measure of labour reallocation than just (changes in) employment levels, and has measured the differences between worker and job flows. In the sequel, evidence on worker and job flows was collected for many other countries. Over time, several stylized facts emerged from this literature which is nicely summarized in this chapter by Gómez-Salvador, Messina and Vallanti.

In empirical cross-country studies, comparability of datasets is always an important issue. When datasets differ across countries, one always runs the risk of confounding actual cross-country differences and pure data measurement and sampling features. One of the main contributions of the present chapter is its use of the internationally homogeneous database 'Amadeus' collected by Bureau van Dijk (BvD) which serves as the basis for comparisons in job flows of firms in 15 European countries.

The focus of the chapter is on the importance of sector characteristics for labour market flows. In a second step, the sectoral features of job flows are sliced-up into size, capital intensity and average productivity effects of the firms in the given sector. In the last step, the role of institutional features in the dynamics of job creation and job destruction in European labour markets is examined.

The main results of the chapter are that employment protection reduces labour market flows, although this effect is partially counterbalanced through the use of temporary employment contracts, the latter effect driven in particular by Spain. On the other hand, and also consistent with theoretical insights by Bertola and Rogerson (1997), unionized labour markets exhibit higher job flows. Further interesting results pertain to the distinction between industrial and service industries: firing restrictions have a much sharper effect on the dynamics of job flows in industrial than in service sectors; temporary contracts facilitate the creation of jobs more clearly in the industrial sector. The distinction between industrial and service sectors is important in particular in view of the fact that many studies exclusively focus on manufacturing. However, to put those last results into perspective it should be noted that the Amadeus database only includes companies with operating revenues equal to at least 1.5 (1) million euro, total assets equal to at least 3 (2) million euro, and number of employees equal to at least 15 (10). Figures are for the UK, Germany, France and Italy (figures in parentheses for all the other countries). Since firms are typically smaller in the service sector and at the same time smaller firms have a higher turnover (see Table 5.9), the data for the service sector are relatively less representative than the data for the industrial sector.

A Plea for a European Establishment Panel

Existing studies on job flows, including this chapter, have either of two strengths: many studies give a detailed account of job reallocation patterns in single countries while other studies take a cross-country perspective and allow for exploitation of cross-country variation in institutional features, which is possible with single-country data only to the extent that there is sufficient within-country variation (for example across regions). The weakness of single-country studies is that their results may not necessarily be generalized to other countries. Although the knowledge accumulated over the last 15 years in the many single-country studies is quite impressive, results would be even more robust if data collection was more standardized so as to exclude measurement issues as an explanation for cross-country differences. Existing cross-country studies are less numerous and crucially depend on the availability of comparable data. Only very few cross-nationally comparable data sources are available at the moment, one of the richest being the Amadeus database analysed here.

This chapter constitutes an important step forward in understanding the importance of labour market institutions to job creation and job destruction and is the broadest study on these issues to date. It confirms many of the key facts that have been found in single country studies, which is good news.

It is therefore natural to ask what can be done to continue along the lines of this chapter and other cross-country studies and to prove the robustness of their results. The issue arises because in addition to its strengths, the Amadeus database has some limitations for which the authors can obviously not be blamed. First, births and deaths of firms – which according to other studies account for at least one quarter of the estimated job flows – cannot be identified. Second, the data are at the firm level and not at the establishment level. In general, firm-level studies differ from establishment level studies in the following respect: employment dynamics *across* plants *within* firms are not observed. Countries with a tendency to organize in huge corporations instead of legally independent units, may thus seem to have more limited job flows if measured at the firm level instead of the plant level. This may be erroneously attributed to labour market institutions instead of the legal environment if the latter is not adequately controlled for. On the other hand, changes in ownership may be measured as a firm start-up if the (same) plant is given the new owner's firm identifier. This may overstate job flows. Third, the majority of firms are small and are not sampled in the Amadeus database (and similar cross-country databases). To give an idea, 2.9 million out of 3.2 million firms – that is, *more than 90 per cent* of all firms – in Germany have fewer than 10 employees. To the extent that much of the turnover in labour markets is related to small firms, the true extent of job reallocation may be understated by any database that omits smaller firms.

Empirical research could provide even deeper insights into the dynamics of the labour market if cross-national data were collected at an establishment level, that is, at the level of the most basic business units. Since in many countries establishment panels are now available, the infrastructure for collecting a cross-national establishment panel, for example at the European level, is in place. The final, crucial, step consists, as always, in coordinating the data collection such as to ensure data comparability. A European establishment panel should definitely contain information on company structures, in order to allow researchers to control for company-specific effects and identify job reallocation *between* plants *within* firms.

A European establishment panel would allow us to get a complete picture of job turnover in Europe and fill the gaps left by existing databases: firm births and deaths, turnover across *all* plant and firm sizes and a representative sectoral coverage. Such a database would also allow us to identify the impact of labour market institutions on the creation of (initially small) firms and, their potential to advance.

Taking the above thoughts further, the ultimate aim should be to add another dimension of job flows, namely the nature of jobs created and destroyed. While establishment surveys could in theory ask this information, a more detailed, if not the best possible, picture would arise from linked employer–employee data (see for example Abowd et al. 1999).

References

Abowd, J., F. Kramarz and D. Margolis (1999), 'High wage workers and high wage firms', *Econometrica*, **67** (2), 251–333.
Bertola, G. and R. Rogerson (1997), 'Institutions and labour reallocation', *European Economic Review*, **41**, 1147–71.
Davis, S.J. and J. Haltiwanger (1992), 'Gross job creation, gross job destruction and employment reallocation', *Quarterly Journal of Economics*, **107**, 819–63.

6. The effect of home-ownership on labour mobility in the Netherlands[1]

Michiel van Leuvensteijn and Pierre Koning[2]

1. INTRODUCTION

The European labour market is often characterized by its low mobility, both within as well as between countries. Since the introduction of EMU this problem has become more prominent as the mobility of labour is one of the few short-term adjustment mechanisms still left. One reason for the low labour mobility in Europe is that there are cultural and linguistic barriers. This, however, does not explain the differences in interregional mobility within a country or changes in labour mobility through time. One of the explanations for this may be that home-ownership diminishes labour mobility and increases unemployment. The idea is that homeowners will not move to other regions when faced with an economic downturn, as they are more attached to their home. Also, they may be faced with decreases in housing prices. Thus, the probability of unemployment would be higher for homeowners.

Although the idea that home-ownership has a positive effect on unemployment is based on microeconomic assumptions, most studies addressing the effect of home-ownership on labour mobility and unemployment use macro- or mesoeconomic data. With aggregated data for the USA, Green and Henderschott (2001) show that home-ownership indeed constrains labour mobility and thus increases unemployment for middle-aged classes due to the high transaction and moving costs involved. Using data from the OECD countries, Nickell (1998) finds similar results. However, these studies do not reveal the underlying behaviour of individuals. For example, it may well be that lower job mobility of homeowners results from higher job commitment, also reducing the risk of unemployment. Obviously, this cannot be measured in meso or macro studies.

Instead of using macro- or mesoeconomic data, we choose longitudinal data of individual employees. This helps us to correct for spurious relationships and identify effects of home-ownership on labour mobility, and vice versa. Both the movements on the housing market and on the labour market are examined to estimate the impact of home-ownership on job mobility as well as the probability of becoming unemployed. We apply longitudinal data that are collected by the Dutch tax department (Income Panel Research data 'IPR', for 1989–98). In the IPR about 75 000 individuals are followed over time. These individuals can change between jobs, between unemployment and employment, between homes and between regions. In modelling these transitions, several variables in the IPR may be useful: age, income, the number of children, gender, home-ownership, job tenure and housing duration.

Our analysis contributes to the literature on labour and housing market mobility in a number of ways. First, the IPR provides us with a rather unique panel allowing us to link the individual labour and housing market histories of a large sample of employees. The IPR data are comparable with the British Household Panel Survey, which also combines both types of information (see for example Boeheim and Taylor 2000). Second, and in contrast to many other empirical studies on job mobility, we also explicitly model the probability of home-ownership so as to correct for endogeneity bias. To minimize the biasing impact of distributional assumptions, this is done in a nonparametric fashion. Third, we analyse not only the impact of home-ownership on job-to-job mobility, but also (and simultaneously) on the risk of becoming unemployed or non-participant. This means we estimate a job duration model with multiple ('competing') risks.

The further structure of the chapter is as follows. Section 2 describes the literature on the relationship between the housing market and labour mobility. Section 3 presents the empirical model, whereas the data are described in Section 4. In Section 5 and 6 the estimation results and conclusions are presented.

2.   THEORY AND REVIEW

There are two strands of literature describing the relationship between the housing market and the labour market, depending on the macro- or microeconomic focus. Contributions in the first strand mostly try to explain labour migration. Here the starting point is the Harris–Todaro model. In Harris and Todaro (1970) a neoclassical model is developed in which (international) migration is caused by geographic differences in the supply and demand for labour. Regions with a limited supply of labour will have a relatively high expected wage, which is the product of the complement of the unemployment rate and the wage if employed. High expected wages will attract a large inflow of labour from low-wage regions. This inflow of labour is mirrored by an outflow of capital.

Green and Henderschott (2001) add to this the role of home-ownership to explain high unemployment and low labour migration. There are a number of ways in which home-ownership influences labour migration. First, in regions with an economic downturn homeowners are faced with a drop in house prices, making homes highly illiquid assets. Moving to another region to find a job may therefore be costly for homeowners. Second, high interest rates in times of recession may also result in a lock-in to below market-rate mortgages, with similar consequences for labour mobility. Third, high transaction costs may cause a decrease in labour mobility.

Various macro studies address the relationship between home-ownership and unemployment empirically. For example Nickell (1998) analyses the relationship between home-ownership and unemployment using a panel of 20 OECD countries from 1989 to 1994. With these data Nickell shows that unemployment is (seemingly) positively correlated with home-ownership, with an elasticity of 0.13. This means that a rise of home-ownership of 10 percentage points results in an increase in unemployment of 1.3 per cent. Green and Henderschott (2001) estimate an elasticity of 0.18, using aggregated data for the different states of the USA for the period 1970 to 1990. This estimate is close to that of Oswald (1999), with an elasticity equal to 0.2. He analyses the relationship between home-ownership and unemployment using panel time-series data from 19 OECD countries from 1960 to 1990. This relationship is not only found between countries but also between the regions of France, Italy, Sweden, Switzerland, the USA and the UK.

For the Netherlands, Hassink and Curvers (1999) show that regions with high home-ownership rates do not have high unemployment rates when tested on a mesoeconomic level. They estimate the relationship between the unemployment rate and home-ownership for 348 regions for the period 1990 to 1998, and find home-ownership to have a negative impact on unemployment. This suggests a simultaneity problem: workers in regions with high economic growth and low unemployment will have higher incomes and therefore will be more likely to buy a house. Apparently this is what is picked up in the estimation of the model.

The relationship between labour mobility and the housing market is also studied in a microeconomic context. Van Ommeren et al. (2000) develop a theoretical search model in which the acceptance of a job offer not only depends on the direct gain in wage utility but also on the once-only costs associated with moving residence and search costs. These on-the-job search costs are modest for most professions compared to the once-only costs associated with moving residence. The once-only costs associated with moving to another residence depend strongly on housing status (see for example Van den Berg 1992).

Recently, various empirical studies have addressed the relationship between the housing market and labour mobility, making use of individual longitudinal data. With the British Household Panel Survey, Henley (1998) finds for the UK that unemployed are less likely to move than employed workers. Using the same data, Boeheim and Taylor (2000) arrive at a similar result. Using probit models with pooled data for the UK they find that regions with high unemployment show less home mobility. Also, they find that homeowners change less from jobs than tenants. For the Netherlands Van Ommeren (1996) estimates a search model for job-movers with (retrospective) panel data from the beginning of the 1990s. He finds homeowners to be less likely to move to another home than tenants are. Also, he finds no evidence that job and residential moves are mutually related. Van der Vlist (2001) concludes that homeowners are less likely to move to another home and to change jobs.

To sum up, the two strands of literature portray different, but not necessarily contradictory, pictures. Macro studies, using variations between countries or regions over time, suggest that high home-ownership rates may lead to higher unemployment, in particular in periods of economic downturn. Micro studies, utilizing (longitudinal) data of individuals or households, find home-ownership to be associated with lower residential mobility and lower job-to-job mobility. This suggests that homeowners have more job commitment and thus also may have a lower risk of unemployment. However, little is known on the exact causality of these effects. The question remains, to what extent home-ownership is driven by job commitment and to what extent the reverse holds.

3. THE EMPIRICAL MODEL

Our empirical model consists of two parts: the job duration model and the housing model. In the job duration model we explain the individual labour market histories of a flow-sample of employees. With this information we identify the impact of various explanatory variables, including housing state on labour mobility. Also, since individuals are followed over time, we control for unobserved heterogeneity. Within the context of duration models this means that we assume a (nonparametric) distribution of random effects. The same principle holds for the housing model. Here we explain a sequence of housing states measured on a yearly basis. These data allow us to estimate a random effects logit model.

Initially the job duration and the housing model are treated separately and without the inclusion of random effects. As a result the estimated impact of housing state on job mobility may be biased. Next we estimate a simultaneous model where the job duration and the housing model are linked by the possible correlation of their random effects.

3.1 The Job Duration Model

In this paper we use hazard-rate or – stated differently – duration models to examine the impact of home-ownership on job spells. The hazard rate is defined as the rate at which an event takes place over a short period of time, given that this event has not occurred so far. The hazard rate θ measures the probability of leaving a job or over a specific (small) time interval $[T, T + dt]$, given that one occupies this job up to T:

$$\theta = \Pr(T < t < T + dt | t \geq T) \tag{6.1}$$

In the job duration model the time interval dt is normalized to one month. Three types of transitions may take place: that into another job, of becoming unemployed or of becoming non-participant. Therefore the hazard rate out of employment is modelled into three possible competing risks. The impact of several exogenous variables, such as age, gender or income, may vary with respect to these risks.

The competing risks have a *proportional* (or *loglinear*) structure (see for example Lancaster 1990). b denotes the index of a particular risk ($b = 1, 2, \ldots, B$). Thus the risk into b at time t can be described as:

$$\theta_b(t | y_t, X_t) = \exp [\alpha_b\, y_t + \beta_b\, X_t + \Psi(t)] \tag{6.2}$$

with

$$b = 1, 2, 3$$

in which y_t equals one if the individual is a homeowner at time t (and zero if renting) and X_t is a matrix representing individual covariates that may change over time t. Some of these characteristics do not vary over time but are defined at the beginning of the duration spell. Obviously the most relevant variable – that of the housing state y – is time-dependent. Ψ denotes the impact of duration dependence. In the estimation of the model we use a (nonparametric) step function for Ψ. Further, take notice that the variables that change over time only do so on a calendar-year base. Therefore residential transitions may coincide with job movements within a calendar year, whereas the exact sequence of events is unknown.

3.2 The Housing Model

We assume the housing state y to follow a logit specification:

$$\Pr(y_t = 1 | X_t, h_t) = \frac{\exp[\gamma X_t + \Phi(t) + \delta h_t]}{1 + \exp[\gamma X_t + \Phi(t) + \delta h_t]}$$

$$\Pr(y_t = 0 | X_t, h_t) = 1 - \Pr(y_t = 1) \tag{6.3}$$

As becomes apparent from (6.3) we assume the housing probability to be driven by the same time-varying covariates as the job duration model X_t. In addition to this we use the regional home-ownership rate h_t as an instrumental variable, only affecting the housing status. In our data we have 538 regions. Also, since h_t pertains to average group behaviour, it should be noted at this point that the assumptions for identification here are stronger than in models where instruments are measured on an individual basis (see Manski 1993). We will discuss these assumptions in detail in Section 5 when we come to the estimation results. Further, similar to (6.2), $\Phi(t)$ denotes a step function describing the impact of job tenure.

3.3 Unobserved Heterogeneity

The IPR data that we use provide us with a limited amount of registered individual information. Obviously more characteristics may be relevant in explaining the differences in, for example, the risk of unemployment or that of moving to another home. In particular, job commitment, which is approximated by the job tenure variable, may be measured imperfectly. The more important the impact of such unobserved heterogeneity, the larger the potential biasing impact of endogeneity effects. Endogeneity may arise if the choice of buying or renting a home is correlated with the risk of job transitions, becoming unemployed or non-participant.

Within the context of duration models, several methods have been developed to allow for unobserved heterogeneity. To minimize the impact of distributional assumptions, we adopt a nonparametric method which has been introduced by Heckman and Singer (1984). They assume that a sample consists of two or more (unobserved) subsamples with different levels of time-invariant unobservable effects. Then, for all subsamples the corresponding weights are estimated as well as the impact of unobserved differences on the hazard. This mass-point methodology is also used for the housing model. The unobserved differences in both models can then be linked, so as to allow for cross-correlation.

To allow for the presence of unobserved heterogeneity we specify the risks (with index b) as a so-called mixed proportional hazard (MPH) structure.

The mixing is with respect to v, which can be interpreted as a time-invariant random effect:

$$\theta_b(t|y_t, X_t, v_b) = \exp[\alpha_b y_t + \beta_b X_t + \Psi(t) + v_b] \qquad (6.4)$$

where

$$b = 1, 2, 3.$$

We also extend the housing model with random effects u:

$$\Pr(y_t = 1|Z_t, u) = \frac{\exp[\gamma X_t + \Phi(t) + \delta h_t + u]}{1 + \exp[\gamma X_t + \Phi(t) + \delta h_t + u]}$$

$$\Pr(y_t = 0|Z_t, u) = 1 - \Pr(y_t = 1) \qquad (6.5)$$

To correct for endogeneity bias we allow v_1, v_2, v_3 and u to be correlated. Similar to Heckman and Singer (1984), we do this by modeling K combinations of mass points for $\{v_1, v_2, v_3, u\}$ with probability weights $P_1, P_2, \ldots, 1 - P_1 - \ldots - P_{k-1}$, respectively. Thus, the unknown distribution of $\{v_1, v_2, v_3, u\}$ is represented by a nonparametric distribution with a finite number of points of support. The first point of support is normalized to $\{0, 0, 0, 0\}$. Thus, in this specification one has to estimate the parameters $\{\alpha, \beta, \gamma, P_1, P_2, \ldots, P_{K-1}\}$ as well as $K - 1$ combinations of $\{v_1, v_2, v_3, u\}$. We do this by using maximum likelihood estimation. We start by estimating the model without unobserved heterogeneity ($K = 1$, where there is only one point of support and $P_1 = 1$). Subsequently we increase the number of points of support K iteratively so as to improve the fit of the model. We perform a likelihood ratio test to determine the optimal K, that is, the number of points of support where the inclusion of an additional point of support $\{v_1, v_2, v_3, u\}$ together with an additional weight improves the likelihood significantly.

Correlation between the v's and u is not explicitly specified in the model but follows from the combination of mass points. In principle 4^{K-1} points of support allow for all possible forms of correlation between the four random effects. However, this makes the empirical model computationally very burdensome. Therefore, with increasing K we add a fixed point of support for $\{v_1, v_2, v_3, u\}$. For $K = 2$ this means that we only allow the random effects of the v's and u to be fully correlated. For $K > 2$, however, the model becomes more flexible.

The mass-point methodology we use resembles that of Abbring (1997) and Holm (2002) who both estimate a bivariate model with limited dependent or duration data. Abbring studies the impact of punitive sanctions on the job-finding rate of unemployed employees. Both the job-finding process as well as the risk of being sanctioned are influenced by random effects that may be correlated. Analogously, Holm (2002) studies the effect of training on search durations. He also uses a random effect approach, both in the training allocation model as well as in the hazard rate model of finding a job.

3.4 The Likelihood

As stated before, if we do not allow for time-invariant (unobserved) heterogeneity, the likelihood function of the model consists of two model parts that can be estimated separately. For ease of exposition we first derive these two likelihood contributions, conditional on the unobserved components $\{v_1, v_2, v_3, u\}$. Next we integrate with respect to the unobserved mass points so as to obtain the joint likelihood of the model.

Basically our model explains two types of information.

Elapsed job durations

- T = the elapsed job duration, starting from the moment of inflow in the IPR sample.
- d = a censoring indicator which equals one if the job duration is right censored, and zero otherwise.
- b = the destination that follows the job duration spell. This destination can be another job ($v = 1$), unemployment ($v = 2$) or non-participation ($v = 3$).

Housing state

- y_t = a dummy indicator which equals one if an employee is a homeowner at time t, for $t = 1, \ldots, T$.

We assume that the censoring times are stochastically independent of the corresponding job durations, that is, we assume that censoring is independent. Since the job durations are exponentially distributed, conditional likelihood of $\{T, b\}$ of a particular individual can be described as:

$$f_T(T, b|y, X, v) = \exp[-\Sigma_t^T\{\theta_1(t) + \theta_2(t) + \theta_3(t)\}]$$
$$\times [\theta_1(T)^{I(b=1)} \times \theta_2(T)^{I(b=2)} \times \theta_3(T)^{I(b=3)}]^{(1-d)} \quad (6.6)$$

where $I(b = 1, 2, 3)$ is an indicator function of the event between parentheses. In particular, this concerns the destination following the jobs spell. The first part of (6.6) represents the survival probability. Within the context of our model, this is the probability of not having found another job, having become unemployed or having become non-participant, up to time T. If T is censored ($= 1$), the likelihood of $\{T, b\}$ equals the survival probability. If T is uncensored ($= 0$), Equation (6.6) consists of two parts: the probability of survival until T and the likelihood of a transition, either into another job ($b = 1$) or unemployment ($b = 2$) or non-participation ($b = 3$).

The individual conditional likelihood of y – consisting of a sequence of housing states over the job spell of an individual – that follows from the (panel) logit model (6.5) is:

$$\Pr(y|X, h, u) = \Pi_t^T \Pr(y_t = 1|X_t, h_t, u)^{I(y(t)=1)} \times \Pr(y_t = 0|Z_t, h_t, u)^{I(y(t)=0)}$$

(6.7)

The joint individual likelihood of the observed variables – given the unobserved variables v and u – is obtained by multiplying (6.6) and (6.7). For the unobserved variables we have K combinations of mass points for $\{v_1, v_2, v_3, u\}$ with probability weights $P_1, P_2, \ldots, 1 - P_1 - \ldots - P_{k-1}$, respectively. Thus, the joint integrated likelihood can be written as:

$$L = \Sigma_i^K [P_i \times f_T(T, b|y, X, v_i) \times \Pr(y|X, h, u_i)]$$

(6.8)

where i indicates the mass point combination. This expression is maximized with respect to $\{\alpha, \beta, \gamma\}$ as well as K mass points of $\{v_1, v_2, v_3, u\}$. Obviously, more combinations of mass points may help in increasing the fit of the model. As stated before, we use a likelihood ratio test to determine the optimal number of combinations.

4. DATA

The IPR database consists of a sample of about 75 000 individuals who are followed yearly by tax authorities over the period 1989–98. In the IPR a number of possible housing and labour market states are distinguished. The states for the labour market are based on individual income states, such as social assistance (SA) benefits, unemployment insurance (UI) benefits, income and no income. From these income states one can derive the data at which a person becomes unemployed (SA- or UI-benefit) or non-participant (no income or disability benefits). Further, since we know the identity of the employer it is possible to keep track of job-to-job changes. Moving behaviour can be derived from address changes. Housing market states consist of rental housing, home-ownership or other types (for example, housing for the elderly). These are observed on a yearly basis. For each individual we observe a complete or incomplete job spell, together with various individual characteristics.

Our data consist of a flow sample of employees. This means that we select individuals entering into a job, avoiding the problem of left censoring. This leaves us with 9426 observations of individual spells. The construction of a flow sample has one major advantage: for each employee we observe the exact job tenure. Obviously this variable is crucial to identifying the impact of job commitment, in particular the impact of (negative) duration dependence.

We also select employees who are homeowners and/or tenants during the time span covered by the interviews. Thus, employees living in 'other house types' are left out of the sample. As the vast majority of individuals in this category are students or pensioners, this does not reduce the size of our sample (consisting of employees) substantially.

Given the IPR, the following variables are used in the empirical analysis:

(1) age at time of moment of entry in the sample;
(2) gender;
(3) higher or university education (this (proxy) dummy variable indicates whether a person has recently received a scholarship for higher or university education at the moment of inflow in the sample; thus, this level of education is not observed for older employees);
(4) having children who receive child support, or not;
(5) having a partner who earns income, or not;
(6) marital state: being married or not;
(7) wage in logs.

In Table 6.1 we present the characteristics of employees at the end of 1998. The majority of the employees are male (59 per cent), 40 per cent have a working partner, 32 per cent have children and 7 per cent have studied recently. As we have a flow sample, a large fraction of the sample consists of employees who are more likely to switch jobs and/or start their labour market career. Consequently, on average, employees are rather young (34 years) and job durations relatively short (almost 20 months). The mean percentage of homeowners is 53 per cent. In the first year of a job spell we observe a mean percentage of homeowners of about 25 per cent. Thus, a large fraction of employees is observed to buy a home during their job spell.

As we have yearly observations of housing state (measured at the end of calendar years) and monthly observations of labour market state, this may cause measurement problems. For example, an employee becoming unemployed may be faced with a drop in income and therefore have to sell his home and move to a rental home. Suppose this employee is registered as being a tenant for the whole year, the new housing state may be misperceived as having caused an increase in job mobility. Similar problems arise if, for example, an employee decides to move to another region and only temporarily moves to the rental sector. If then, after a while, the tenant becomes a homeowner again, the new housing state may seem to have

Table 6.1   Description of variables (mean and standard deviation)

	Employees mean	Standard deviation of mean
		Fractions*
Job duration (including censored; in days)	596.250	7.440
Percentage of right censored	0.232	0.004
Female	0.475	0.005
Working partner	0.345	0.005
Children	0.310	0.005
High education	0.176	0.004
Age (years)	30.600	0.106
Married	0.410	0.005
Wage	4.470	0.050
Percentage of homeowners	0.530	–
Number of observations	9426	–

Note: *Unless defined otherwise.

caused an increase in job mobility. Thus, measurement errors may occur in some cases. However, there are no strong a priori beliefs that this will lead to a strong bias in our estimation results.

5. ESTIMATION RESULTS

Initially – as we have stated before – the job duration model and the housing model are estimated separately and without the inclusion of time invariant random effects. This is the model for $K = 1$. Obviously no possible interaction exists between the job duration and the housing model when unobserved heterogeneity is not included in the model. Thus, the comparison between the two models helps us to identify the possible impact of endogeneity effects. Endogeneity can be tested by examining the difference in the coefficient estimates of home-ownership in the two models – the null hypothesis being that this difference equals zero and there is no endogeneity (see for example Wooldridge 2002). At the end of this section we will employ this endogeneity test.

We first assume that the hazard of leaving a job is not affected by duration in a job. Then, as we have a flow sample of employees, we allow for the presence of (negative) duration dependence in both models. The results of these two model versions are presented in the first two pairs of columns of Table 6.2.

Table 6.2 The (simultaneous) job duration and housing model, without and with unobserved heterogeneity (N = 9426)

	Without unobserved effects; no job tenure included		Without unobserved effects; job tenure included		With unobserved effects; job tenure included	
	Estimates	Std. err.	Estimates	Std. err.	Estimates	Std. err.
Parameters of job duration model						
Risk of job changes						
Constant	−0.8905	0.0302	−0.1830	0.0406	−0.1747	0.0550
Homeowner	−0.3460	0.0374	0.0397	0.0459	−0.0084	0.0555
1–2 years tenure			−1.7229	0.0583	−1.7199	0.0585
3–5 years tenure			−2.2921	0.0660	−2.2853	0.0661
More than 5 years			−2.7514	0.1365	−2.7302	0.1356
Age 25–35 years	−0.0575	0.0395	−0.2032	0.0512	−0.1903	0.0521
Age 35–45 years	−0.3181	0.0522	−0.4333	0.0667	−0.4333	0.0678
Age >45 years	−0.5873	0.0691	−0.8013	0.0838	−0.8046	0.0849
Women	−0.1929	0.0310	−0.0988	0.0393	−0.0974	0.0395
Children	−0.2055	0.0380	−0.1682	0.0476	−0.1741	0.0478
Working partner	−0.0061	0.0389	−0.0482	0.0483	−0.0369	0.0484
High education	0.2504	0.0412	0.1184	0.0546	0.1139	0.0549
Log wage	−0.3727	0.0152	−0.1769	0.0182	−0.1757	0.0183
Married	−0.0356	0.0454	−0.0748	0.0562	−0.0727	0.0563
Random effects: 2nd point of support: v_{21}					0.0893	0.0624
3rd point of support: v_{31}					−0.0820	0.0733
Risk into non-participation						
Constant	−1.6860	0.0455	−0.9838	0.0543	−0.9509	0.0758
Homeowner	−0.3392	0.0553	0.0119	0.0630	0.0529	0.0800
1–2 years tenure			−1.8735	0.0841	−1.8745	0.0841
3–5 years tenure			−2.2942	0.0941	−2.2983	0.0943
More than 5 years			−2.5341	0.1765	−2.5410	0.1774
Age 25–35 years	−0.1669	0.6430	−0.2977	0.0737	−0.3073	0.0749
Age 35–45 years	−0.4199	0.0800	−0.5153	0.0919	−0.5267	0.0932
Age >45 years	−0.1159	0.0878	−0.2640	0.1042	−0.2774	0.1062
Women	−0.0449	0.0443	0.0455	0.0515	0.0454	0.0515
Children	−0.0271	0.0514	0.0230	0.0607	0.0222	0.0608
Working partner	−0.1483	0.0584	−0.1505	0.0664	−0.1536	0.0664
High education	0.3523	0.0553	0.2045	0.0653	0.2075	0.0656
Log wage	−0.5847	0.0172	−0.4100	0.0201	−0.4103	0.0201
Married	0.1658	0.0708	0.1185	0.0807	0.1134	0.0809
Random effects: 2nd point of support: v_{22}					−0.0813	0.0838
3rd point of support: v_{32}					−0.0580	0.1018
Risk into unemployment						
Constant	−2.2779	0.0655	−1.5910	0.0722	−1.3931	0.0926
Homeowner	−0.8687	0.0785	−0.5837	0.0844	−0.3745	0.1173

Table 6.2 (continued)

	Without unobserved effects; no job tenure included		Without unobserved effects; job tenure included		With unobserved effects; job tenure included	
	Estimates	Std. err.	Estimates	Std. err.	Estimates	Std. err.
1–2 years tenure			−1.6169	0.1051	−1.6199	0.1051
3–5 years tenure			−2.1531	0.1211	−2.1690	0.1214
More than 5 years			−3.3230	0.3584	−3.3640	0.3585
Age 25–35 years	0.2200	0.0802	0.0958	0.0868	0.0365	0.0885
Age 35–45 years	0.1971	0.0960	0.1342	0.1042	0.0431	0.1078
Age > 45 years	0.2077	0.1137	0.0447	0.1232	−0.0628	0.1275
Women	−0.0387	0.0646	0.0480	0.0692	0.0495	0.0694
Children	−0.0600	0.0746	−0.0247	0.0807	−0.0344	0.0810
Working partner	−0.2873	0.0786	−0.2796	0.0835	−0.2838	0.0836
High education	−0.0782	0.0960	−0.2122	0.1038	−0.1984	0.1045
Log wage	−0.2840	0.0383	−0.0941	0.0401	−0.0926	0.0402
Married	0.0366	0.0855	0.0180	0.0925	−0.0073	0.0926
Random effects:	2nd point of support: v_{23}				−0.3365	0.1119
	3rd point of support: v_{33}				−0.4086	0.1224
Unobserved heterogeneity: probability masses						
P_1: 1st point of support					0.2863	0.0055
P_2: 2nd point of support					0.3184	0.0099
P_3: 3rd point of support					0.3953	0.0100
Parameters of housing model						
Constant	−3.2909	0.0175	−3.3851	0.0179	−9.1951	0.0904
1–2 years tenure			0.3334	0.0513	0.4922	0.0616
3–5 years tenure			0.7746	0.0297	1.4827	0.0475
More than 5 years			1.5174	0.0367	3.3260	0.0768
Age 25–35 years	0.3752	0.0103	0.4036	0.0104	1.1249	0.0327
Age 35–45 years	0.9179	0.0112	0.9332	0.0113	2.1337	0.0458
Age > 45 years	0.9872	0.0123	1.0296	0.0124	2.5575	0.0558
Women	0.3133	0.0075	0.2991	0.0076	0.3186	0.0252
Children	0.1062	0.0079	0.1008	0.0079	0.0219	0.0329
Working partner	0.6068	0.0073	0.6115	0.0074	0.6808	0.0297
High education	−0.2631	0.0155	−0.2315	0.0157	−0.4934	0.0352
Log wage	0.2885	0.0038	0.2446	0.0039	0.1837	0.0132
Married	0.9347	0.0087	0.9405	0.0088	1.4555	0.0395
% homeowners	2.7560	0.0264	2.7399	0.0267	1.7655	0.0935
Random effects:	2nd point of support: u_2				7.6423	0.0685
	3rd point of support: u_3				4.8388	0.0585
Mean log likelihood	−7.1992		−6.8322		−5.0056	

From the first pair of columns we may conclude that homeowners indeed experience fewer job-to-job transitions, but they also have a smaller risk of becoming either non-participant or unemployed. Obviously, as will be shown below, these findings may be biased for various reasons.[3] Further, most coefficients are in line with economic intuition. That is, the probability of job-to-job transitions decreases with age and the wage level. Also, we find that women, as well as married employees, show less job-to-job mobility than other employees do.

The risk into non-participation first decreases and then increases with age. Students often have temporary jobs, which explains the relatively high inflow into non-participation of younger employees. On the other hand, older employees often enter into disability insurance or pre-retirement schemes. Remarkably, we find the 'higher education' dummy to have a positive impact on the risk of becoming non-participant. This reflects the fact that this dummy is measured only for employees who are students or have studied in the recent past. Again this group often works in temporary jobs.

Less pronounced effects are found for the risk into unemployment. Here the (negative) impact of home-ownership appears to be substantial, compared to the other variables. The higher the wage that is earned, the lower the probability of becoming unemployed. Employees with children have a significantly higher risk of becoming unemployed. It may be that these employees often work in part-time jobs, to combine formal and informal labour activities, and are more vulnerable to unemployment.

Generally the estimation results of the housing model are in line with economic intuition: the probability of being a homeowner increases with job duration, age and the wage level. In addition to this, individuals having children, being married or having a working partner are more likely to own a home. Students often live in rental homes. Remarkably, women are more likely to live in owned homes than men are. It may well be that the female coefficient captures a difference in the education level – which we only observe to some extent – between men and women. In the Netherlands the labour market participation of women is still relatively low compared to other countries, and women that do participate are, on average, more highly educated than men. As a result, the coefficient of women may be overestimated.

5.1 Duration Dependence and Job Commitment

Until now we have abstracted from the role of job tenure. Obviously job commitment is crucial in understanding the decision to buy a home, as well as labour mobility. As job commitment and job security grow, individual employees will have a lower risk of becoming unemployed. Also, increasingly they will be faced with the risk of losing the returns to job-specific investments. Thus less time will be spent searching for other jobs. The attachment to a job also reduces the probability of moving, which makes buying a home more attractive.

The results in the first and second pair of columns of Table 6.2 illustrate the importance of job tenure as a proxy of job commitment, which is included as a (nonparametric) step function. The fit of the model increases dramatically and all risks show that the job hazard strongly declines with tenure. A similar pattern is found in the housing model: the larger the job commitment, the more likely it is that one owns a home. This indicates that the decision to buy a home is strongly influenced by job commitment. Using job tenure as a control variable helps in reducing the estimation bias: we no longer find a significant impact of home-ownership on job-to-job mobility. Also, the risk of non-participation is no longer affected by the home-ownership dummy. For the risk into unemployment we still find a (smaller) significant negative impact. These findings suggest that the housing market is affected by the labour market, in particular the tenure of workers, rather than the reverse.

The conclusion that there is no impact of home-ownership on the risk of job changes may be peculiar to densely populated areas where people can change jobs without changing residence. Also, moving costs may have been relatively low for homeowners. In the Netherlands housing transactions are taxed by about 6 per cent, but it may well be that – in the time span covered by the data – these costs were compensated by strong increases in housing prices. From the perspective of tenants, in particular those in the social renting sector, the costs of moving are often high; rental prices are kept artificially low, leading to long waiting lists. Once a new job in another region is accepted and one has to move to another region, one may be faced with much higher rental prices in the private sector.

Thus, it seems that individual employees decide to change jobs without changing residence. In contrast to this, we do find a negative coefficient describing the effect of home-ownership on the risk of becoming unemployed. In a way this is not surprising; the consequences of this event may lead to a far more substantial and unanticipated decrease in income. Homeowners are not entitled to social assistance if they have capital and therefore have to break into their housing equity. Also, tenants are (partially) insured against loss of income, as they may receive higher rent subsidies to compensate for this. Thus, homeowners have higher incentives to prevent unemployment by investing more in job-specific capital.

5.2 The Simultaneous Model

Clearly, the inclusion of duration dependence helps in obtaining a better understanding of labour market dynamics as well as the role of the housing market. Also, it helps us in disentangling duration dependence and the mixing distribution. If unobserved effects are important in the duration model, this means that the impact of genuine duration dependence is overestimated.

As becomes apparent from the third pair of columns of Table 6.2, unobserved time invariant effects are indeed important. The simultaneous model, which is estimated with three points of support (up to $K=3$ the likelihood of the model increases significantly), again shows a dramatic increase of the fit of the model. However, take notice that this increase is almost fully confined to the housing model; random effects are important in explaining housing state. This becomes apparent from the size and the significance of the coefficients of the parameters u_1 and u_2, the random effects in the housing model. Following the estimation results, three types of employees can be distinguished (at the three points of support), having unobservable characteristics that make them more or less likely to own a home. As a result of these characteristics, 32 per cent are very likely to own a home (P_2) and 29 per cent very unlikely to own a home (P_1).

In contrast to this, in the job duration model the impact of unobserved time invariant characteristics is mostly found to be small. All coefficients, except for those of the risk into unemployment (which are denoted by v_{23} and v_{33}), are found to be insignificant. Moreover, for all risks the pattern of duration dependence seems to be unaffected. Not surprisingly, the estimated coefficients of the home-ownership dummy remain almost unchanged. Thus, following a Hausman test on the difference between the coefficients for the two model versions, the null hypothesis that there is no endogeneity cannot be rejected (with p-values of 0.252 and 0.343 for the home-owner-ship coefficient of the risks of job changes and into non-participation, respectively). These findings suggest that the potential biasing impact of unobserved, time-invariant characteristics is not important.

Random effects, however, do matter with respect to the risk into unemployment. Employees with hidden characteristics that make them less (more) vulnerable for unemployment or non-participation have a higher (lower) probability of owning a home. This seems to result in endogeneity effects: comparing the home-ownership coefficients for the unemployment risk in the two models, we find (weak) evidence that the difference is significant (p-value = 0.074) – suggesting the presence of endogeneity effects. The intuition behind this result is that the lower the risk of a decrease in income, the higher the possibilities of buying a home. This effect may be reinforced by banks' selection criteria to grant mortgages. However, we still do find a significant (negative) impact of home-ownership on the risk of becoming unemployed. This means that the unemployment risk is affected negatively by home-ownership. As explained earlier, this can be driven by the stronger incentives homeowners have to invest in their jobs.

5.3 The Regional Home-ownership Rate as an Instrumental Variable

In our model, the instrumental variable 'regional home-ownership' serves as an important variable for identification, in particular for the simultaneous model. This rate is observed for 538 regions in the Netherlands. We find the regional home-ownership rate to have a strong impact on individual housing status: the higher the regional proportion of homeowners, the higher the individual probability of being a homeowner. However, there still are some conditions to be met for this variable to be used as a proper instrument. Clearly, the regional proportion of homeowners is a variable pertaining to average group behaviour. As shown by Manski (1993), the identification of causality effects with these variables may be problematic for various reasons. Three types of effects may lead to estimation biases: endogenous effects, exogenous effects and correlated effects.

Endogenous effects occur when the propensity of an individual to behave in a certain way is influenced by the behaviour of the group. Within the context of our model, individual homeowners may compare their social status with that of other homeowners in their neighbourhood and thus tend to invest in their careers. As a result, labour mobility of the individual homeowner, as well as the unemployment risk, may be small. In that case, the regional proportion of homeowners would not be a valid instrument that is fully exogenous. However, in our model such endogeneity effects are not likely to be important, as the proportion of homeowners is measured at the level of regions and not at the level of (relevant) neighbourhoods.

Exogenous (or contextual) effects occur if the propensity of an individual to behave in some way varies with exogenous characteristics of the reference group. Within the context of our model these effects may result from individuals having a strong labour market position and earning a high income, moving to regions with high home-ownership rates. To a large extent these exogenous effects are controlled for in our model, in particular by the income variable. Still, as far as some exogenous effects are not fully captured in our model, it is likely that most variation is between individuals within regions and not variation between regions. Thus, exogenous effects will be considerably smaller for the instrumental variable.

Correlated effects arise if individuals in the same group tend to behave similarly because they face similar institutional settings. In the context of our model this would mean that unobserved neighbourhood characteristics affecting job mobility are correlated with the home-ownership rate. In particular, good employment perspectives may be concentrated in rich regions with a high proportion of homeowners. These effects are – by using income as a control variable – largely taken into account by the heterogeneity in our model. Further variation in job mobility between regions may be associated with differences in regional institutional settings, such as property taxes set by local authorities, but these are not very likely to be related to the proportion of homeowners.

All in all, it seems that all three types of effects will not be substantial, as home-ownership is measured at the level of communities and not (smaller) neighbourhoods. Also, to a large extent the home-ownership rate is regulated by local authorities and we control for various variables so as to avoid exogenous or correlated effects. Thus we conclude that this variable can be used as a valid instrument for identification.

6.   CONCLUSIONS

To sum up, our estimation results suggest that the housing decision is strongly affected by job commitment; the estimated impact of home-ownership strongly decreases if we control for this effect. Thus, the housing market is affected by the labour market, rather than the reverse. In particular, we do not find evidence of home-ownership affecting the risk of job changes or the risk of non-participation. Also, and not surprisingly, endogeneity effects are not likely to be important for these risks. Individual employees decide to change jobs, irrespective of their housing status, and there are various explanations for this. First, given the population density in the Netherlands, people often change jobs without changing residence. Second, strong increases in housing prices may have compensated the moving costs of homeowners. And third, the regulation of the social renting sector may result in high moving costs for tenants.

Similar to the risk of job mobility, we find no impact of home-ownership on the outflow of the labour force. To a large extent this concerns employees getting pensioned or becoming disabled. It seems these transitions are not driven by housing state and do not (directly) affect moving behaviour.

In contrast to job-to-job changes and the probability of becoming non-participant we do find a negative effect of home-ownership on the probability of becoming unemployed. The explanation for this is that the decrease in income that comes with unemployment is far more substantial for home-owners than for tenants. In principle, homeowners are not eligible for social assistance and have to break into their housing equity. Moreover, tenants are (partly) insured against loss of income due to the rent subsidy system. Thus, homeowners have a higher incentive to reduce the risk of becoming unemployed, in particular by investing more in job-specific capital.

To conclude, home-ownership seems to stimulate job commitment in one way (lower risk of unemployment), but not at the cost of less job-to-job mobility. However, from these findings alone we cannot conclude that home-ownership does not affect labour market mobility at all. Institutional settings in the rental sector – in particular rental subsidies and low prices in the social rental sector – may discourage labour mobility. From that perspective, labour mobility may be too low, both for homeowners and tenants.

NOTES

1. Reprinted from *Journal of Urban Economics*, Vol. 55, Michiel van Leuvensteijn and Pierre Koning, 'The effect of home-ownership on labor mobility in the Netherlands', 580–596, Copyright (2004), with permission from Elsevier.
2. The authors would like to thank Rob Alessie, Casper van Ewijk, Bas van der Klaauw, Jos van Ommeren, Gusta Renes, and two anonymous referees for valuable comments. Statistics Netherlands is gratefully acknowledged for providing access to the IPR data. Of course, the usual disclaimer applies. Both authors are affiliated with the CPB Netherlands Bureau for Economic Policy Analysis, P.O. Box 80510, 2508 GM, The Hague, The Netherlands, tel: + 31 70 338 3488 or + 31 70 338 3489, fax: + 31 70 338 3350. Pierre Koning is also affiliated with the Utrecht School of Economics (USE). E-mail addresses: mvl@cpb.nl; pwck@cpb.nl.
3. For all model versions we also tested for possible biases stemming from the fact that job tenure is measured in months, and housing statuses on a yearly basis. In particular, we delayed the observed housing status with one year. This did not change our results substantially.

REFERENCES

Abbring, J.H. (1997), *Essays in Labor Economics*, Amsterdam: Thesis Publishers.
Boeheim, R. and M. Taylor (2000), 'Residential mobility, housing tenure and the labour market in Britain', Institute for Social and Economic Research and Institute for Labour Research, University of Essex Working Paper.
Green, R. and P. Henderschott (2001), 'Home ownership and unemployment in the US', *Urban Studies*, **38**, 1509–20.
Harris, J.R. and M.P. Todaro (1970), 'Migration, unemployment and development: a two sector analysis', *American Economic Review*, **60**, 126–42.
Hassink, W. and Ch. Kurvers (1999), 'De invloed van woningbezit op werkloosheid: Oswald's these voor Nederland bezien' [The influence of home-ownership on unemployment: Oswald's thesis analysed for the Netherlands], mimeo, University of Utrecht.
Heckman, J.J. and B. Singer (1984), 'A method for minimizing the impact of distributional assumptions in econometric models for duration data', *Econometrica*, **52**, 271–320.

Henley, A. (1998), 'Residential mobility, housing equity and the labour market', *Economic Journal*, **108**, 414–27.

Holm, A. (2002), 'The effect of training on search durations: a random effects approach', *Labor Economics*, **9**, 433–50.

Lancaster, T. (1990), 'The econometric analysis of transition data', Econometric Society Monographs, no. 17, Cambridge: Cambridge University Press.

Manski, C.F. (1993), 'Identification of endogenous social effects: the reflection problem', *Review of Economic Studies*, **60** (3), 531–42.

Nickell, S. (1998), 'Unemployment: questions and some answers', *Economic Journal*, **108**, 802–16.

Oswald, A.J. (1999), 'The housing market and Europe's unemployment: a nontechnical paper', mimeo, University of Warwick.

Van den Berg, G.J. (1992), 'A structural dynamic analysis of job turnover and the costs associated with moving to another job', *Economic Journal*, **102**, 1116–33.

Van Ommeren, J.N. (1996), 'Commuting and relocation of jobs and residences', PhD thesis, Tinbergen Institute Research Series.

Van Ommeren, J.N., P. Rietveld and P. Nijkamp (2000), 'Job mobility, residential mobility and commuting: a theoretical analysis using search theory', *Annals of Regional Science*, **34**, 213–32.

Van der Vlist, A.J. (2001), 'Residential mobility and commuting', PhD thesis, Tinbergen Institute Research Series.

Wooldridge, J.M. (2002), *Econometric Analysis of Cross Section and Panel Data*, Cambridge, MA: MIT Press.

DISCUSSION

Anna Sanz-de-Galdeano

This chapter by Van Leuvensteijn and Koning is a nice contribution to the growing literature on the interaction between housing tenure and the labour market. Most previous studies have attempted to assess the effect of home-ownership on job mobility and unemployment by using macroeconomic data (Green and Henderschott 2001; Nickell 1998), generally finding that home-ownership reduces labour mobility and increases unemployment. This paper relies on longitudinal data on individuals in order to assess whether the observed negative association between home-ownership and job-to-job mobility reflects a causal relationship or if home-ownership is rather driven by job commitment.

Van Leuvensteijn and Koning use data collected by the Dutch Tax Department (Income Panel Research database) covering the period 1989–98. Job transitions and home-ownership are modelled jointly in a nonparametric fashion and in order to account for the potential endogeneity of housing decisions, random effects are allowed to be correlated across the housing and labour mobility equations. The main finding of the chapter is that homeowners do not appear to change jobs less than tenants. The authors conclude that housing decisions are driven by job commitment, or, in other words, that the housing market is affected by the labour market, rather than the reverse.

While it seems to be well established that housing decisions are determined by institutional characteristics to a large extent, there is little discussion concerning the institutional setting in the Netherlands (housing policies, tax incentives related to housing, financial markets and so on). In this respect, cross-country comparisons can be very informative and there is actually an interesting related paper that the authors do not include in their references; Barceló (2003) uses longitudinal data on individuals to analyse the impact of housing tenure on unemployed workers' labour mobility in five European countries (France, Germany, Italy, Spain and the UK) taking into account their institutional differences. To this purpose, she uses a discrete unemployment duration model with two exits to employment (associated with a residential change or not), jointly modelling housing tenure and unemployment duration and allowing for the presence of unobserved heterogeneity potentially correlated across the two decisions.

There is also very little discussion regarding the potential source of endogeneity of the home-ownership decision. The authors propose one possible source of endogeneity: job commitment. Alternatively, it could be that

Table 6D.1   *One-year job turnover random effects logit coefficient estimates*

	(1)	(2)	(3)
Constant	−1.047	0.516	1.934
	(−15.54)	(1.02)	(3.51)
Homeowner	**−0.284**	**−0.197**	**−0.119**
	(−3.28)	(−1.95)	(−0.95)
Female		−0.261	−0.317
		(−1.60)	(−1.94)
Primary education		0.157	0.219
		(0.88)	(1.21)
Secondary education		−0.232	−0.181
		(−1.22)	(−0.95)
Married		−0.022	−0.086
		(−0.14)	(−0.54)
Age 25–34		0.010	−0.091
		(0.05)	(−0.42)
Age 35–44		−0.281	−0.483
		(−1.17)	(−2.00)
Age 45+		−0.342	−0.532
		(−1.32)	(−2.04)
Log (net hourly wages)		−0.573	−0.424
		(−4.30)	(−3.01)
Kids < 12		0.249	0.295
		(1.71)	(2.02)
Job sat. with earnings			**0.031**
			(0.62)
Job sat. with work			**−0.153**
			(−3.03)
Job sat. with security			**−0.257**
			(−6.55)
Log-likelihood	−1859.3	−1425.1	−1381.9

Notes: N = 2881. The dependent variable takes value one if the employee leaves his/her job in the next 12 months and zero otherwise. t-statistics are reported in parentheses. Additional control variables are year dummies.

risk-averse individuals are both more likely to invest in housing and less likely to change jobs. One way to shed some light on this issue is to use one or more variables that are believed to be good proxies for job commitment, such as job satisfaction indicators.[1] In order to do so I use data for the Netherlands from the 1994–2001 waves of the European Community Household Panel, ECHP.

I select a flow sample of employees who started their jobs at most two years before the interview date and then estimate a job mobility equation by using a random effects logit model and including a similar set of covariates to those considered by the authors. The results of this analysis are reported in Table 6D.1. Column (1) displays uncontrolled estimates of the impact of home-ownership on job mobility. Consistent with previous studies it is found that home-ownership has a negative and statistically significant impact on the probability of changing jobs. As a next step I include of a set of control variables which are very similar to those employed by the authors (see column (2)). The estimated coefficient on the home-ownership dummy remains negative, although its magnitude is somewhat reduced.

Finally I add job satisfaction indicators to the job turnover equation.[2] These indicators are meant to be considered as a proxy for job commitment in order to investigate whether job commitment is indeed the driving force behind housing and mobility decisions. The results of this analysis, reported in column (3), appear to be in line with this hypothesis, since the home-ownership coefficient estimate is substantially reduced (in absolute value) and far from statistically significant at standard levels once the job satisfaction indicators are introduced. Therefore this evidence can be interpreted as one further robustness check of the authors' hypothesis that the driving force behind housing and mobility decisions is job commitment.

Notes

1. Several studies have found that job satisfaction predicts future quits (Freeman 1978; Clark et al. 1998) and that job satisfaction responses are negatively correlated with absenteeism and positively correlated with workers' productivity (Mangione and Quinn 1975; Clegg 1983).
2. The job satisfaction questions in the ECHP ask workers to give an integer response on a scale of one to six that best described how satisfied or dissatisfied they are with several specifc facets of their present job, with one representing the lowest level of job satisfaction and six the highest.

References

Barceló, C. (2003), 'Housing tenure and labour mobility: a comparison across European countries', CEMFI Working Paper 0302.

Clark, A.E., Y. Georgellis and P. Sanfey (1998), 'Job satisfaction, wage changes and quits: evidence from Germany', *Research in Labor Economics*, **17**, 95–122.

Clegg, C.W. (1983), 'Psychology of employee lateness, absence and turnover: a methodological critique and an empirical study', *Journal of Applied Psychology*, **68**, 88–101.

Freeman, R.B. (1978), 'Job satisfaction as an economic variable', *American Economic Review*, **68**, 135–41.

Green, R. and P. Henderschott (2001), 'Home-ownership and unemployment in the US', *Urban Studies*, **38**, 1509–20.

Mangione, T.W. and R.P. Quinn (1975), 'Job satisfaction, counterproductive behaviour and drug use at work', *Journal of Applied Psychology*, **60**, 114–16.

Nickell, S. (1998), 'Unemployment: questions and some answers', *Economic Journal*, **108**, 802–16.

7. The impact of credit constraints on household formation

Nuno C. Martins and Ernesto Villanueva[1]

1. INTRODUCTION

There are striking differences in household composition within European countries. Around two-thirds of Spanish young adults between 18 and 30 years of age, more than three-quarters of Italian and about 70 per cent of Portuguese young adults live with their parents. The corresponding number for the USA is 43 per cent (Manacorda and Moretti 2003). Recent work has argued that the extent of co-residence in Southern Europe reflects a lack of workers' mobility, a problem specially important at a moment in the life cycle in which individuals are relatively more mobile (Bentolila and Ichino 2003). To the extent that market failures such as credit constraints cause this pattern of household structure, public policy that eases access to long-term debt can encourage young adults to take up new jobs in other regions and increase labour market mobility. Understanding co-residence is also important in assessing the distributional impact of policies that help the elderly, as these policies may end up subsidizing the consumption of young co-residing adults. This paper studies whether or not limited access to mortgage markets explains co-residence.

Previous studies have addressed the determinants of co-residence in Europe. Martínez-Granado and Ruiz-Castillo (2002) show that the probability of co-residence increases among the unemployed, and with regional housing costs.[2] Manacorda and Moretti (2003) argue that co-residence is a normal good among Italian parents, and that they buy this service by giving transfers that may only happen within the household. Becker et al. (2004) use cross-country variation to argue that co-residence is related to job insecurity for children and parents. They also experiment with micro data from Italy, finding evidence that children are less likely to 'leave the nest' if their parents hold more secure jobs. Finally, Giuliano (2004) argues that cross-country variation in co-residence patterns is associated with changes in preferences across countries.

This chapter argues that co-residence is linked to limited access to the market for mortgage debt. In that sense, we follow on previous work by Chiuri and Jappelli (2003) who document that the peak in the age of home-ownership occurs later in Southern European countries than in Northern ones. Chiuri and Jappelli also find evidence that countries with tighter liquidity constraints have delayed access to home-ownership. While cross-country evidence is suggestive, it presents well-known problems of omitted variable biases. The reason is that many institutional country-specific characteristics correlated with aggregate measures of liquidity constraints may bias the results. Our chapter uses a quasi-experimental set-up to test the link between limited availability of credit and the probability of co-residence. To this end, we exploit a reform in a large programme in Portugal, called Credito Bonificado (CB). The CB programme provided subsidies of up to 26 per cent on interest rate payments on mortgage borrowing. The programme targeted young individuals in the lower three quartiles of the income distribution. A reform in 1998 introduced a ceiling on the price of the house that could be financed by the programme. The ceiling was uniform all over the country. We argue that the reform was most likely to affect eligible young individuals living in areas with high housing costs. To analyse the effect of interest rates (and availability of credit) on young adult co-residence, we use the large discontinuity in incentives to borrow introduced by the reform. Our approach exploits three sources of variation to identify the effect of interest rates on co-residence: time variation (pre- and post-reform periods), geographical variation (high and low-price areas) and cross-sectional variation (eligible versus non-eligible young adults).

In our opinion, there are four main reasons why the analysis in the present work is an interesting set-up for analysing the impact of changes in the availability of mortgage debt on the probability of co-residence. The first is that the CB programme targeted young individuals and individuals in the lower part of the income distribution, that is, the group who are most likely to live with their parents. Second, the CB programme provided subsidies at the source, that is, the debtor did not have to pay the installment before getting the subsidy. Such a feature is a real-world counterpart of an effective fall in the interest rate. The third reason is that the CB programme provided four different subsidies to eligible individuals, a feature that allows us to examine the responses of several treatment groups to the change in incentives. Fourth, while tax incentives may not be effective because individuals lack the relevant information about financial markets, or about the tax code (see Jappelli and Pistaferri 2002, 2003), the CB programme was well used in Portugal. In 1998, two out of three new mortgages signed were subsidized by the CB programme.

The data used are the 1998–2001 waves from the National Employment Survey in Portugal (Inquérito ao Emprego). Our empirical findings suggest that the effects of the removal of the subsidy vary over the income distribution. The effect is basically zero at the lower part of the income distribution, eligible for a 26 per cent subsidy. For the higher-income group, eligible for the 16 per cent subsidy, our preferred estimate indicates that the propensity to live with parents increased by 12 percentage points.

The structure of the chapter is as follows. Section 2 reviews some of the country-level statistics on co-residence. Section 3 provides details on the Credito Bonificado programme and its likely impact on co-residence patterns. Section 4 describes our data and the empirical specification, and Section 5 discusses our empirical results. In Section 6 we test the empirical methodology and discuss the extent to which the subsidized programme was passed on to real estate prices. Finally, Section 7 presents the main conclusions.

2. TRENDS IN HOUSEHOLD FORMATION IN EUROPE AND THE MARKET FOR CREDIT

Becker et al. (2004) document that in 1997 there was a wide dispersion on co-residence rates across European countries. At one extreme were Southern European countries (Italy, Spain, Greece and Portugal), where the vast majority of young adults lived with their parents. At the other extreme were Northern European countries, such as the UK, France or (West) Germany.

These differences, at least regarding Southern European countries, have been relatively stable over time. Jurado (1999) documents that in 1990 the proportion of young adults between 20 and 24 years of age living with their parents was highest in Southern European countries. The countries with the highest rates of co-residence were Italy (88.3 per cent of young adults lived with their parents), Spain (75.2 per cent), Ireland (72.4 per cent) and Portugal (68.9 per cent). The countries with the lowest degrees of co-residence were Denmark (27.9 per cent), France (42.2 per cent) and the UK (49.1 per cent). The comparable magnitude in 1995 still suggests that Portugal, Spain and Italy were the European countries in which a highest proportion of young adults lived with their parents. Co-residence in Italy remained almost constant at 87 per cent, and in Portugal and Spain, the proportion of young adults between 20 and 24 years of age living with their parents increased slightly, to 82 per cent and 89 per cent, respectively.

The features of credit markets also differ across countries. In a study on home-ownership rates across European countries, Chiuri and Jappelli (2003) document a wide variation across OECD countries in the availability of long-term credit, as measured by (a) outstanding mortgage loans over GDP, (b) mortgage maturity and (c) the downpayment ratio. In all these dimensions, Spain and Italy have the lowest measures of availability of long-term credit debt, with countries such as the USA or the UK having the highest availability. Chiuri and Jappelli use household-level data to regress the probability of being a homeowner on country-level measures of the availability of mortgage credit. They find that individuals living in countries with thicker credit markets become homeowners earlier in the life cycle.

Chiuri and Jappelli's study does not include Portugal. We used data from the Statistical Bulletin of the Banco de Portugal and found that the average outstanding mortgage loan as a percentage of yearly GDP for the 1986–96 period (same time sample used in Chiuri and Jappelli) is 14.11 per cent. This aggregate figure fits better with the characteristics of the Italian and Spanish credit markets (5.49 and 15.01 per cent, respectively) than with figures in countries with lower levels of co-residence such as the UK or Germany (51.87 per cent and 28.92 per cent, respectively).

3.   THE CREDITO BONIFICADO PROGRAMME[3]

In 1986 the Portuguese Government enacted the Credito Bonificado (CB), a programme intended to stimulate the access to home-ownership among young and low-income individuals. The CB programme provided various types of interest rate reductions at source to eligible households who financed with a mortgage loan either (a) the purchase of the house of residence with a mortgage or (b) the construction or repairs of the house of residence or (c) the purchase of land towards the construction of the house of residence. Only households with taxable income below a given threshold and who were not currently holding any type of mortgage debt were eligible for the programme. The amount of the loan could not exceed the total value of the house. A person who purchased a house financed with a CB loan was not allowed to sell it within a period of five years: a condition that was waived if the transaction was motivated by a job change.[4]

The CB programme subsidized a proportion of the monthly interest rate payments of a mortgage loan. The subsidy was given by the Portuguese Ministry of Finance directly to the lending institution, so that any household receiving the subsidy had its monthly payment effectively reduced from the first installment on. The subsidized proportion was constant for the first two years of the loan, fell at a 1 per cent rate during the subsequent three years of the life of the mortgage loan and at a 2 per cent rate thereafter, until exhaustion. The proportion subsidized depended negatively on the taxable income of the family, following an adjustment for family size for married individuals.[5]

The programme offered a 44 per cent subsidy on interest rate payments during the first two years of the loan to households whose (adjusted) taxable income was less than 3.25 times the statutory minimum wage (on an annual basis) (class 1). The corresponding starting subsidy was 32.5 per cent for households with taxable income between 3.25 and 3.50 times the minimum wage (class 2). Households with taxable income between 3.5 and 4.25 times the minimum wage (class 3) had an initial subsidy of 21 per cent of interest rate payments, and for those with taxable income between 4.25 and 4.75 times the minimum wage (class 4) the initial subsidy was 10 per cent of the interest rate payment. According to our sample (see Section 4), 73 per cent of non-self-employed adults between 18 and 35 years of age with earnings above the minimum wage qualified for the maximum subsidy, 8 per cent qualified for the class 2 subsidy, and 8 per cent qualified for the class 3 and 4 subsidies.

Table 7.1 illustrates an example of the savings associated with the CB programme. We assume an initial mortgage loan of 48 000 euro with 25-year maturity and a constant interest rate of 8 per cent. The second column shows the evolution of the amount of outstanding debt. The third column shows the (constant) stream of payments. The fifth column presents the stream of payment in period-zero euro which, by construction, must add up to the initial loan amount of 48 000 euro. The sixth column presents the annual percentage of subsidy for a family in class 1 subsidy and the seventh column the actual yearly payment. Discounting the stream of payments to the moment in which the mortgage was granted and summing up the amounts yields 36 408 euro which represents 76 per cent of the amount paid by an individual with an identical mortgage, but without the subsidy. Similar analyses for the other classes of subsidy show that individuals in classes 2, 3 and 4 would pay respectively, 84 per cent, 92 per cent and 97 per cent of the baseline 48 000 euro. Aggregate evidence suggests that the subsidy was effective, in the sense that it was not passed on in higher interest rates.[6]

The subsidy provided by the CB programme could potentially have a significant impact on household net income. Using the 2000 wave of the Inquérito ao Patrimonio e Endividamento das Familias (IPEF), we have estimated that monthly mortgage payments represented, on average, 21 per cent of total net household income.[7] This means that the subsidy on mortgage loans could represent up to 9.3 per cent of monthly net income at the period of maximum subsidy for class 1 households.

In the last quarter of 1998 the Portuguese Government reformed the programme. To be eligible for the subsidy, households satisfying the income requirements could not purchase a house above a ceiling price. The particular limit depended on the taxable income and on the family size of eligible households, but not on the place of residence.[8] For example, a two-person household with income of less than 3.25 times the statutory minimum could only be subsidized for the purchase of a house whose price was below

Table 7.1   Savings associated to the CB programme, an example

Panel A: Example of stream of payments with and without the CB subsidy

Age loan	Debt stock	Yearly (non-CB) payment	1/(interest rate)	Yearly (non-CB) payment, euro age 0	% Subsidy class 1	Yearly (CB) payment
	(1)	(2)	(3)	= (2)*(3)	(4)	= (2) − subsidy
0	48 000	–	–	–	–	–
1	47 400	4440	0.926	4111	0.44	2751
2	46 751	4440	0.857	3807	0.44	2772
3	46 051	4440	0.794	3525	0.43	2832
4	45 295	4440	0.735	3264	0.42	2893
5	44 478	4440	0.681	3022	0.41	2955
6	43 596	4440	0.630	2798	0.39	3053
7	42 643	4440	0.583	2591	0.37	3150
8	41 614	4440	0.540	2399	0.35	3246
9	40 503	4440	0.500	2221	0.33	3342
10	39 303	4440	0.463	2057	0.31	3436
11	38 007	4440	0.429	1904	0.29	3529
12	36 607	4440	0.397	1763	0.27	3619
13	35 095	4440	0.368	1633	0.25	3708
14	33 463	4440	0.340	1512	0.23	3795
15	31 699	4440	0.315	1400	0.21	3878
16	29 795	4440	0.292	1296	0.19	3959
17	27 738	4440	0.270	1200	0.17	4035
18	25 517	4440	0.250	1111	0.15	4107
19	23 118	4440	0.232	1029	0.13	4175
20	20 527	4440	0.215	953	0.11	4237
21	17 729	4440	0.199	882	0.09	4293
22	14 707	4440	0.184	817	0.07	4341
23	11 443	4440	0.170	756	0.05	4382
24	7918	4440	0.158	700	0.03	4413
25	4111	4440	0.146	648	0.01	4434
26	0	4440	0.135	600	0.00	4440
Discounted payment stream (euro year 0):				48 000	–	36 408

Panel B: Fraction of the original mortgage paid by individuals with the subsidy, by class

Class 1	**0.76** = (36 408/48 000)
Class 2	**0.84**
Class 3	**0.92**
Class 4	**0.97**

Notes: Computations assume an interest rate of 8%; maturity of the loan: 25 years; no inflation; constant interest rate.

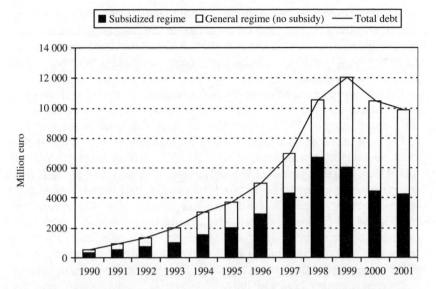

Notes: Shaded box: total amount of mortgages subsidized by the programme, by year; white box: amount of mortgages subsidized by the programme, by year; line: sum of the previous two components by year.

Figure 7.1   *Total value of new long-term debt contracts for the three types of debt commitments*

63 500 euro (in 1998 euro). If the value of the purchased house exceeded the value of the ceiling by 1 euro, the household was no longer eligible for any type of subsidy (aside from the standard income tax deduction, which is very small in Portugal). The reform was effective in the second quarter of 1999 and hereafter we refer to it as the '1999 reform'.

We have used the IPEF 2000 to compute the average values of the houses for the various eligible classes and compare them to the 1999 ceilings. According to our own calculations from the IPEF 2000, the average (median) value of a house bought before 1999 by households eligible for the maximum subsidy was 71 028 euro (62 350 euro). We have estimated that the limits introduced by the reform were in the 60th percentile of the distribution of the value of houses bought by eligibles before the 1999 reform.

Figure 7.1 shows the evolution of the value of mortgages created during the period spanning 1990 and 2001.[9] Probably due to the steady decrease in the interest rates over the decade and to the increase in competition in the commercial banking sector, mortgage loans significantly increased after 1994.[10] Between 1994 and 1998 the aggregate value of mortgage loans increased from 3 billion euro to 12 billion euro. In 1994, half of all new euro of mortgage debt were borrowed under CB loans. In 1998 the proportion rose to two-thirds. After 1999 the total amount of mortgage debt and the relative proportion created through the CB loans decreased dramatically. In 2000 only 43 cent out of each euro of new mortgages were borrowed through the programme.[11]

The evolution of the total number of mortgages is similar to the evolution of the total value of loans. In 1994, 84 445 mortgages were issued, with an average value of 35 702 euro. Among these, CB loans accounted for 43 875 contracts with an average value of 34 141 euro per loan. By 1998 the total number of new mortgages was 216 631 (with an average value of 48 351 euro). In that year the CB programme contributed to 130 335 loans, with an average value of 51 239 euro. By the end of 2001 the number of new loans decreased to 153 134 (with an average value of 64 425 euro), this included 67 351 CB loans, with an average value of 63 115 euro. The pattern described above suggests that the 1999 reform had a substantial effect on the borrowing behaviour of households. We use this reform to estimate the effect of a change in the interest rate on co-residence, using micro data from the period spanning 1998 and 2001.

3.1 Predicted Effects of the Reform

The 1999 reform should have affected the budget constraint of an eligible young adult considering the purchase of their home of residence in a rather non-linear way. Holding housing prices constant, the price of a unit of housing services financed with a mortgage loan would only vary if the individual wanted to purchase services above the ceiling established by the reform. If the young adult wanted to purchase housing services below the threshold, then the pre- and post-reform cost of the marginal unit of housing services would be the same. Conversely, if the young adult wanted to purchase above the ceiling, the marginal price of an extra unit would increase by between 8 per cent (the group eligible for the third-class subsidy) and 26 per cent (the group eligible for the highest subsidy). Additionally, the price of the inframarginal units would also increase, creating a non-convex budget constraint.

There are several possible responses to the reform by young adults considering purchasing their own house and establishing their own household. The first is still to profit from the subsidy, purchasing a house whose price is below the limit established by the law. The 1999 reform should have little effect on co-residence patterns for these individuals. Second, individuals with preferences for more expensive housing will postpone the decision of 'leaving the nest' if the reservation utility of continued co-residence with parents is larger than the utility of purchasing a house financed by the CB programme. The last response would be 'leaving the nest', but renting a house (instead of purchasing one). Perhaps for historical reasons, the latter choice is a not popular in Portugal. The housing rental market in Portugal is small: less than 5 per cent of young adults between 18 and 35 years of age rent a house in Portugal.

Thus, the effects of the CB programme are likely to be heterogeneous for different eligible groups. One source of heterogeneity may come from unobserved variation in preferences for higher housing services. Due to a lack of data we do not pursue that approach. Rather, our strategy exploits cross-county variation in housing prices, where county refers to the NUTS-III classification of regions. Given that the pre-reform prices of housing changed substantially across Portuguese counties, the impact of the establishment of a uniform ceiling should bite differently in different counties. In other words, we assume that it is more difficult to find a house that can be financed at a low-interest rate in a county in which the price of houses was already high before the reform than in a county with low (pre-reform) prices. Thus, the reform should particularly affect eligible young adults living in high price counties.

Our empirical strategy is to estimate the proportion of adults between 18 and 35 years of age living with their parents and eligible for the programme in high price counties before and after the reform. That is our treatment group. The control group are individuals who are also eligible for the programme but who lived in counties with low housing prices prior to the reform. We identify the effect of the change of interest rate on the proportion of adults living with their parents from the differential trend in co-residence patterns between these two groups. Second, to control for any other differential effect between low and high price regions in the period spanning 1998 and 2001 we subtract from the previous estimate the corresponding difference among non-eligible individuals who should not be directly affected by the reform in the programme.

Finally, this strategy leads to a reduced form estimate of the impact of changing access to credit on the probability of living with parents. The reduced form estimates may also pick up general equilibrium effects in housing prices. As a robustness check we run regressions of changes in prices on the proportion of individuals who live with their parents, finding little impact of the passing of the reform on uncorrected prices of real estate.

4. THE DATA

The main source of data is drawn from a quarterly rotating panel called Inquérito ao Emprego (IE), from 1998 to 2001. The IE follows respondents for at most six consecutive quarters, and includes information on the educational level of the individual, labour force status, occupation, industry and demographics. This survey would be the Portuguese version of the Current Population Survey (CPS) in the USA.

Given that claimants for the CB programme had to present their last tax return to be eligible for the programme, the unit of observation in our analysis is the combination 'taxpaying unit' year. The taxpaying unit coincides with the household in the case of married individuals, as in Portugal married couples must file jointly. Hence, each married couple or each single individual living in their own household and earning income above the minimum yearly wage, contributes one observation per year. Individuals above the age of 18, living with their parents and whose labour earnings exceed the minimum wage, contribute another observation per year.

Also, we construct our sample in the following way. The time unit of the IE is the quarter, so the combined sample consists of 13 quarterly surveys. Given that the variation between individuals in a given year is not really informative about their co-residence decisions (as young adults are no longer interviewed once they leave the parental home), we pooled observations from all the quarterly surveys and kept one observation per individual per year.

We restrict the initial sample to taxpaying units in which the main earner is between 18 and 35 years of age, is not self-employed and whose reported income exceeds the minimum yearly wage. To determine eligibility, in the case of married individuals we add the earnings of both spouses.[12] When computing family size, we exclude individuals in the household who are 18 years or more and report positive income. Each individual contributes at most one observation per year and we use information from three years: 1998, 2000 and 2001 (1999 is excluded, given that it was a transitional year). Note that the rotation scheme may make individuals contribute two observations to the sample.

The dependent variable takes a value of zero if the individual was not the head of his or her household during the four quarters of the survey year, and one if he or she was the head of the household. In the Portuguese Inquérito ao Emprego the 'head of the household' is the person who is the main earner. Hence, our measure of co-residence actually captures as non-co-residents young adults who are the main earners and live with their parents. While that measure is potentially misleading, the average proportion of co-residents coincides with that in other work, for example, Manacorda and Moretti (2003). In further work we plan to experiment with alternative measures of co-residence. Our sample contains 11 375 observations of young individuals between 18 and 35 years of age. The summary statistics of the sample are described in Table 7.2. A vast majority of young individuals (89 per cent) were eligible for some type of subsidy,

Table 7.2 Descriptive statistics of the main sample

Number of observations:	Class 1 8256 72.6%		Class 2 929 8.2%		Classes 3 and 4 909 8.0%		Non-eligible 1281 11.3%		Whole sample 11375 100%	
	Mean	St. Dev.	Mean	St. Dev.	Mean	St. Dev.	Mean	St. Dev.	Mean	St. Dev.
Lives with parents	0.73	0.44	0.68	0.47	0.65	0.48	0.54	0.54	0.69	0.46
Gross income	8306	2414	13039	2159	15697	2631	27864	17827	11486	8949
Age	25.75	4.77	26.98	4.29	27.24	3.92	28.81	4.04	26.31	6.50
Does not read	0.04	0.18	0.02	0.14	0.01	0.09	0.00	0.04	0.02	0.14
Completed 6th grade	0.54	0.50	0.33	0.47	0.25	0.43	0.13	0.34	0.46	0.50
Basic school	0.23	0.42	0.22	0.42	0.19	0.39	0.13	0.33	0.22	0.41
At least high school or equivalent	0.19	0.40	0.42	0.49	0.55	0.49	0.74	0.44	0.30	0.46
Works for public sector	0.06	0.23	0.12	0.32	0.13	0.34	0.22	0.41	0.09	0.29
Part-time	0.02	0.15	0.02	0.13	0.01	0.10	0.02	0.14	0.02	0.14
Lived in high price county	0.20	0.40	0.24	0.43	0.27	0.44	0.34	0.47	0.22	0.41
Female	0.35	0.48	0.30	0.46	0.29	0.45	0.30	0.46	0.33	0.47

Notes: Gross income denotes pre-tax earnings in constant 1999 euro. Married individuals contribute one observation, and the report of age, education or labour market situation corresponds to the main earner. 'Lived in a high price county' refers to the year prior to the interview. 'Lived in a high price county' takes value one if the NUTS-III place of residence one year before the interview contained the main city in one of the districts in Portugal. 'Basic school' is a binary variable taking value one if the individual completed primary school, and zero otherwise. 'At least high school or equivalent' takes value one if the individual at least completed high school or professional training, and zero otherwise.

221

and 73 per cent were eligible for the maximum subsidy. In addition, and by construction, eligibility is strongly (negatively) correlated with the earning potential of the taxpaying unit. Current income is three times larger among non-eligibles than among eligibles. Co-residence is also positively correlated with eligibility. Among eligibles for the maximum subsidy, 54 per cent of young male adults live with their parents. The corresponding number among non-eligibles is 35 per cent.

As discussed in Section 3, an important variable in our analysis is whether an individual lives in a high price county prior to the passage of the 1998 reform. In this draft we assign main cities in the district as 'high price counties'. Main cities in districts had prices in 2001 (the first year for which the Portuguese Statistical Agency collected prices) on average 30 per cent higher than the rest of the villages and cities in Portugal.

4.1   The Empirical Methodology

We present estimates of the following triple differences (DDD) model:

$$1(COR_i = 1) = \beta_0 + \delta_1 ELIG\_1_i {}^* H\_P_i {}^* AFTER_t + \delta_2 ELIG\_2_i {}^* H\_P_i {}^* AFTER_t$$

$$+ \delta_3 ELIG\_3_i {}^* H\_P_i {}^* AFTER_t + \sum_{j=1}^{j=3} \beta_j ELIG\_J_i + \beta_4 AFTER_t$$

$$+ \beta_5 H\_P_i + \sum_{j=1}^{j=3} \beta_{5+i} ELIG\_J_i {}^* AFTER_t$$

$$+ \sum_{j=1}^{j=3} \beta_{8+i} ELIG\_1_i {}^* H\_P_i + \beta_{11} AFTER_t {}^* H\_P_i + \gamma X_{it} + \eta_{it} \quad (7.1)$$

The dependent variable takes value one if the young adult lives with his or her parents and zero otherwise. $ELIG\_1_i$, $ELIG\_2_i$ and $ELIG\_3_i$ are binary variables indicating whether or not the individual is eligible for the programme, and which eligibility class the individual belongs to.[13] The omitted group includes individuals who are not eligible for the programme. $AFTER_t$ is a binary variable that takes value one if the observation belongs to the post-reform periods of 2000 and 2001 and zero if the individual is observed in 1998. H_P_i denotes that the county of residence of the individual is 'high price', measured as 'main city in the district'. X_{it} contains demographics affecting the individual's propensity to co-reside, such as a polynomial in age, education intercepts and the logarithm of earnings.

The parameters of interest are δ_1, δ_2 and δ_3, the coefficients of the interaction between $AFTER$, eligibility dummies $ELIG\_1$, . . . $ELIG\_3$ and the dummy of main city of the district H_P. The interpretation of δ_1 is the difference between the change in the propensity to co-reside during the

1998 and 2001 periods for eligibles for class 1 subsidy and the corresponding change for non-eligibles. Given the discussion in the previous subsection, we expect δ_1, δ_2 and δ_3 to be positive: the elimination of the subsidy to purchase highly priced houses resulted in an increase in the probability of living with parents. To avoid biases caused by individuals moving to a low price region in response to the reform, we use the county of residence one year prior to the interview.

The specification in our model uses three sources of variation to identify the effects of changes in interest rate on the probability of living with parents. First it exploits the time variation from the reform of the programme. Second it exploits the variation in interest rate subsidies across eligible groups, and finally it permits differential effects for high price counties. The main advantage of this specification is that it uses eligibles in low price counties as a control group for eligibles in high price counties. Both groups are similar in income, age and other demographics.

5.   EMPIRICAL RESULTS

This section presents triple-differences evidence of the effect of the 1999 reform on the propensity to live with parents. Next, it presents a conditional analysis.

5.1   Triple Differences Evidence

Tables 7.3 and 7.4 illustrate the triple-differences estimates of the 1999 reform in Credito Bonificado. First we examine individuals eligible for the maximum subsidy and then we examine individuals eligible for the second-highest subsidy. The top panel in Table 7.3 compares the change in the propensity to live with parents among young individuals eligible for the maximum subsidy, in main cities of the district and in other cities. The bottom panel shows the evolution of the propensity to co-reside among our control group: non-eligibles. Table 7.3 documents a 2 per cent increase in the stock of co-resident young adults among the eligible in 'expensive' areas. It is very similar to the corresponding increase in 'cheap' areas. That evidence suggests little effect of the reform among the largest group of eligibles, those eligible for the maximum subsidy. In the bottom panel of Table 7.3 we examine the corresponding evolution of the probability to co-reside among non-eligibles for the programme. Non-eligibles are less likely to live with their parents than eligibles (50 per cent compared to 70 per cent prior to the reform). As expected, the group of non-eligibles in the main cities did not significantly change their behaviour: the probability of co-residence

Table 7.3   Triple differences for first eligible group (class 1)

Location/period	Time difference		
	Before 1999 reform	After 1999 reform	For location
A. Treatment individuals: eligible for the first subsidy, 18–35 years			
Main city in the district	0.71	0.73	0.02
	(0.02)	(0.01)	(0.02)
Place of residence is not main city	0.70	0.74	0.04
	(0.03)	(0.01)	(0.01)
Location difference at a point in time	0.01	−0.01	−
	(0.02)	(0.02)	−
Difference in difference	−	−0.02	−
	−	(0.02)	−
B. Control group: non-eligibles, 18–35 years			
Main city in district	0.50	0.51	0.01
	(0.035)	(0.03)	(0.05)
Place of residence is not main city	0.55	0.57	0.02
	(0.02)	(.02)	(0.03)
Location difference at a point in time	−0.05	−0.06	−
	(0.04)	(0.04)	−
Difference in difference	−	−0.01	−
	−	(0.058)	−
DDD	−	−0.01	−
	−	(0.07)	−

Notes: Cells contain mean proportion of co-residents. Standard errors are presented in parentheses. Years before the 1999 reform include 1998, years after the reform are 2000 and 2001.

increased by 1 per cent. The corresponding trend is very similar among non-eligibles who, prior to the reform, lived in places other than the main city of the county (an increase of 2 per cent of co-residents). At face value, this evidence suggests that the reform did not affect the first group of eligibles (those who could get discounts on their mortgage lending of about 26 per cent).

In Table 7.4 we perform a similar exercise for the second group. That group has higher incomes, but they are still eligible for the programme, at a lower subsidy (16 per cent, rather than 25 per cent). Before the reform 54 per cent of eligibles in high price areas lived with their parents. The estimate in the second column, first row of Table 7.4 is 0.67. This implies that 67 per cent of young adults lived with their parents after the reform. On the contrary,

Table 7.4   Triple differences for second eligible group (class 2)

Location/period	Time difference		
	Before 1999 reform	After 1999 reform	For location
A. Treatment individuals: eligible for the second subsidy, 18–35 years			
Main city in the district	0.54	0.67	0.13
	(0.05)	(0.04)	(0.06)
Place of residence is not main city	0.70	0.70	0.001
	(0.03)	(0.03)	(0.03)
Location difference at a point in time:	−0.15	−0.026	–
	(0.05)	(0.04)	–
Difference in difference	–	0.13	–
	–	(0.07)	–
B. Control group: non-eligibles, 18–35 years			
Main city in district	0.50	0.51	0.01
	(0.035)	(0.03)	(0.05)
Place of residence is not main city	0.55	0.57	0.02
	(0.02)	(0.02)	(0.03)
Location difference at a point in time	−0.05	−0.06	–
	(0.04)	(0.04)	–
Difference in difference	–	−0.01	–
	–	(0.058)	–
DDD	–	0.14	–
	–	(0.09)	–

Notes: Cells contain mean proportion of co-residents. Standard errors are presented in parentheses. Years before the 1999 reform include 1998, years after the reform are 2000 and 2001.

eligibles for the second highest subsidy who lived in cheaper cities did not experience any change in their co-residence rate. The difference in the increase of the stock of co-residents among eligibles for the second highest subsidy is about 13 per cent. This asymmetry in the co-residence trends is consistent with the notion that the 1999 reform established a national-level ceiling, most likely to affect individuals who want to leave their parents' house and live in high price areas. The bottom panel in Table 7.4 provides the comparison group of non-eligibles, whose behaviour did not change significantly after the passing of the reform (the percentage of co-residents fell by a point among this group). The triple differences estimate is the difference between the 13 per cent increase among eligibles in high price areas and the 1 per cent relative decrease in co-residence among non-eligibles. The estimate is 14 per cent, significantly different from zero at the 10 per cent confidence level.

Overall we draw two conclusions from the analysis in Tables 7.3 and 7.4. The first is that changes in availability of debt had different effects on different eligible groups. Eligibles for the highest subsidy do not seem to be affected by the decrease in the availability of mortgage debt. Nevertheless, higher income groups who were limited in their access to subsidized mortgage debt were indeed affected, and reacted to the reform by staying in their parents' home. Of course, many objections can be raised to this type of analysis. First, co-residence is strongly correlated with age, income and other variables of the young individual, for which we did not control. Hence, we turn to a conditional analysis in the next subsection.

5.2 Regression Analysis

This subsection presents regression estimates of Equation (7.1). Table 7.5 uses a probit specification and reports the marginal impact of the independent variables on the stock of co-residents. The standard errors are corrected for heteroskedasticity and correlation among the observations from the same individual. The coefficients of interest are the interactions between *ELIG_*1..3, *AFTER*, and *HIGHPRICE*.

The specification in the first column contains no controls. The estimate of the interaction between *ELIG_*1, *AFTER* and *HIGHPRICE* is negative and large, but very imprecise. It suggest a reduction in the propensity to co-reside by 5 per cent, but the standard error is large (.08). That means that among eligibles for the 26 per cent subsidy the proportion of co-residents decreased by 1.5 per cent, contrary to what one would expect. The coefficient of the interaction between *ELIG_*2, *AFTER* and *HIGHPRICE* is about 12 per cent, rather similar to the triple-differences estimate in Table 7.4.

The second specification in Table 7.5 introduces a dummy for each age of the individual (head of the household, in the case of married households) between the ages of 19 and 35, and education intercepts. The pattern of the age coefficients (not shown) displays a strong monotonic relationship between the probability of living with parents and the age of the individual. The relationship is concave from the origin. At earlier ages, increasing age by one year diminishes the probability of living with parents by less than a percentage point. At age 30, one extra year of age diminishes the probability of living with parents by between 3 and 4 percentage points. Nevertheless, these estimates mix cohort, time and age effects, and should be taken with care. We also find a strong positive effect

Table 7.5   *The effect of interest rates on the probability of living with parents*

Specification method: probit	(1) Basic covariates	(2) Limited covariates	(3) Including income
ELIG_1*AFTER*HIGHPRICE	−0.015	−0.011	−0.015
	(0.064)	(0.064)	(0.068)
ELIG_2*AFTER*HIGHPRICE	0.119	0.133	0.128
	(0.069)*	(0.056)**	(0.055)**
ELIG_3*AFTER*HIGHPRICE	0.028	0.064	0.064
	(0.086)	(0.075)	(0.074)
ELIG_1*AFTER	0.022	0.016	0.027
	(0.035)	(0.034)	(0.038)
ELIG_2*AFTER	−0.018	−0.022	−0.021
	(0.051)	(0.049)	(0.051)
ELIG_3*AFTER	0.007	0.019	0.022
	(0.049)	(0.046)	(0.047)
ELIG_1*HIGHPRICE	0.051	0.063	0.084
	(0.041)	(0.039)	(0.038)*
ELIG_2*HIGHPRICE	−0.105	−0.107	−0.083
	(0.072)	(0.078)	(0.075)
ELIG_3*HIGHPRICE	−0.022	−0.049	−0.037
	(0.068)	(0.071)	(0.070)
ELIG_1	0.148	0.131	−0.304
	(0.026)**	(0.027)**	(0.021)**
ELIG_2	0.121	0.112	−0.200
	(0.028)**	(0.026)**	(0.047)**
ELIG_3	0.082	0.052	−0.194
	(0.031)**	(0.031)	(0.045)**
AFTER	0.019	0.015	0.045
	(0.033)	(0.031)	(0.036)
AFTER*HIGHPRICE	−0.013	−0.020	−0.018
	(0.057)	(0.057)	(0.061)
HIGHPRICE	−0.048	−0.062	−0.085
	(0.041)	(0.041)	(0.044)
Does not read nor write	–	0.036	−0.025
	–	(0.032)	(0.038)
First cycle of primary education	–	−0.112	−0.108
	–	(0.012)**	(0.012)**
Omitted group: second cycle of primary education			
Secondary education or above	–	0.113	0.112
	–	(0.015)**	(0.015)**

Table 7.5   (continued)

Specification method: probit	(1) Basic covariates	(2) Limited covariates	(3) Including income
Logarithm of income	–	–	−0.452
	–	–	(0.022)**
Age dummies	No	Yes	Yes
Number of observations	11 375	11 375	11 375

Notes: Reported estimates are marginal effects, evaluated at sample means. Standard errors account for heteroskedasticity and correlation within observations of the same individual.

HIGHPRICE takes value one if the county of residence one year prior to the survey is main city in the district.

AFTER takes value one if the observation corresponds to year 2000 or 2001.

Income denotes earnings in 1999 euro.

Columns (2) and (3) include a dummy for each age of the individual between ages of 19 and 35, excluding 25.

The sample contains males and females between 18 and 35 years of age. *, ** denote that the estimate is significantly different from zero at the 10 and 5 per cent confidence level, respectively.

of education on the probability of living with parents, even after controlling for the income of the young adult. The impact of education on the probability of living with parents is surprisingly positive, as individuals with high school or higher education are 11 points more likely to live with their parents. The effect could be due to longer stays in the parental home by young adults who take college studies (universities in Portugal do not provide accomodation and young adults tend to attend the university in the place where their parents live). We have re-run the regression including only young adults above 26 years of age. The dummy for 'high school or more' is 0.14 (standard error: 0.02) positive and significant. This result is somewhat hard to interpret.

Once we control for age, the estimate of the interaction between *ELIG_1*, *AFTER* and *HIGHPRICE* is −0.037, again negative and not significantly different from zero. The corresponding estimate for *ELIG_2*, *AFTER* and *HIGHPRICE* is positive and significantly different from zero at the 5 per cent confidence level. The point estimate indicates that, among eligibles for the second highest subsidy, the proportion of co-residents increased by 12 per cent, very close to the DDD estimate in the previous subsection. The corresponding estimate for the third group is basically zero. This group is somewhat heterogeneous, as it mixes two types of subsidies, one of which is negligible. Hence, we do not comment on those results in detail. Finally, specification (3) includes the logarithm of household income as a regressor. The estimates of the parameters of interest remain unchanged.

Overall, the analysis using the stock of co-residents points to unequal effects of the programme over the income distribution. Our estimation results point at no effects for the co-residence decisions of the majority of the population targeted by the subsidy. Nevertheless, higher income groups did react to the limit in the access to mortgage debt, in a way that is consistent with what consumer theory would predict. Possible explanations for this pattern of behaviour are that the first eligible group (class 1) is very heterogeneous and contains individuals with very low incomes who are unlikely to get a mortgage even with the substantial discount implied by the programme. Another possibility is that we should focus on a different parameter: the probability of individuals leaving their parents' home, rather than on the stock of co-residents. A third possibility is that eligibles with lower income levels found housing services at the ceiling more 'palatable' than higher income adults. Martins and Villanueva (2003) document that the probability of signing a loan at the maximum level for eligibles for the highest subsidy increased between 1999 and 2001. When more data on the cancellation of the programme (in 2002) are available, we plan to disentangle these three possibilities.

6.   ROBUSTNESS CHECK: DID THE CB PROGRAMME AFFECT REAL ESTATE PRICES?

Subsidies to housing are often criticized for resulting in higher prices of real estate without increasing access to home-ownership. The reason is that the supply in this market is either inelastic (Glaeser and Shapiro 2002) or adjusts slowly (Poterba 1984). The CB programme could well have resulted in increases in real estate prices, especially in the type of housing demanded by eligibles. This section discusses the impact of the CB programme on real estate prices in two different ways. First, we discuss the aggregate relationship between measures of use of the CB programme and the evolution of real estate prices. Second, we examine the county-level relationship between the evolution of real estate prices in the 1995–98 period and eligibility for the CB programme.

Figure 7.2 presents the evolution of the (quality-unadjusted) price of real estate and of the nominal interest rate between 1989 and 2001. The figure suggests a steady increase in the price of real estate over the decade, together with the fall of the interest rate. Two conclusions from the figure lead us to think that the CB Programme did not result immediately in higher real estate prices. First, according to Figure 7.2 the period of higher increase in

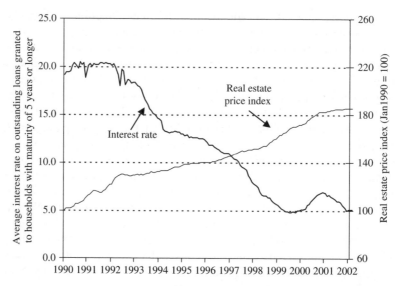

*Figure 7.2   Real estate price index and average interest rate on long-term
loans*

the value of new debt corresponds to relatively moderate increases in the
real estate prices. From 1995–98 the amount of new loans increased at an
average annual rate of 41 per cent, while the average yearly increase for the
1991–2001 period was 32 per cent. On the other hand, real estate prices
increased at an annual rate of 6.2 per cent over the 1990–2001 period and
3.2 per cent during the 1995–98 period. Second, after the 1999 reform real
estate prices continued to increase despite the decrease in the value of total
loans, which is not consistent with the assumption of a rigid supply of real
estate. Figure 7.2 documents an annual increase of 6.4 per cent in real estate
prices during the 1999 to 2001 period, while, as highlighted in Figure 7.1,
there was a significant decrease in the annual amount of new loans after the
reform (the amount of new loans decreased by 12.7 per cent in 2000 and by
5.6 per cent in 2001).

The previous analysis reflects only country trends and does not quantify
the relationship between real estate and the use of the CB programme. We
have analysed the relationship between eligibility for the CB programme
pre-reform and the increase in the price of real estate between 1995 and
1998 – the years of expansion of the CB programme – using variation in
the proportion of eligibles across counties. Our identifying assumption is
that if the CB programme had an impact on the prices of real estate, counties with a higher proportion of eligibles should experience overall higher

growth in house prices, holding income of the county constant. For this regression, we use information on 86 counties, the proportion of eligibles in the county, and the average income in the county in 1998, all computed using the Inquérito ao Emprego. The information on prices is obtained from a Portuguese real estate agency that computed inflation for selected counties in Portugal.

The results of the regression are presented in the following specification, where standard error of the estimated coefficients are shown in parentheses:

$$\frac{PRICE\_98}{PRICE\_95} = -0.005(0.004)PELIG\_1 + 0.024(0.04)PELIG\_2$$
$$+ 0.07(0.07)PELIG\_3 + 0.143(0.069)INCOME$$
$$- 0.004(0.011)POPULATION - 0.0003(0.00007)*PRICE\_95$$

The number of observations was 86. The R^2 of the regression is 0.38. In the regression *PELIG_1* represents the ratio between the eligibility of class 1 and the non-eligibles in the county (similar definitions for classes 2 and 3). The estimates suggest that income in 1998 is positively correlated with housing inflation and that the original price in 1995 was negatively correlated with inflation. The ratio of eligibles to non-eligibles does not explain much of the growth.

In summary we interpret that (a) there were three trends in the 1990s: steady increase in the use of the CB programme, a steady fall in the interest rates and a steady increase in the price of real estate; (b) the sharpest increase in real estate prices occurred at the beginning of the 1990s (when the CB programme was starting to develop, but was by no means at its highest) and after 1999 (when the programme was cancelled); and (c) regional variations in eligibility do not seem to explain differences in the increase of real estate prices. We infer that the increase in housing prices from 1990–2001 has been general across all counties, independently of the proportion of the eligible group of individuals living in a particular county. Hence, our strategy of allowing for a time trend should capture the effect of the increase in prices on the propensity to co-reside.

7.   CONCLUSIONS

The aim of this chapter is to uncover a causal link between access to debt markets and co-residence in a Southern European country. For this purpose, we exploit a reform in a large programme in Portugal that implied a dramatic change in the incentives to borrow among young low income groups. The analysis focuses on the stock of co-residents as the dependent variable. Our results point to a negative impact of increased access to mortgage debt on the probability of living with parents. The effect is large and significant among less poor eligibles (those with higher incomes). The effects among the lowest income groups are imprecise.

Regarding the policy implications of this exercise, given current concerns about the lack of mobility in Europe, we find that public policy aimed at achieving easier access to credit markets may promote the mobility of workers from certain income groups. It is worth noting that these results are unlikely to be specific to Portugal. Southern European countries share a large proportion of co-residing young adults and limited access to credit markets.

NOTES

1. Correspondence addresses: Nuno C. Martins, Banco de Portugal, Av. Almirante Reis, 71, 1150-012 Lisbon, Portugal; e-mail: nmartins@fe.unl.pt; Ernesto Villanueva, Research Department, Banco de España, Alcalá 50, 28014 Madrid, Spain; e-mail: ernesto.villanueva@upf.edu.
2. Rosenzweig and Wolpin (1993, 1994) find that, for the USA, co-residence is most likely following bad income shocks for the child.
3. This is discussed fully in Martins and Villanueva (2003).
4. If the house was sold before the time limit, the individual would be obliged to return the amount subsidized plus a premium. Under some circumstances, such as moving to another region for work-related circumstances, the government could waive the obligation to return the subsidy (decree-law n. 328-B/86, 30 September, 1986).
5. The adjustment consisted in deducting an amount from the taxable income of the family. The deduction depended on family size.
6. Aggregate records of average interest rates by loan type provided by the Portuguese Ministry of Finance show that in February 2001 the average interest rate charged to a person with a CB loan was 7.59 per cent, while the average interest rate charged to a non-CB loan was 7.43 per cent. From February 2001 until May 2002 the difference in the charged interest rates never exceeded 16 basis points. See Devereux and Lanot (2003) for evidence on the incidence of MIRS (Mortgage Interest Relief at Source) on mortgage financial costs.
7. The IPEF is a survey on wealth holdings of Portuguese households, conducted for the first time in the year 2000.
8. The limit was established according to the decree law n. 349/98, 11 November, 1998. For eligibles of class 1 the limit was 62 350 euro, 68 585 euro, 81 055 euro or 87 290 euro if the family size was 1, 2, 3 or 4 and above, respectively. Conditional on family size, households eligible for the class 2 subsidy had higher limits: 69 832 euro (one individual), 76 815 euro (two individuals), 90 781 euro (three or four individuals) and 97 764 euro (five or more individuals). The corresponding limits for class 3 were: 77 314 euro, 85 045 euro, 100 508 euro and 108 239 euro, and finally, for class 4 the limits were: 84 796 euro, 93 275 euro, 110 234 euro and 118 714 euro.
9. Source: Portuguese Ministry of Finance (http://www.dgt.pt/informacoes/default.htm).
10. Between the end of 1994 and the end of 2001 the country aggregate interest rate implicit on outstanding household loans with a maturity of five years or longer decreased from an average of 13 per cent to 5 per cent. During this period, the six-month interest rate benchmark (Lisbor) decreased from 11.3 per cent to 2.64 per cent by May 1999. It increased to 3.57 per cent by the end of 2001.

11. According to our calculations from IPEF 2000 the take-up rate of the CB programme among eligible households was 51 per cent. However, this number could be biased as the eligibility class is measured in the year 2000 when the household is interviewed, but not at the moment of signing the loan. This take-up rate would be comparable to the take-up rate of 401(k) (a widely studied tax-favoured savings vehicle in the USA) in the USA during the mid-1980s (see Engen and Gale 2000).

12. Eligibility for the CB subsidy depends on family income and family size. The Inquérito ao Emprego contains information on monthly net labour income for salaried workers, business income for the self-employed, unemployment benefits for the unemployed and pension income for retirees. We use only salaried workers, unemployed or retired individuals, and impute pre-tax labour income from the standard withholding rules in the Portuguese law. We do not have direct information on transfer income or asset income. Hence, the eligibility measure could be subject to measurement error. We have computed the proportion of household income that comes from labour earnings using the 2000 IPEF survey, and this amounts to 93.4 per cent of total earnings. The proportion of eligibles in both samples is similar.

13. We decided to pool together eligibility classes 3 and 4. The reason is that there are a relatively small number of individuals in these groups.

REFERENCES

Becker, S., S. Bentolila, A. Fernandes and A. Ichino (2004), 'Does job insecurity affect youth emancipation decisions', mimeo, European University Institute.

Bentolila, S. and A. Ichino (2003), 'Unemployment and consumption: why are job losses less painful than expected near the Mediterranean?', CEPR Discussion Paper 2539.

Billari, F.C., D. Philipov and P. Baizán (2001), 'Leaving home in Europe: the experience of cohorts born around 1960', *International Journal of Population Geography*, 7 (5), 339–56.

Chiuri, M. and T. Jappelli (2003), 'Financial market imperfections and home ownership: a comparative study', *European Economic Review*, 47, 857–75.

Devereux, M. and G. Lanot (2003), 'Measuring tax incidence: an application to mortgage provision in the UK', *Journal of Public Economics*, 87 (7–8), 1747–78.

Engen, E. and W.G. Gale (2000), 'The effects of 401(k) plans on household wealth', NBER Working Paper 8032.

Giuliano, P. (2004), 'On the determinants of living arrangements in Western europe: does cultural origin matter?', mimeo, International Monetary Fund.

Glaeser, E. and M. Shapiro (2002), 'The benefits of home mortgage interest deduction', Harvard Institute of Economic Research Discussion Paper 1979.

Jappelli, T. and L. Pistaferri (2002), 'Incentives to borrow and the demand for mortgage debt: an analysis of tax reforms', CSEF Working Paper 90, University of Salerno.

Jappelli, T. and L. Pistaferri (2003), 'Tax incentives and the demand for life insurance: evidence from Italy', *Journal of Public Economics*, 87 (7–8), 1779–99.

Jurado, T. (1999), 'Youth in transition: housing, employment, social policies and families in France and Spain', thesis read at European University Institute.

Manacorda, M. and E. Moretti (2003), 'Intergenerational transfers and family structure: why do most Italian youths live with their parents?', mimeo, UCLA.

Martínez-Granado, M. and J. Ruiz-Castillo (2002), 'The decisions of Spanish youth: a cross-section study', *Journal of Population Economics*, 15, 305–30.

Martins, N. and E. Villanueva (2003), 'The impact of interest-rate-subsidies on long-term household debt: evidence from a large programme', Universitat Pompeu Fabra Working Paper 713.

Poterba, J. (1984), 'Tax subsidies to owner-occupied housing: an asset market approach', *Quarterly Journal of Economics*, **99** (4), 729–52.

Rosenzweig, M. and K. Wolpin (1993), 'Intergenerational support and the life-cycle incomes of young men and their parents: human capital investments, co-residence, and intergenerational financial transfers', *Journal of Labor Economics*, **11** (1), 84–112.

Rosenzweig, M. and K. Wolpin (1994), 'Parental and public transfers to young women and their children', *American Economic Review*, **84** (5), 1195–212.

DISCUSSION

Pierre Koning[1]

Until now, in the literature little is known on the effectiveness of housing subsidies such as the Credito Bonificado programme (CB) in Portugal. Similar to other types of tax deductions, for policymakers it is important to know whether such measures have led to income transfers only, and to what extent behavioural effects occur. Martins and Villanueva provide a welcome first step towards answering these questions, at least for the Credito Bonificado programme in Portugal. They present a straightforward, accessible empirical analysis of the effect of a large housing subsidy programme on the co-residence of young adults. Both the framework for analysis, as well as the empirical strategy – triple differencing so as to correct for various (potential) endogeneity biases – are intuitively appealing. Still, many interesting questions in this strand of literature remain unanswered, in particular when addressing the role of liquidity constraints. In what follows, I will discuss some of these.

The first question is: how important are liquidity constraints really? To test for the link between liquidity constraints and access to the housing market in a proper way, the authors use a quasi-experimental set-up, using data on co-residence and information on tax incentives induced by the reform of the CB programme. However, testing the effectiveness of this programme in terms of co-residence is not informative on the importance of liquidity constraints per se. Young adults may respond to tax incentive measures, just like older adults, irrespective of the existence of liquidity constraints. Stated differently, programmes like the CB can be just as effective or ineffective in Northern European countries where the access to mortgage markets for young adults may be less limited than in Southern European countries. Thus, in order to test for the importance of liquidity constraints, a different research design is needed. One may think of measuring the effect of the CB programme in terms of substitution of the tax deduction: if liquidity constraints are important, one may expect tax deductions to result in higher mortgages. Analogously, when liquidity constraints are not important, tax deductions will lead to a reduction in private mortgage expenses to the same extent (substitution).

The second question is: why is it that liquidity constraints are especially important for Southern European countries like Portugal, and how 'bad' is this? In many studies, the existence of liquidity constraints in Southern European countries such as Portugal is treated as exogenous and undisputed. However, the argument that the high co-residence of young adults reflects (cultural) preferences in Southern European countries, seems just as likely to me. Related to this, the main argument against liquidity constraints is that it hampers labour mobility. But again, if high co-residence of young adults reflects (cultural) preferences to remain attached to their family and their social network, then low labour mobility is not an argument per se for programmes like the CB.

The third and last question is: how reliable are the difference in difference estimates? Or more specifically: what are the exact assumptions underlying the identification of programmes like the CB, using (exogenous) variation from different sources? In the literature, these assumptions are often not listed explicitly – in those cases, reference is made to some vague notion that endogeneity and selection effects will cancel out when using difference in differences transformations. The analysis of Martins and Villanueva does not seems an exception to this. In particular, they exploit three sources of (exogenous) variation to identify the CB reform effect: pre- and post-reform, geographical variation in housing prices and eligible versus non-eligible young adults. Within the context of their model, this means that the effect of the CB reform is over-identified: the effect can be estimated following a difference in difference approach either on the combination of pre- and post-reform variation and geographical variation, or on the combination of pre- and post-reform variation and eligibility versus non-eligibility variation. This over-identification of the model is not mentioned explicitly and both difference in differences estimates are not estimated separately. However, the comparison of both estimates can be used as a check on the robustness of the results.

In sum, in the literature various questions still have been left unanswered, and Martins and Villanueva are no exception to this. Still these authors make an important contribution to a strand of literature that has largely been unexposed until now: young not-so-poor adults do respond to housing subsidy incentives by leaving their parental nest earlier.

Note

1. Correspondence address: CPB Netherlands Bureau for Economic Policy Analysis, P.O. Box 80510, 2508 GM, The Hague, The Netherlands; e-mail: pwck@cpb.nl.

Index